The Pleasure of Poetry

READING AND ENJOYING BRITISH POETRY
FROM DONNE TO BURNS

NICOLAS H. NELSON

Westport, Connecticut
London

Library of Congress Cataloging-in-Publication Data

Nelson, Nicolas H., 1940–
    The pleasure of poetry : reading and enjoying British poetry from Donne to Burns /
Nicolas H. Nelson.
      p. cm.
    Includes bibliographical references and index.
    ISBN 0–275–99137–7 (alk. paper)
    1. English poetry—Early modern, 1500–1700—History and criticism. 2. English
poetry—18th century—History and criticism. 3. Poets, English—Early modern,
1500–1700—Biography. 4. Poets, English—18th century—Biography. 1. Title.
PR541.N46 2006
821'.409—dc22   2006009799

British Library Cataloguing in Publication Data is available.

Library of Congress Catalog Card Number: 2006009799
ISBN: 0–275–99137–7

First published in 2006

Praeger Publishers, 88 Post Road West, Westport, CT 06881
An imprint of Greenwood Publishing Group, Inc.
www.praeger.com

Printed in the United States of America

The paper used in this book complies with the
Permanent Paper Standard issued by the National
Information Standards Organization (Z39.48–1984).

10 9 8 7 6 5 4 3 2 1

To
Eveline
With love and gratitude
And
To
The memory of my parents

Contents

Preface

This is a book for the general reader, or anyone who has an interest in poetry. It is meant to be an introduction to some of the finest poems written in England and Scotland in the two centuries between 1600 and 1800. Some of these can be difficult for modern readers, but, perhaps surprisingly, most are not. With a little help in understanding unfamiliar words and some distant events, these poems can live again for us today.

I have written this book, then, in the hope that readers may discover here some new delights in an older poetic tradition. I have chosen what I believe to be some of the most accessible and appealing poems from John Donne to Robert Burns, a period that is central to the growth and development of British poetry. I discuss them in some detail but without entering into the problems in the texts, the many allusions, or the often complicated sources. I have provided glosses in the margins for some of the words (underlined) that may be difficult for readers today. My goal is to convey something of the beauty and significance in the poems, along with pointing out various techniques the poets have adopted in composing them, without getting distracted by the issues in them. My hope is that readers will then proceed to read further in the poets of this period with increased confidence, pleasure, and understanding. The "Further Reading" section contains lists of other poems to sample by these poets, as well as books about them and the period in which they wrote. Exploring more deeply in poet or period can be continually rewarding.

My readings of these poems are meant as general guides and broadly suggestive explanations rather than as definitive or exhaustive accounts.

Readers will, of course, form their own interpretation of these poems and have their own favorites. This is as it should be. Poetry is much too personal to pronounce absolute determinations of worth or meaning. My goal is to remind those who have already read some poetry in the past of pleasures they may have experienced before but forgotten, or to introduce others who did not have such experience to some things they have missed. It is never too late to take up something new and discover enjoyment and satisfaction in it.

I take pleasure here in thanking all those teachers, authors, and students who have taught me along my way. I wish to cite especially Professors Phillip Harth and Howard Weinbrot of the University of Wisconsin for their exceptional scholarly and critical guidance. I also remember with gratitude the books, essays, lectures, and editions by such scholars as Cleanth Brooks and Maynard Mack, who join wisdom with insight, learning, and eloquence. And I must not neglect to mention some of the great teachers I had many years ago, from Frank O'Connor, the Irish short story writer whose classes in modern literature were a human delight, to Alvin Whitley, one of the great university lecturers in the Johnsonian tradition.

I wish also to thank Kathy Wendland, a wonderful editor and dear friend, for her careful reading of my manuscript and her many excellent suggestions. Without her help and encouragement, this book would not have been possible. Any errors that remain are, of course, wholly my own responsibility.

My greatest debt is in the dedication.

A Note on Sources

The primary source of the poems cited in this book is the two-volume anthology edited by M. H. Abrams and Stephen Greenblatt, *The Norton Anthology of English Literature*, 7th ed. (New York: Norton, 2000). For Milton's *Samson Agonistes* I have used Merritt Y. Hughes's edition, *John Milton: The Complete Poems and Major Prose* (Indianapolis: Bobbs-Merrill/Odyssey, 1957). For Dryden's *Religio Laici* I have used Keith Walker's edition, *John Dryden* (The Oxford Authors) (Oxford: Oxford University Press, 1987). For Swift's poetry (except for "A Description of a City Shower" and "Verses on the Death of Dr. Swift," which are in the *Norton Anthology*), I have relied on Pat Rogers's edition, *Jonathan Swift: The Complete Poems* (New Haven, CT: Yale University Press, 1983). For Burns's "John Anderson My Jo" I have used Carol McGuirk's edition, *Robert Burns: Selected Poems* (London: Penguin, 1993).

CHAPTER 1

Introduction to Reading Poetry

Poetry is something for everyone to enjoy, not just a select few. Anyone who reads at a high school level should be able to take pleasure in it with a minimum of aid. As surprising as it may seem to modern readers, given the difficulty of much poetry since the early twentieth century, most poets throughout history have actually been interested in communicating with their readers, not in baffling them or putting them off. Occasionally, of course, a poet will write primarily for a limited audience, a few insiders or an educated elite, but overall, poets wish to be understood and appreciated, if for nothing more than to sell their books.

In the poetry that follows, readers will find much to interest them, from a surprising variety of ideas to a wide range of emotion, sharp wit, verbal music, and an abundance of imaginative delight. In addition, the lives and times of the poets will be briefly considered in order to provide a useful context for the reader. Poems are not written in a vacuum, of course, but often refer to historical events or figures that may not be familiar to us today, as well as to personal concerns of the poet. Such topical references that occur will be briefly described and their relevance to the poetry explained, so the reader may readily understand and appreciate the poet's point. The pleasure of reading this poetry should not be lost for lack of a few pertinent historical or biographical facts.

The broad subject of this book is the major poetry written in English from 1600 to 1800. This period is not as well known as some others, such as the Renaissance with Shakespeare or the Romantic period in the early nineteenth century. Still, there is much to enjoy in the poetry of this era, much even that is surprisingly contemporary in its concerns. Some of the greatest poets in English, like John Milton and Alexander Pope, wrote during this time but are practically unknown today. Yet they are brilliant handlers of the language with a wonderful variety of poems, many of which are quite accessible to modern readers. The first part of this period, to the middle of the seventeenth century, is usually characterized as one dominated by the so-called Metaphysical Poets, a name that suggests they reveal a strong philosophical interest in their poetry. The most important Metaphysical Poets we will consider are John Donne and Andrew Marvell, but we will see that, despite the name, they are not always very serious or interested only in philosophical themes. Moreover, there are other poets at this time, like Ben Jonson and Robert Herrick, who do not fully share their concerns. The later period, once called the Neoclassical Age but now more accurately termed the Restoration (roughly from 1660 to 1700) and the eighteenth century, was dominated first by satire and later by themes of sympathy and sensibility. Still, as we shall see, other themes and kinds of poetry than these were written and enjoyed. Diversity is clearly one of this poetry's main features.

These two hundred years or so in England were often turbulent and occasionally marred by violent conflict. In the seventeenth century the country was moving from a largely feudal society to a freer, more capitalistic economy and a somewhat more constitutional form of monarchy. It was sharply divided in the middle of the century by a civil war that pitted the king (Charles I) against the Parliament, Puritan against Anglican, community against community, and brother against brother. The issues were serious and of continuing relevance: among these were such problems as the nature and scope of the freedoms of worship and speech, the rights of citizens versus the royal prerogative, the powers of Parliament, and the relation of church and state. The repercussions of these conflicts and changes lasted into the next century, though, after a brief interruption when Oliver Cromwell ruled, England reestablished its monarchy on a firm constitutional basis with Parliament taking on a more prominent role than it had before. In the eighteenth century the English expanded their trading activities, enriching themselves, but also bringing them into conflict with other countries, as well as with some of their own colonies, most notably the one that became the United States. The industrial revolution began later in this century, a movement that was to transform England and later the world. The poetry written during these years does not usually deal specifically with these events, but the poet may allude to them or incorporate them indirectly into the poem. These references will be explained as needed, either in the margin of the text or in the discussion itself.

Today, it seems, few people read poems for pleasure, especially the older sort, in part because they have never had much exposure to poetry and in part because they do not see its relevance. Yet the basic principles for reading poetry are few and well known. In fact, they are not much different from those for reading prose. Poetry is not a mystery, though it may deal with the mysterious and the haunting, or the ambiguous and the elusive as well as the beautiful and the ugly. All of life is its province. What follows here is a brief review, for those who feel the need for it, of some of the basic principles intended to help in reading this poetry with greater understanding and pleasure.

The first principle in reading poetry is to realize that it is generally indirect. That is, poetry often makes its point or introduces its subject not by stating it directly but through figures of speech, which are nonliteral expressions meant to evoke the subject in a certain way or for a particular response. A poet, for example, may employ comparisons to unexpected objects or un- usual things that do not at first seem relevant. Such comparisons (called metaphors or similes) characterize the subject in ways that enhance our un- derstanding or appreciation of it. Poets rarely call a spade a spade, because they want to dig deeper than the literal object can go. When Robert Burns writes, "O my Love's like a red, red rose / That's newly sprung in June," he wants us to see how beautiful his beloved is and to sense how deep his feel- ing is for her. The word "like" makes the comparison between love and a rose explicit; this is called a simile. The rose, everyone knows, is a traditional symbol for love as red is a symbol for passion. The repetition of "red" un- derscores the depth of the color as well as of the poet's affection, while the second line, with its associations of spring and new life, furthers the idea of his beloved's freshness, vitality, and beauty. In just a few words the poet evokes a powerful feeling of love that we might otherwise think is inde- scribable. The lilting rhythm and songlike sounds of his lines reinforce this effect as well.

Sometimes poets will not signal the comparison being made, but create a kind of equation between two things to suggest that this one equals, or is identical to, that one, or they may let the equation remain implicit. This metaphorical comparison is less obvious than with a simile, but nevertheless is usually clear enough, especially as the poem develops. When John Donne writes in one of his Holy Sonnets (No. 6), "This is my play's last scene," we know that he means his life is drawing to a close. It is not just "like" a drama, it is one. Comparing one's life to a play was commonplace in the Renais- sance, as in Shakespeare's "All the world's a stage, / And all the men and women merely players" (Jaques in *As You Like It*, 2.7.139–140). Donne con- tinues in his sonnet with other metaphors for his life, comparing it to a pilgrimage as well as to a race, both again in the final moments before reaching their goal. Donne uses these metaphors to convey his sense of his own life as an active and dynamic experience coming to a climax: poets often dramatize their lives in highly expressive terms that convey more to a reader than a flat statement of fact would do. We feel, not just think, that their lives are about to end.

Another common figure of speech used by poets is personification, that is, when an object or an idea is given human attributes. Thus Ben Jonson, in his "Epitaph on S. P." (a young actor he knew who had recently died), says that "Heaven and Nature seemed to strive / Which owned the creature" (lines 7–8), as if these two abstract concepts were able to struggle like people over possession of the young boy, who had been favored by both. It is a way of exalting S. P.'s value if God and Nature appear to desire to retain him for their own realms. In the same poem, Jonson refers to Death and the Fates as if they were human and capable of specific intentions, motives, and feelings. "Death's self," he says, "is sorry" for causing S. P.'s death, and the "Fates turned cruel" to bring about this tragic end. For the reader, personification makes such concepts come alive to act with energy, purpose, and impact in the world, even though we may not believe in the literal reality of these forces.

Exaggeration or hyperbole, another common figure of speech, occurs when a poet makes his point by inflating it beyond a reasonable or literal possibility. Andrew Marvell does this in "The Garden" to suggest the abundance of food in his rural retreat, a kind of Garden of Eden, where the fruit seems to seek to be eaten: "The nectarine and curious peach / Into my hands themselves do reach" (lines 37–38). The poet does not even have to go pick them for himself. Personification also plays an implicit role in these lines, which treat the fruit as if they have human motives. The two figures of speech clearly work together to create a more forceful expression. In Jonathan Swift's "Verses on the Death of Dr. Swift," a poem in which he imagines his own death and the reaction to it among his friends and acquaintances, the poet suggests that he is very jealous of Pope's power as a poet: "In Pope I cannot read a line, / But with a sigh I wish it mine" (lines 47–48). We know that Swift admired Pope's poetry, but we need not take this literally to see his point. Surely not every line by Pope makes him sigh with envy, but the statement makes us smile at the absurd exaggeration without detracting from its compliment to Pope's great powers as a poet. Humor often adds to our pleasure in these figures of speech.

A further technique for the poet to convey meaning and feeling indirectly is through allusion, the reference to events or people outside the subject that help in some way to characterize it. Classical myths provide a fund of allusions for poets in the seventeenth and eighteenth centuries, since they were an integral part of the education of the time. Among the more familiar mythological figures are Apollo, the god of poetry; Bacchus, the god of wine and inspiration; Aurora, the goddess of the dawn; Jove (or Jupiter or Zeus), the king of the gods; the nine Muses, the daughters of Jove who inspire the various arts on earth; and many more. In "His Farewell to Sack," Robert Herrick says that even Apollo and the nine Muses could not find inspiration without the benefit of sack, a sherry wine from Spain:

> 'Tis not Apollo can, or those thrice three
> <u>Castalian</u> sisters sing, if wanting [lacking] thee. *their sacred spring on*
> *Mt. Parnassus*
> (29–30)

Herrick, of course, uses such an allusion to these divine figures in the Greek pantheon for humorous exaggeration. Classical writers and their works (e.g., Homer, *The Iliad*), and major historical events (the Trojan War or the Spanish Inquisition) furnish more sources for allusions. Clearly, one needs to know some mythology, as well as some classical literature and history, in order to comprehend these references. But one can usually catch the drift of a passage even if the specific references are not clear. A good encyclopedia or an edition with annotations will provide the basic information needed to understand such references. It is, of course, also true that the more one reads, the more one will begin to recognize such allusions.

A second concept important to reading poetry is the voice or persona in the poem. Who is supposedly writing and speaking in the poem, the poet himself or herself, or someone else? Today we tend to see poetry as self-expression, but in the seventeenth and eighteenth centuries that was not usually the case. In fact, most of the time poets would have been scorned if they had written directly about their own feelings. Poets, like other writers, were expected to write about subjects of general concern, such as aspects of human nature or life in their society. Occasionally, though, even in the era under consideration a poet will dramatize the plight of a historical person by adopting his or her voice to speak about a specific situation. Pope's "Eloisa to Abelard" (1717) is a poem depicting the love of a twelfth-century nun for her teacher, a well-known philosopher who returned her love. The poet becomes the tortured Heloise (the more common spelling of her name today), who writes about her continuing passion for Abelard despite their years of separation and her confinement in a convent. Her passion has been reignited after a letter he wrote to a friend explaining their love came into her hands. The poem begins:

In these deep solitudes and awful cells,
Where heavenly-pensive contemplation dwells,
And ever-musing melancholy reigns;
What means this tumult in a vestal's veins?
Why rove my thoughts beyond this last retreat?
Why feels my heart its long-forgotten heat?
Yet, yet I love!—From Abelard _it_ came,   *the letter*
And Eloisa yet must kiss the name.   (1–8)

In the rest of the poem Pope depicts Eloisa's mind trying to come to grips
with her feelings as she struggles to reconcile her passionate earthly love with
her love for God. Such a point of view was about as far from Pope, an
eighteenth-century gentleman and poet, as one can imagine. Yet the woman's
fate clearly fascinated Pope, prompting him to write a powerful poem about
her internal struggle from the inside, as if he were she. Eloisa's reaction to the
letter is tumultuous as she recalls the details of their affair and realizes that
she still loves Abelard as passionately as before.

Using such a specific voice will sometimes imply a certain situation that
involves more than one character, as Eloisa evokes Abelard, their exchange of
letters, and the whole of their love affair. Her rediscovery of her continuing
passion is a moment of great power with a long history behind it, a confusing
and melancholy present, and an uncertain future. She describes all this in her
long letter to Abelard that recalls the highlights of their love, the opposition
of her father, and their resulting separation and retirement into different
monasteries. Eloisa concludes her letter by imagining their being reunited in
death and being mourned not only by other loving couples, but also by a
later poet (or bard) who can understand their terrible fate because he, too,
loves one from whom he is irretrievably separated:

And sure if fate some future bard shall join   *pronounced "jine"*
In sad similitude of griefs to mine,
Condemned whole years in absence to deplore,
And image charms he must behold no more,
Such if there be, who loves so long, so well,
Let him our sad, our tender story tell;
The well-sung woes will sooth my pensive ghost;
He best can paint 'em, who shall feel 'em most.   (359–366)

In these lines Pope clearly suggests that he, too, may have been suffering
similar pangs of frustrated love (a point much debated by scholars), but

whether true or not this is only a minor complication of the whole history of Eloisa's love as evoked by the poet in this poem. Pope's poem is no doubt more elaborate than most poems using a first-person narrator (it runs to 366 lines), but it shows us clearly what poets can do in adopting someone else's voice.

Readers of poetry naturally need to be especially attentive to the kind of language employed by the author. Poets will normally adapt their diction to their subject, unless they wish to mark a contrast or juxtapose the language to the context. For example, Milton, in composing his epic, *Paradise Lost*, generally employs an elevated, formal language for his profoundly serious work. In describing what God did to Satan after the archangel rebelled against Him, Milton says:

> Him the Almighty Power
> Hurled headlong flaming from th'ethereal sky
> With hideous ruin and combustion down
> To bottomless perdition, there to dwell
> In adamantine chains and penal fire,
> Who durst defy th'Omnipotent to arms.   (1: 44–49)

With such formal, polysyllabic words as ethereal, combustion, perdition, and adamantine, Milton suggests this is no common event that he is describing, but something huge and momentous. He begins his sentence with the object instead of the subject (an inversion of normal syntax), which adds to its formality and unusual emphasis, and focuses our attention on Satan as the target of God's wrath. On the other hand, poets will occasionally employ slang or "low" words to characterize the subject they are attacking or mocking. John Dryden, in his satire on a fellow dramatist called "Mac Flecknoe," slips in a few such words when he describes the area around a training school for actors, which also harbors brothels:

> Where their vast courts the mother-strumpets keep,
> And, undisturbed by <u>watch</u>, in silence sleep.   *police*
>   (72–73)

Nearby is the building, a "Nursery" (training school)

> Where unfledged actors learn to laugh and cry,
> Where infant <u>punks</u> their tender voices try...   *prostitutes*
>   (76–77)

Dryden's picture of this area is clearly derogatory, especially since much of his description uses more formal diction and elegant language: the association of "mother-strumpets" with courts, which are usually linked rather with royalty, undercuts any dignity the school may have had. Here the poet plays on the sharp contrast between high and low language, contributing to the ridicule of his target and to his mock-epic form. The connotations of the poet's words are often more important than their denotation, so that historical notes on the language may be necessary to alert readers to any nuances or shades of meaning in the poem.

Another important part of the language poets employ are the images (i.e., concrete references to the things of this world) to evoke their subject. The images they select and the way they treat them help determine the effect they produce in the poem. For example, Pope in "Eloisa to Abelard" focuses on the gloomy, solitary situation of the convent, with its "Relentless walls" and "rugged rocks" (lines 17, 19), its surrounding "grots and caverns shagged with horrid thorn" (line 20), to suggest the feelings of isolation and imprisonment that Eloisa has in her convent. It is not just description for its own sake, but a vivid projection of her mental state and her perception of her situation. In George Herbert's poem "Time," the focus is on the Grim Reaper's scythe, which the speaker says is not as keen as it should be, that Time should sharpen it so that people can die more readily and thus go to Heaven to rejoin God. Perhaps long ago, the speaker thinks, people did not want it to be sharp:

> "Perhaps some such of old did pass,
> Who above all things loved this life;
> To whom thy scythe a hatchet was,
> Which now is but a pruning knife.
>   Christ's coming hath made man thy debtor,
>   Since by thy cutting he grows better."   (7–12)

The speaker calls it a "pruning knife" instead of a "hatchet" because it improves man's growth in holiness and leads to salvation. The hatchet is merely brutal and inefficient. At the end of the poem, Time concludes, ironically, that the speaker wants more time in life rather than less. Herbert raises the specter of death to debate the idea of wanting to leave this life in order to escape its suffering and sins to find eternal rest and peace and joy with God. As in several of his poems (e.g., "The Altar," "The Pulley," and "The Collar") Herbert wittily plays with a single object or image around which to focus our attention.

Poets occasionally use a special kind of image, a symbol, to concentrate or enhance their meaning. A symbol is generally an object that stands for something else, like a flag for a country or the swastika for Nazi Germany. Often, it is enough just to mention the object to convey the significance or feeling one intends. Thus, John Donne uses directions for important symbolic meanings in "Good Friday, 1613. Riding Westward." Here he describes how he is "carried towards the West / This day, when my soul's form bends toward the East" (lines 9–10), to suggest how his body is moving toward the setting sun, or death, as he rides toward a friend's house, while his soul goes in the opposite direction, toward the rising sun (the Son, Christ, a common pun) and eternal life. The contrasting movement of body and soul, of physical deterioration versus spiritual yearning and growth, is suggested by these directions and embodies one of the central themes of this poem.

Conversely, in the eighteenth century Thomas Gray invokes specific historical figures from the previous century in the following stanza from his "Elegy Written in a Country Churchyard" (1751) to stand for certain achievements:

> Some village Hampden, that with dauntless breast
>   The little tyrant of his fields withstood;
> Some mute inglorious Milton here may rest,
>   Some Cromwell guiltless of his country's blood.   (57–60)

These were all famous people from the seventeenth century in England who were prominent during the conflict between the king and Parliament. John Hampden was a Parliamentary leader who led the political fight against the arbitrary rule of Charles I; Milton was not only a great poet, but an eloquent voice who argued forcefully for freedom and republicanism in many prose writings; and Oliver Cromwell was an outstanding military leader for Parliament in the English Civil War, who eventually became England's ruler. They all emerged from relative obscurity to become significant historical figures during this time. Simply by naming them they become symbols for the kind of achievement no longer possible for those in the cemetery Gray laments, who have died without reaching their full potential. Symbols can embody certain values and emotional associations that enable poets to concentrate their significance into a single word, always a useful feature.

Symbols may also be put together into a coherent narrative or extended description to form an allegory. This becomes a complex action in which characters and events represent certain ideas or values, as well as their own reality. Dryden's *Absalom and Achitophel*, as we will see, is a kind of historical allegory using biblical characters and episodes, whereas Dante's *Divine Comedy* is perhaps the most elaborate allegory in all of poetry, as Dante the character takes his arduous spiritual journey all the way from Hell through Purgatory to Paradise. There are not many allegories in the poetry we will discuss, but occasionally one will be found as part of a larger whole. Such a passage occurs in William Cowper's *The Task* (1785), when the poet starts with a metaphor for his life but expands it into a mini-allegory:

> I was a stricken deer, that left the herd
> Long since; with many an arrow deep infixed
> My panting side was charged, when I withdrew
> To seek a tranquil death in distant shades.
> There was I found by one who had himself
> Been hurt by the archers. In his side he bore,
> And in his hands and feet, the cruel scars.
> With gentle force soliciting the darts,
> He drew them forth, and healed, and bade me live.   (3: 108–116)

Here Cowper describes his own personal experience of being wounded by life but finding someone who shared his pain and suffering and was able, through his own strength, to heal Cowper's serious depression. His savior, at least on the worldly level, was probably John Newton, an Evangelical preacher and author of "Amazing Grace," who helped Cowper renew his faith and return to a fuller, more productive life, at least for some years. On a spiritual level, of course, Jesus Christ would have been his true savior. But the poem clearly reflects the poet's deepest feelings about his own life, a more common subject of poetry as we approach the Romantic age.

Most of the poets in this book use rhyme and other special sound effects to enhance the music of their verse. Such elements are part of the more technical side of poetry, but certainly add something to the pleasure we receive in reading their work. End rhyme is only one aspect of the music of poetry, though perhaps the most obvious one. Readers will find all sorts of rhyme schemes in this survey, from the simple couplet (two lines in succession that rhyme) to a variety of complex stanzas. The important point to note is that rhyme not only is pleasing in itself through the repetition of similar sounds, but also is an enhancement of the meaning of the line. Rhyme is not simply an end in itself, but a way to emphasize certain words, and thus their meanings and connotations. End rhyme is, of course, commonly noted by using small letters to stand for the final sound in a group of lines, as a quatrain with alternating rhyme is marked *abab*. Other musical devices include alliteration, assonance, and consonance, which are the repetition of consonant or vowel sounds within a line (or in successive lines) of verse. A few lines from John Dryden's "Alexander's Feast" (1697) in which Alexander the Great's musician, Timotheus, proves he can evoke practically any emotion he wants in his audience through his flute playing, will illustrate how intensely musical verse can be:

> The <u>mighty master</u> smiled to see   *Alexander the Great*
> That love was in the next degree;
> 'Twas but a kindred sound to move,
> For pity melts the mind to love.
>   Softly sweet, in <u>Lydian</u> measures,   *sad, plaintive music*
> Soon he soothed his soul to pleasures.   (93–98)

Here we see (and hear) the prominent end rhyme, the alliteration and consonance of the *m* sound and the assonance of the long *i* in the first line, the continuing alliteration of *m*s and *ss*, and the assonance of the *oo* sound in the later lines. This passage is a melodious feast meant to underscore music's power over our hearts and minds. Poetry and music have long enjoyed a close association, and Dryden here displays it subtly but abundantly.

Another part of the appeal of any poem is in its rhythm, which has to do with the movement of its sounds. The rhythm of a poem is partly a function of its basic meter (or lack thereof) and all the variations from the norm in the line. All the poets in this book compose metrical verse. This means that they employ a pattern of stressed and unstressed syllables (the natural pattern in English but not in all languages) to give a certain rhythm to their poems. The most common pattern is a unit composed of an unstressed syllable followed by a stressed syllable (called iambic), with the lines usually having eight or ten syllables in all. Thus there are generally four or five stressed syllables in each line (called tetrameter and pentameter respectively). Although each poem will have a dominant metrical pattern, most of the lines in each will have some sort of variation on it, usually for emphasis. Here are a couple of examples with the stresses marked. The first is from Andrew Marvell's "Upon Appleton House" (1681), where he describes the estate of Sir Thomas Fairfax, who was a prominent parliamentary general during England's Civil War:

> Withìn this sòber fràme expèct
> Wòrk of no fòreign Àrchitèct,
> That ùnto càves the qùarries drèw,
> And fòrests dìd to pàstures hèw.   (1–4)

Marvell is praising the simple construction of the buildings on the estate, which had been part of an ancient monastery and blended readily into the surrounding landscape. The stresses in the first line are regularly iambic as indicated, but in the second line the first word is clearly stressed, not the short and unimportant "of." The word "foreign" then has somewhat greater stress on its first syllable, perhaps to underscore the fact that the estate has its foundation in native design. Any change in the metrical pattern usually means that the poet wishes to emphasize the word receiving the stress. The rest of the line continues the regular iambic pattern, as do the two lines that follow. With the eight syllable lines and their four stressed syllables the poem is in iambic tetrameter. It also is made up of couplets (two successive lines that rhyme) in mainly end-stopped lines (where the sense of the phrase or clause is completed at the end of each line). Like the architecture of Fairfax's estate, the poem is calm, regular, and orderly. It should be noted, however, that different readers will sometimes find somewhat different stress patterns in any given poetic line, though they will usually agree on the overall meter in the poem.

In a skilled poet's hands, the tetrameter line is a highly flexible medium and may be used for various purposes. Dialogue might seem to be difficult to fit into this relatively short line that is further crimped by end rhyme, but Jonathan Swift shows what can be done with it in the following passage from his "Verses on the Death of Dr. Swift" (1739). Here he imagines some of his friends talking just at the point of his passing away (he had been dean of St. Patrick's Cathedral in Dublin for many years):

> Behold the fatal day arrive!
> "How is the Dean?"—"He's just alive."
> Now the departing prayer is read.
> "He hardly breathes"—"The Dean is dead."
> Before the passing bell begun,
> The news through half the town has run.
> "Oh! may we all for death prepare!
> What has he left? And who's his heir?" (147–154)

The brief sentences in this passage suggest a breathless and not so pious suspense in the attitudes of those who are supposed to be his friends. Needless to say, it is a satiric portrait of the mock concern among these people who are anything but devastated by his death. Their real interest is brought out in the last line of the passage. The fragmented rhythm represents the events as they happen and as the people react in often breathless and urgent fashion.

Here the iambic tetrameter line clearly serves quite a different function than in the passage from Marvell.

The iambic pentameter line with its normal pattern of five stressed syllables allows the poet to develop his thought more fully. This is the line commonly used in more serious verse, at least in the two centuries we are surveying in this book. Few poets can match Samuel Johnson's use of this line in the "Vanity of Human Wishes" (1749) to sound the organ tones of doom as he surveys the social scene in contemporary England, but his criticism of the values dominant in the society around him should not seem unfamiliar to us today:

> For gold his sword the hireling ruffian draws,
> For gold the hireling judge distorts the laws;
> Wealth heaped on wealth, nor truth nor safety buys,
> The dangers gather as the treasures rise.   (25–28)

Through repetition, the inversion of normal word order, and an accumulation of examples, Johnson evokes the disastrous effects of greed joined with prosperity. The first two lines of the passage are regular iambic pentameter, while the last two lines contain variations that help suggest his dark vision of England. The metrical stresses on both "wealths" as well as on "heaped" provide special emphasis on the corruptive power of riches being piled up for their own sake. Johnson's tone and focus are much different from Swift, though both are effective satirists.

One special example of the pentameter line is worth mentioning. John Milton uses it in *Paradise Lost* (1674), but without the end rhyme. This is called blank verse, or unrhymed iambic pentameter, the kind of verse Shakespeare uses in most of his plays because of the greater freedom it gave him to develop his dialogue. Milton employs it for everything in his great epic, from dialogue to narrative, from description to prophetic laments, satiric portraits, and lyric celebration. In the following passage Milton describes Satan's inner turmoil as he prepares to seduce human beings away from obedience to God's commands. Satan, the fallen angel, cannot help but reflect on his glorious past and his sad present as he goes to spoil God's most recent creation. Thus, as he muses,

>   horror and doubt distract
> His troubled thoughts, and from the bottom stir
> The Hell within him, for within him Hell
> He brings, and round about him, nor from Hell

One step no more than from himself can fly
By change of place: now conscience wakes despair
That slumbered, wakes the bitter memory
Of what he was, what is, and what must be
Worse; of worse deeds worse sufferings must ensue.   (4: 18–26)

Note how Milton uses run-on lines (where the sense moves on to the next line without stopping) to mirror the chain of torturing thoughts that cascade through Satan's mind as he contemplates what he is about to do and feels the Hell within him. Milton's complex psychological portrait of this once magnificent being, a former archangel who cannot escape what he once was and is still subject to the call of conscience and even despair, is remarkable. The lines are less regular metrically than Johnson's, though the iambic pattern is still dominant. Because of its flexibility, blank verse is one of the most important poetic forms in English, used by practically all our great poets as well as by many lesser ones.

Two other important aspects of rhythm may be noted: the caesura, or pause in the movement, and the end-stopped or run-on lines. These may seem like trivial details, but poets consciously work with them to enhance their meaning. The pause may be a full stop, as with a period, or a slight slowing down, as with a comma. Some lines from Alexander Pope's *Rape of the Lock* may be considered to illustrate both the pause and the end-stopping. Near the beginning of the poem the poet describes the scene as Belinda, a beautiful society girl and "heroine" of the story, awakes from sleep on the fateful day:

Sol through white curtains shot a timorous ray,
And oped those eyes that must eclipse the day.
Now lapdogs give themselves the rousing shake,
And sleepless lovers, just at twelve, awake.   (13–16)

The sun seems only to dare a timid ray to intrude on the sleeping beauty since it presumably knows that it will soon be outshone by her brilliant eyes. Note that the sense continues to the end of each of the first three lines without a pause. These are firmly end-stopped. In the fourth line, however, there are two slight pauses with the commas around a short phrase. Why does Pope make this interjection stand out? Probably because he wants the reader to note that the lovers are waking up at twelve noon, which is obviously very late, and perhaps will make us realize that the lovers are really sleeping very well, not "sleepless." He underscores this because the world he is describing

is one of late-night parties and late awakenings, not one of many significant
responsibilities or regular daily obligations. This is Belinda's world, and she
fits right in, to her eventual detriment. Pope wishes to satirize this world,
though not harshly, because he wants the reader to see the moral consequences of living such a life. There is much more of this as the poem proceeds, but we can see him beginning to set the tone early on.

On the other hand, some poets like to slow down the movement of the
verse for other effects. Ben Jonson is notable for using a much slower paced
line, as he does in the following passage from "Inviting a Friend to Supper,"
where he describes some of the food he will serve if his friend will only join
him. The poet pulls out all the stops to entice him:

> Yet shall you have, to rectify your palate,
>   An olive, capers, or some better salad
> Ushering the mutton; with a short-legged hen,
>   If we can get her, full of eggs, and then
> Lemons and wine for sauce; to these, a <u>coney</u>   *rabbit*
>   Is not to be despaired of for our money;
> And though fowl now be scarce, yet there are <u>clerks</u>,   *scholars*
>   The sky not falling, think we may have larks.
> I'll tell you of more, and lie, so you will come...   (9–17)

Only one line is not interrupted by a caesura, and several have two. Three
lines are run-on (10, 12, and 13), stopping not at the end of the line but in
the middle. All these give a somewhat choppy rhythm to his lines, in contrast to the smooth flow of Pope's. Jonson, here, does this to emphasize the
different types of food he will serve and to sound more colloquial, like a real
human voice that is describing a special banquet. There is definitely humor
in the exaggerated delicacies he suggests are possible, but they reflect the
strong desire on the poet's part to have his friend with him this evening, as does
the fact that he will go to any length, including lying, to lure him. Jonson
goes on to tempt him further with the promise of an intellectual feast, with
readings from classical authors and a free discussion of ideas to go along with
the food. They will pursue their conversation with moderation, innocence,
and delight, he urges, and thus will not have to worry about the consequences
tomorrow. This is the humanist ideal of shared pleasure in the discussion and
exchange of ideas over a meal, which Jonson evokes in part through the slow
and thoughtful movement of the lines.

Most readers are probably aware that poems are often classified according
to their overall form or genre. Thus, a poem is called an ode if it celebrates

a public (or sometimes special private) event, either with a formal, elaborate structure (like the odes of Pindar, an ancient Greek poet) or with a relatively simple, straightforward structure (like those of Horace, an ancient Latin poet). Occasionally, poets will themselves identify their poem with a certain type, as Gray does with his "Elegy Written in a Country Churchyard." The elegy was a common type of poem, often formal and elaborate like the ode and reflecting about life, generally written to commemorate someone who had recently died. One of the most popular poetic forms in the late Elizabethan period was the sonnet. It was a fourteen-line poem in iambic pentameter usually about love, and came in two main types. The first was the English (or Shakespearean) with its three quatrains (rhyming *abab cdcd efef*) and a couplet (*gg*). The other was the Italian (or Petrarchan) with its division into two parts, the octave (rhyming *abba abba*) and the sestet (rhyming *cdecde* or *cdcdcd*). We will see in sonnets by Donne and Milton how the poet adapts the structure of his form to the sense and the development of the imagery, the rhythm, and other poetic features. There are, of course, many other kinds of poems, like the epic, the ballad, and the epigram, along with a number of variants and subgenres (like the pastoral elegy), which may be found defined and illustrated in collections of literary terms (e.g., M. H. Abrams, *A Glossary of Literary Terms* and, more comprehensively, William Harmon and C. Hugh Holman, *A Handbook to Literature*). These forms provide structure and discipline to the poets in developing their subjects, challenging them to see if they can compose something meaningful and worthwhile within their confines.

Finally, a few practical suggestions for reading poetry are in order. A poem should always be read at least three times before you make a definite judgment about it. The first time through you discover its subject and something of the poet's attitude toward it. The second time you begin to understand what the poet has done to organize and develop the subject. The third time you should be able to assess the whole in the light of what you have discovered about it, to see it clearly and accurately, even though some of the details may remain obscure. An annotated edition or a reference book may help with the obscurities. Reading a few poems carefully is generally more satisfying than reading many that you only partially, if at all, understand. Worthwhile poems will amply repay and reward such patient attention.

Figures of speech, poetic voice and situation, language, imagery and symbols, and rhythm and rhyme are just a few of the elements of poetry that will help you understand and appreciate it more fully. They are not difficult concepts and should enable practically anyone to read all poetry, old or new, with pleasure and insight. As we consider various poets and a few of their poems from the seventeenth and eighteenth centuries, we will discuss these elements as they appear in each work. The interpretations offered here are not meant to be exhaustive or definitive. They are starting points, designed to provide a general framework or point of view for further individual exploration and analysis, a process that can continue for a lifetime. Part of the joy of poetry is in the continual discovery of its different facets the more one reads and reflects on it.

Readers should realize, moreover, that poets are not always perfectly clear, but can be ambiguous or elusive, sometimes on purpose as they try to imitate the ambiguity or complexity of life itself. Part of their brilliance may be to suggest the contradictoriness of human beings who live their lives from day to day with little thought of being consistent or coherent. Poets may depict other characters, or themselves (or their feelings), sometimes fully and with many sides and sometimes simply and baldly, without offering clear-cut or definitive answers to the questions they raise. But if poets are allowed to speak in their fullness to us through their works, they will help sharpen our understanding of human nature and, in the process, give us great pleasure in their handling of language, form, and ideas. The poets that follow offer a feast of linguistic, psychological, and imaginative delight, even in their dark or gloomy poems. Some are solid and meaty, others are light and refreshing, sweet or sour or even intoxicating. All tastes should find something to satisfy themselves. Enjoy!

CHAPTER 2

John Donne (1572–1631):
Poet of Secular and Sacred Love

To begin with, a little background will be helpful to put the poets and their poetry in perspective. Our story begins in 1572 when the first two poets we will consider, John Donne and Ben Jonson, were born in or near London. Queen Elizabeth ruled England, after succeeding to the throne in 1558 on the death of her half sister Mary. Mary had attempted to reinstate Catholicism by force in England, but Elizabeth led the country to adopt a compromise in the ongoing struggle between Catholicism and Protestantism that made up the Reformation. Taking elements from both religious traditions to form the Church of England, the queen and her bishops managed to resolve at least temporarily the disputed issues, though conflict continued to simmer just below the surface. Elizabeth eventually became one of the most revered monarchs in her nation's history, especially after the decisive victory of her navy over the Spanish armada in 1588, when the Spanish tried to reclaim England for the Catholic Church. Just a few years after this event, in the early 1590s, William Shakespeare emerged as one of the country's leading dramatists, helping to establish the public theater, a recent creation, as one of the central cultural institutions of the age. Though some of the luster of Elizabeth's reign had dimmed by the time of her death in 1603, the Elizabethan Age, with its growing sense of national identity, its new prominence in Europe, and its flourishing literary scene, remains one of the high points in English history.

It was a dynamic, confident time for the English, who were sending their merchant ships around the world and plundering Spanish ships returning from the New World with gold and goods. Though no one had been officially designated her successor when Elizabeth died, the political leaders of the time invited the Scottish king, James, Elizabeth's cousin (with whom they had been in correspondence for several years), to become their monarch, since the queen had never married and had no direct heir. At first James I was a popular king, especially after the discovery of the Gunpowder Plot in 1605, in which several men led by some Catholic militants tried to blow up Parliament on the day that the king was to open its first session in the fall. The conspirators had secretly moved some thirty-six barrels of gunpowder into the basement of the Houses of Parliament where all the political leaders of England would be assembled. A lesser member of the conspiracy, Guy Fawkes, was left to guard the cache of explosives, but the night before Parliament was to meet, the plot was discovered and the conspirators were arrested. Several were tried and executed for their attempted terrorist act. This incident set off a wave of anti-Catholic feeling in England, and ever since, England has celebrated Guy Fawkes Day, November 5, as one of their most important holidays, with fireworks and bonfires.

James's popularity, however, did not last, since he began to govern more and more through favorites, and less and less through Parliament, which kept antagonizing him with objections to his policies and practices, especially his belief in the divine right of kings. James also alienated his new subjects by spending lavishly on his favorites, on entertainment, and on hunting, despite being deep in debt. Moreover, he foolishly tried to bring a rapprochement with Spain by opening negotiations for his son to marry the Spanish princess, despite the English people's deep mistrust of that Catholic nation. The Puritans, the more rigorous wing of the Protestants, were gradually gaining strength in England, although some were leaving to go to other lands, including the New World, where they sought to establish their own way of life and live free of religious persecution. When James's son Charles became king in 1625 on his father's death, he tried to strengthen the high church wing (the more Catholic side) of the Anglican Church under Bishop Laud, and he married a French princess (still Catholic, however) instead of a Spanish one. After objecting to Parliament's Petition of Right (1628) that demanded he respect the traditional laws against arbitrary seizure and martial law, Charles attempted to rule without Parliament, because of its increasingly vehement opposition to his schemes for special taxes and his plans for the Church. Charles's relationship to his country gradually deteriorated until military conflict became inevitable. Our first two poets, Donne and Jonson, however, died before the worst had come to pass.

John Donne began life as the son of a prosperous London merchant who died when he was only four. His mother, a strong Catholic and daughter of

John Heywood, a well-known writer and dramatist, and granddaughter of Sir Thomas More, the former Chancellor of England who was beheaded by Henry VIII, brought up her son in her own church. Donne, however, after much soul-searching, eventually renounced his family's religion when he came to adulthood. As a young boy, he was an excellent student, going to Oxford University at the age of 12 (not an unusual age at the time) and possibly Cambridge later, as well as Lincoln's Inn, one of the law schools of the time. Donne did not become a professional poet, since he could not gain a livelihood that way unless, like Shakespeare, he wrote for the theater. Donne actually published only a few poems during his lifetime, but circulated copies of his many works in manuscript to his friends, a common practice of the time. He also served in a couple of military expeditions against the Spanish at Cádiz and in the Azores in 1596 and 1597 along with a number of young English bloods and returned to England in late 1599 to become secretary to Sir Thomas Egerton, Lord Keeper of the Great Seal, one of the highest political positions in the land. In 1601 Donne secretly married Egerton's niece, forcing Sir Thomas to dismiss him as a result of this serious breach of social ethics, which caused Donne to be arrested and briefly imprisoned. This effectively ended Donne's chance for higher public service, as he discovered afterwards in seeking different positions. Donne dearly loved his wife, who bore him many children, but they lived in relative poverty and difficult circumstances for a good many years. Finally, in 1615 Donne, at the urging of King James and others, became a clergyman in the Church of England, then dean of St. Paul's Cathedral (in 1621), and eventually one of the most famous preachers in London. To Donne's great sorrow, his wife died in 1617 after giving birth to a stillborn child (they had had twelve children that lived at least for some time). After having been seriously ill for several weeks and having given his final sermon at court, Donne died on March 31, 1631, and was buried in St. Paul's Cathedral. His poetry was first published in a collected edition by his son John two years later.

Though much admired as a poet by his friends and peers in the society of his time, Donne was little read during the eighteenth and nineteenth centuries because of his occasional obscurities, his penchant for extravagant images, and his sometimes harsh and irregular verses. He came back into favor in the early twentieth century with the support of poets like T. S. Eliot and other modernists. Since then, he has maintained his position as one of the most admired poets in English literature. Donne's characteristic poetic voice consists in developing subtle, witty arguments in support of his theme, introducing unusual images and figures of speech (or "conceits" as they are called), imagining dramatic situations, and employing colloquial language that was rarely chosen for its beauty or musicality. Early on, his poems were often meant to shock and astonish rather than to please. As befitting the young man about town that he was in the 1590s, Donne's early poetry centers on love in all its forms: physical, cynical, and ideal. He rejected the conventional strain of Elizabethan love poetry in order to inject new life and vigor into it. As Samuel Johnson said in a famous passage, in Donne's love poems, the "most heterogeneous ideas are yoked by violence together" (*Lives of the Poets* 1: 14) to express various feelings and attitudes about it. Extremes of emotion and image are typical, as Donne explores many different themes and points of view in his poetry. He was a master of the baroque style, with its interest in emotion, in extravagant images, and in theatrical encounters. He is often identified as the first and greatest of the Metaphysical Poets, so-called because of their apparent concern with philosophical ideas and figures of speech drawn from esoteric fields. Donne can be difficult, especially in his language and conceits, but, in his finest poems, he remains delightfully imaginative and amusingly bold and passionate. As a result, his poems can still be read with pleasure and fascination today.

One of his earlier poems is called simply "Song." It is better known by its first line, "Go and catch a falling star," and provides a good introduction to Donne's work since it is relatively straightforward and clear. A song, of course, needs to be fairly simple in order to be understood by its audience, but Donne's poem contrasts in attitude with many of the other songs written in the Renaissance that express in conventional ways either the delight or pains of love or the sorrow of death. This poem was probably set to a melody that already existed, since Donne himself was not a composer. The speaker first addresses an unidentified listener with a series of suggested tasks:

> Go and catch a falling star,
>   Get with child a mandrake root,
> Tell me where all past years are,
>   Or who cleft the Devil's foot,
> Teach me to hear mermaids singing,
> Or to keep off envy's stinging,
>   And find
>   What wind
> Serves to advance an honest mind.   (1–9)

These tasks, it soon becomes clear, are all impossible, even absurd. No one could possibly catch a falling star nor could a mandrake root, though it is forked like the two legs of a human being, ever give birth to a child. Envy exists, of course, but we cannot control or eliminate our "stinging" feelings over the success of others or discover the "wind" that will propel a good person to be rewarded on his or her merits. Everyone knows that such a wind does not exist, that goodness is never properly honored or honesty often rewarded. The stanza concludes on a strong note of cynicism, leaving us to wonder if the poet will continue in this vein or modify it.

In the second stanza the speaker imagines more impossibilities. He addresses a listener who may have special powers to see the invisible and to ride practically forever searching the world for uncommon sights:

> If thou beest born to strange sights,
>   Things invisible to see,
> Ride ten thousand days and nights,
>   Till age snow white hairs on thee,
> Thou, when thou return'st, wilt tell me
> All strange wonders that befell thee,
>   And swear
>   No where
> Lives a woman true, and fair.   (10–18)

Even such a person, the speaker declares, despite his extraordinary powers, will never discover a woman who is both beautiful and faithful. The cynicism clearly continues, though his subject has changed. Even if you make a superhuman effort at exploring the world and lose your youth in the search, the poet maintains, it will be futile to try to find a perfect woman. Note the way he focuses on the absolute confidence that the explorer has in his failure in the short lines where he will "swear" that such a woman can never be found. The short lines and the rhyme underscore this confidence by giving emphasis to the meaning. Thus a pattern has been established. Will the third stanza confirm it?

A change does occur. The speaker actually admits the possibility that such a woman might be found:

> If thou find'st one, let me know,
>   Such a pilgrimage were sweet;
> Yet do not, I would not go,
>   Though at next door we might meet;
> Though she were true when you met her,
> And last till you write your letter,
>   Yet she
>   Will be
> False, ere I come, to two, or three.   (19–27)

But even as the poet raises the possibility, he dismisses it because he believes such fidelity cannot last. In fact, this seemingly perfect woman will be unfaithful several times before he arrives, even if she is nearby. The door is thus slammed shut on the hope in constancy, the sweetness of making a pilgrimage to the shrine of some good and true woman is denied, and the triumph of fickleness is confirmed. No such truly good woman exists or ever will.

But let us not take the poem too seriously. Donne, I believe, is not writing from his heart, but playing with one of the traditional themes of love poetry, the inconstancy of women. Their assumed constancy, he claims, is completely illusory, and he illustrates this idea with fanciful images embodied in a compact stanzaic pattern (note the repeated rhyme scheme and varying line lengths, especially the two lines of two syllables each) that is his own creation. This is Donne the man-about-town being witty and provocative in a conventional form, treating love in a kind of libertine fashion.

Another poem in a similar vein is "The Flea." It is also a dramatic monologue in which the situation is more specific than in the previous poem and the drama more immediate. It has quite a different point than "Song," but it still reflects a libertine poetic tradition. Many poets had written about fleas because they represent an insect associated with love. Fleas were common at the time since personal cleanliness was difficult to achieve, given the conditions of life then. Baths were considered unhealthy if not dangerous because of the lack of heat and running water in homes and the prevalence of dirty water. The occasional bath was the norm. Hence, poets wrote about fleas that may have visited parts of their beloved's body to which they had no access. The speaker here is talking with his mistress about a flea he has just observed:

> Mark but this flea, and mark in this,
> How little that which thou deniest me is;
> Me it sucked first, and now sucks thee,
> And in this flea our two bloods mingled be;
> Thou know'st that this cannot be said
> A sin, or shame, or loss of maidenhead,
>   Yet this enjoys before it woo,
>   And pampered swells with one blood made of two,
>   And this, alas, is more than we would do.   (1–9)

The flea has bitten him and now is biting her. The speaker points out that the effect is the same as if they had made love together. (It was a common belief at that time that blood was mixed during intercourse.) Since there is no shame in the flea's actions, he reasons, why could they not do the same? In response to his urging, his beloved had apparently raised the objection that it would be a sin. So, although it is a dramatic monologue with only one voice speaking, a dialogue is implied. The speaker, clearly, is developing a clever argument for seduction against his lady's protestations. It is logical, witty, and utterly specious. How does his beloved react to it?

We see what she starts to do from the words of the speaker in the second stanza. His voice is urgent when he says:

> Oh stay, three lives in one flea spare,
> Where we almost, nay more than married are.
> This flea is you and I, and this
> Our marriage bed and marriage temple is;
> Though parents grudge, and you, we are met,
> And cloistered in these living walls of <u>jet</u>.   *black*
>   Though <u>use</u> make you apt to kill me,   *habit*
>   Let not to that, self-murder added be,
>   And sacrilege, three sins in killing three.   (10–18)

His mistress is about to kill the flea when he urges her to stop and consider the consequences. They, too, will be killed if she proceeds to action since their blood is mixed in the flea, which embodies their sacred tie. There is nothing she can do about the fact that they are married in the flea, even though she and her parents may object. In fact, he claims it would be "sacrilege" for her to do it since their relationship has been consecrated. Of course this is complete nonsense since their union has not been blessed, but the speaker is mainly concerned with developing a witty, pseudo-logical argument to support his case for seduction.

Does this argument deter his mistress? Not at all. The next stanza opens with the speaker's "emotional" reaction to her bloody act of squashing the flea:

> Cruel and sudden, hast thou since
> Purpled thy nail in blood of innocence?
> Wherein could this flea guilty be,
> Except in that drop which it sucked from thee?
> Yet thou triumph'st, and say'st that thou
> Find'st not thy self nor me the weaker now;
>   'Tis true; then learn how false fears be:
>   Just so much honor, when thou yield'st to me,
>   Will waste, as this flea's death took life from thee.   (19–27)

Note the way the speaker begins with his characterization of his mistress's brutal act against the "innocence" of the poor flea, and couches his reprimand as a question. But she proclaims, according to him, that her act has not harmed either one of them, morally or physically. So he, perhaps unexpectedly, agrees with her, since this shows that making love will have the same result: neither honor nor life will be damaged by it.

The pleasure in the poem lies in the witty way in which the poet develops his argument for seduction starting from a commonplace situation. It is dramatically rendered in the voice of the speaker, and is embodied in a three-stanza poem with a regular rhyme scheme and alternating line lengths. Despite the structural requirements of such a form, Donne manages to make the voice sound real and colloquial. The last three lines inset with their triple rhyme give greater emphasis to his argument, but this only makes it seem more absurd, not serious. It is a poem in which we can appreciate the craft and cleverness, but not one that is meant to proclaim a serious moral philosophy. It is, clearly, chiefly designed to provoke and amuse.

Donne's attitude toward love, even in his early poems, was not always what we have witnessed in these first two works. "The Sun Rising" illustrates just the opposite in fact, the exaltation of love. It takes the form of a salute-to-the-dawn poem that may be found in many collections of love poems of the time. In these, the poet usually greets the dawn warmly at the beginning of another day in which he will again see his beloved. Donne's opening is strikingly different from the usual one:

> Busy old fool, unruly sun,
>   Why dost thou thus
> Through windows and through curtains call on us?
> Must to thy motions lovers' seasons run?
>   Saucy pedantic wretch, go chide
>   Late schoolboys and sour prentices,
>   Go tell court huntsmen that the King will ride,
>   Call country ants to harvest offices;
> Love, all alike, no season knows nor clime,
> Nor hours, days, months, which are the rags of time.   (1–10)

Donne begins abruptly by insulting the sun. Instead of celebrating the beauty of the dawn in conventional terms, the poet chides the sun for shining too bright and interrupting his amours. With great scorn, he says for it to go elsewhere and bother others who are more bound by its rules. Love, he claims, is not subject to duty, weather, or time. The insults the speaker hurls at the sun and the images he evokes of the people who are ruled by the hours of the day, including reluctant boys on their way to school and apprentices unhappy with their work or their masters, indicate the proud defiance he feels at this intrusion, and are summed up in his dismissal of the "rags of time." Such a metaphor forcefully communicates the speaker's contempt. This was a new and striking voice to appear in English poetry, yet one that finds expression within a carefully constructed stanzaic structure with its alternating rhyme and closing couplet. The poem is not the result, clearly, of simple spontaneous combustion.

The second stanza repeats the structure of the first and continues the speaker's diatribe against the sun in the same vein. He dismisses the sun in images equally extravagant and boastful:

> Thy beams, so reverend and strong
>   Why shouldst thou think?
> I could eclipse and cloud them with a wink,
> But that I would not lose her sight so long;
>   If her eyes have not blinded thine,
>   Look, and tomorrow late, tell me,
> Whether both th' <u>Indias</u> of spice and mine   *both East and West*
>   Be where thou leftst them, or lie here with me.
> Ask for those kings whom thou saw'st yesterday,
> And thou shalt hear, All here in one bed lay.   (11–20)

The speaker asserts that the sun's rays are not nearly as powerful as he or others think; they do not even compare to his beloved's eyes, which can blind the sun. Both the valuable spices of East India and the gold of the West Indies are concentrated with him in the person of his beloved. Moreover, all the power of the monarchs that the sun has passed on his day's journey is, in fact, centered with him in the bed where they lie. The exaggeration is amusing, yet serious, in that it suggests the glorious strength of his love.

The third and last stanza confirms this claim. In it the speaker extolls his love beyond everything else in the world:

> She is all states, and all princes I,
>   Nothing else is.
> Princes do but play us; compared to this,
> All honor's mimic, all wealth alchemy.
>   Thou, sun, art half as happy as we,
>   In that the world's contracted thus;
>   Thine age asks ease, and since thy duties be

To warm the world, that's done in warming us.
Shine here to us, and thou art everywhere;
This bed thy center is, these walls thy sphere.   (21–30)

The images here reflect the grandiose ideas the speaker lends his love, giving each of them the highest rank in the political and social realms; still, he and his love transcend them all. We should recall that Donne's world was highly stratified, and class standing was a serious matter based on complicated rules of genealogy and family connection, though the accumulation or loss of wealth, education, and political office could change traditional rankings. Social and political rank, however, was never gained by simple self-assertion, especially for love. The poet does not stop there, but goes on to claim that he and his beloved embody the whole world, that all other values are fake, that their happiness is supreme, and that nothing else matters or even exists. It is extravagant and amusing, with the lovers' bed at the center of the universe and the source of all good in life. Since this represents a new structure to the universe, the speaker changes his attitude toward the sun at the end of the poem, inviting him to "shine here to us" to warm and light up the whole world with much less effort. It is, no doubt, chiefly physical love the poet is celebrating, but his praise goes beyond that to exalt the wonder and power of sublime devotion with a pseudo-metaphysical justification. This is exaggeration taken to new heights.

We should note, however, that the poet has not lost control over his materials, despite the strength of his passion. The poem is a carefully crafted whole, with a repeated pattern of varying line lengths and similar rhyme scheme (*abbacdcdee*) in each of the three ten-line stanzas. The couplet at the end of each stanza provides a neat closure to that unit's thought and feeling. The whole poem makes a delightful, witty, and resounding case for love's glory.

Donne makes a more subdued, yet no less effective, case for love in his "A Valediction: Forbidding Mourning." Here the speaker bids farewell to his beloved, as he leaves on a voyage that will clearly take him from her for some months, if not longer. This poem may have been written for his wife as Donne prepared to go to the continent, but we do not know this for certain. He opens the poem with a simile involving dying:

As virtuous men pass mildly away,
    And whisper to their souls to go,
Whilst some of their sad friends do say
    The breath goes now, and some say, No;

So let us melt, and make no noise,
   No tear-floods, nor sigh-tempests move;
'Twere <u>profanation</u> of our joys   *desecration*
   To tell the laity our love.

Moving of th'earth brings harms and fears,
   Men reckon what it did and meant;
But <u>trepidation</u> of the spheres,   *oscillation*
   Though greater far, is <u>innocent</u>.   *does no harm*
                                                (1–12)

In the Renaissance, the virtuous were thought to die quiet, easy deaths, whereas sinners were thought to die violent, painful deaths. Here the good are eager to escape this life and find their home in heaven. Back on earth the mourners are not sure if the dying person has actually passed away, such is the quiet coming of death in this case. The second stanza makes clear that a particular speaker is addressing his beloved. In addition, the subject of the comparison becomes explicit: we should follow the example of the virtuous and separate in silence without any overt display of sorrow or mourning. At this point we cannot be sure if the poet is talking about death. But there is the definite suggestion of their sharing in the worship of love, of which they are the priests while others are the outsiders, the "laity." They must keep their devotion secret and not expose it to the world that cannot understand it. "Profanation" suggests sacrilege, a violation of something sacred if they do talk about their love, a revelation to avoid if at all possible. It was often assumed that love would be destroyed if it were made public. In the third stanza the speaker brings up a contrast between earthquakes, which can cause tremendous damage and make people wonder why God is angry with them, and the movement of the celestial spheres in the old (Ptolemaic) astronomy, which has little impact on the earth. Though the latter is a cosmic motion, it occurs as part of the normal operation of the heavens and is not destructive or dangerous. Thus, he implies, we should not fear our temporary separation on earth.

   In the next three stanzas the speaker further develops the kind of love they share, as he continues to reassure his beloved. The speaker begins with a contrasting kind or negative example:

Dull <u>sublunary</u> lovers' love   *earthly*
   (Whose soul is sense) cannot admit
Absence, because it doth remove
   Those things which <u>elemented</u> it.   *composed*

But we, by a love so much refined
  That our selves know not what it is,
Inter-assurèd of the mind,   *mutually confident*
  Care less, eyes, lips, and hands to miss.

Our two souls therefore, which are one,
  Though I must go, endure not yet
A breach, but an expansion,
  Like gold to airy thinness beat.   (13–24)

In the first of these stanzas the speaker shows contempt for those whose love
is wholly based on sensory impressions. Such a love cannot last, like everything beneath the moon ("sublunary"), which is subject to the constant
changes in that celestial body. In the Renaissance it was believed that all things
on earth were continually in flux, in contrast to the rest of the universe, which
was permanent and stable. A love that depends upon sight and touch will not
survive when these are absent. Their love, the speaker proclaims, is not
affected by such purely physical elements, even though they hardly understand this themselves. They still feel their love's depth and lasting power even
beyond physical nearness. Thus, the speaker concludes that their separation
will not matter to them because their souls will still be irretrievably linked; the
connection will be stretched, perhaps, but it will not break. The simile of
beaten gold suggests the value of their love as well as its enduring quality in
the event of distancing. Through a simple, but highly effective concrete image,
the speaker confidently maintains that their unity in love cannot be broken.

The last three stanzas develop one of the most famous similes in English
poetry, and cap the speaker's argument about their two souls:

If they be two, they are two so
  As stiff twin compasses are two;
Thy soul, the fixed foot, makes no show
  To move, but doth, if th'other do.

And though it in the center sit,
  Yet when the other far doth roam,
It leans and hearkens after it,
  And grows erect, as that comes home.

Such wilt thou be to me, who must,
  Like th'other foot, obliquely run;
Thy firmness makes my circle just,
  And makes me end where I begun.   (25–36)

If our souls are separate to any degree, the speaker says, they are like the legs of a draftsman's compass that work in tandem. As the one extends out to make a geometrical figure, the other remains stationary at home, but "leans" in sympathy with its partner. As the moving leg returns to its center, the fixed leg returns to its more confident, strong vertical position. The speaker applies this comparison to their relationship in the last stanza, noting how the strength of the stationary leg draws the moving leg back to it, creating a perfect circle of unity and wholeness. This simile, a quiet kind of conceit that provides a concrete analog to the couple's close relationship, captures their love's essence in its depth and strength, enabling it to endure despite separation and distance. If this poem was written for his wife, as seems likely, it should have offered her some substantial comfort in Donne's absence.

The language of this poem is, for Donne, relatively simple and straightforward. So is the four-line stanza with its alternating rhyme scheme and the generally end-stopped octosyllabic lines. The images, too, are, for the most part, clear and down-to-earth, though somewhat unusual. They celebrate love, without sighs or tears and despite an imminent, though temporary, break. It is a picture of calm but deep affection in striking and memorable images. For many, this represents Donne at his best.

The next step in Donne's career was into the church, and, though he wrote less poetry at this time, he still composed some religious poems worthy of attention. Before he took holy orders, Donne had already written several notable ones. One group of these consists of the Holy Sonnets, a series of fourteen-line poems that treat topics like sin and death from a very personal standpoint, using techniques developed by religious writers to meditate on aspects of Christianity in order to understand it more fully. Such techniques emphasize the use of the imagination to grasp concretely Christ's death on the cross, or to raise specific questions about the nature of sin or divine judgment and forgiveness. Donne himself had been raised as a Catholic and was probably familiar with these devotional and educational exercises designed to enhance and deepen one's faith. Here Donne employs them within the sonnet form, which heretofore, as written by Edmund Spenser, Sir Philip Sidney, and William Shakespeare among others, had been primarily used to explore secular love. Donne's Holy Sonnets sometimes depict an individual struggling with his faith or with his sinful nature, and at other times they assert the power of God's love and mercy. They retain many of the features of his secular poems but direct our attention to more spiritual matters.

Among the Holy Sonnets, one of the best known is No. 10 (No. 6 in Helen Gardner's sequence), an address to Death, probably composed with the others in 1609–1610. The speaker begins by boldly challenging the personified figure of Death directly. Here is the entire poem:

> Death, be not proud, though some have callèd thee
> Mighty and dreadful, for thou art not so;
> For those whom thou think'st thou dost overthrow
> Die not, poor Death, nor yet canst thou kill me.
> From rest and sleep, which but thy pictures be,
> Much pleasure; then from thee much more must flow,
> And soonest our best men with thee do go,
> Rest of their bones, and soul's delivery.
> Thou art slave to fate, chance, kings, and desperate men,
> And dost with poison, war, and sickness dwell,
> And <u>poppy</u> or charms can make us sleep as well   *opium*
> And better than thy stroke; why swell'st thou then?
> One short sleep past, we wake eternally
> And death shall be no more; Death, thou shalt die.   (1–14)

Once again Donne employs a dramatic monologue as he confronts the usually terrifying specter of Death. Beginning the poem with four stressed syllables in a row (two spondees), the speaker boldly tells Death that he is not nearly as powerful and fearsome as commonly described. In fact, he cannot really kill anyone, the speaker maintains, despite appearances to the contrary, including himself. The speaker's attitude toward Death is not only exceedingly brash but quite condescending as well, as he calls Death "poor" to suggest its foolish pride and real weakness. Death makes no reply to the speaker here or in the rest of the poem; only the speaker's point of view is presented. The first quatrain, then, presents a radical challenge to the menacing traditional figure of the Grim Reaper. How can the poet make such an audacious assertion?

The second quatrain begins his explanation and defense. He opens the argument by asserting that because the similar experiences of "rest and sleep" give humans pleasure and necessary respite, so death must do so even more because it is only another form of sleep. To treat Death as a form of sleep was a common metaphor found in the Bible as well as in other poems. This connection is confirmed for the poet by the fact that the best people, in their final hours, are often eager to die in order to find peace and salvation. Deliverance from the prison of the body frees humans from their physical limitations and suffering. Death, therefore, must be good, not the evil it is usually considered.

In the third quatrain the speaker asserts that Death's position as the "slave" of all sorts of unsavory characters and forces, from criminals to war and disease, makes him far less worthy of fear and awe than normally suggested. Moreover, the poet claims that drugs and magic can make us sleep better than Death can, so he has no reason to be proud. The speaker's arguments have sometimes been called into question because of his refusal to accept death as a serious human problem and because of the manner of his treatment of death. His "triumphal brassiness," as one reader has put it (Sanders, p. 115), makes it difficult to take the speaker or his fanciful claims seriously. But is not this tone of celebration another example of Donne's love of extravagant claims and pseudo-logic, here to affirm a fundamental Christian belief? Donne deliberately ignores the negative aspects of death, from the suffering and anxiety it can cause to the sinfulness that may damn us eternally, to dwell on the positive side of the ledger. And, according to the Bible and church tradition, Christ's sacrifice and resurrection are a sublime victory over Death, making it essentially powerless. Donne's boldness is, in reality, a witty and provocative assertion of this Christian teaching.

In the couplet that closes the poem the speaker confirms his argument by noting that death is only a "short sleep," a brief nap in the whole reach of time, and once the time for the Last Judgment arrives, we humans will wake to find eternal life. Thus, there will be no more death, so that, after briefly considering death as an idea, the poet turns again in the last half of the last line to the personified Death to address him most emphatically with the stark, unequivocal message that he will die. This paradox, of course, comes from the Bible (see 1 Cor. 15:26), and as such it contains an ultimate truth for Donne. The final four syllables at the end are all stressed (two spondees again) and thus echo the stressed four at the beginning of the poem with the same essential message: Death is nothing to fear because its power is strictly limited. The speaker's clever diminishment of Death, however fancifully done, reminds us of this ultimate Christian reality. Our souls are immortal, and physical death leads to our eternal salvation and bliss with God. Death, however, is mortal and a consequence of sin (and by implication Satan), Donne stresses, while we may live forever in peace and joy. This theme, then, is not Donne's invention, but woven into the very fabric of Christian thought. His dramatization of it, however, is original and striking.

It is worth noting how Donne employs the sonnet structure to develop his argument. We have seen how he uses each quatrain to develop a single primary idea. Following previous poets like Sidney, he constructs a blended version of the Italian and English sonnet forms, with the sense following the English structure of three quatrains and a couplet, while the rhyme scheme is closer to the Italian form with its octave and sestet (rhyming *abbaabbacddcee*). Donne also likes to put pauses in the middle of his lines, reducing the impact of the rhyme at the end of the line and thus the sense of a rigid sonnet form. The firm conclusion is put emphatically within the couplet at the end of the poem, in which the poet underlines the ultimate paradox that is his central point, directing his final pointed remark at Death and its ultimate defeat. The unity and clarity of his message are thus exceptional. Donne's use of the sonnet form to create a sequence of serious religious poems about different aspects of a Christian's spiritual experience helped to make this form available for much more than love and passion. Over the years, the sonnet's brevity and compression have not been a serious limitation on its usefulness for practically any topic. Donne here (as in the other Holy Sonnets) employs it with typical virtuosity.

In December 1623 Donne became seriously ill with a fever that had been devastating parts of London. Although he nearly died, Donne managed to write several works at this time, including at least two poems that express his deeply felt religious convictions. One of his prose works was *Devotions upon Emergent Occasions*, a meditation that contains some of his most famous poetic passages, such as the one arguing that "No man is an island" and the one that suggests we are all beings "For Whom the Bell Tolls." One of the poems he wrote at this time was "A Hymn to God the Father," which he apparently had set to music and loved to hear performed in St. Paul's Cathedral. In it he focuses on his own feelings of guilt and remorse for his sins, and comes to a resolution that may surprise us, especially in some of the techniques he uses.

Donne begins this poem in his characteristic manner by addressing God directly and wondering if He will be able to forgive him all his sins:

> Wilt thou forgive that sin where I begun,
>   Which is my sin, though it were done before?
> Wilt thou forgive that sin through which I run,
>   And do run still, though still I do deplore?
>   When thou hast done, thou hast not done,
>   For I have more. (1–6)

Note that the speaker starts by accepting responsibility for Adam's sin, the original sin, committed long before he lived. This suggests that he assumes all humans have a corrupted nature, a standard Protestant belief. Humans are not born innocent but with a proclivity to sin (i.e., a natural tendency to disobey God's commands and follow their own desires). The speaker then admits that he commits his own sins, too, and wonders if God's forgiveness will extend to him. God, at this point, does not answer these questions with either reassurance or condemnation. And the poet says, perhaps surprisingly, that he is weak and will continue to sin, even though he "deplores" what he is doing. His knowledge that he is sinning, in fact, makes his actions all the more reprehensible. In the last two lines Donne says that his sinning will not stop, nor will his poem or God's mercy. Perhaps the reader has noticed that his use of "done" in line 5 echoes his own name. Could he be playing with it in such a seemingly serious poem? Is there a pattern here?

In the second stanza Donne continues his questioning of God. As in the first stanza the questions occupy the first four lines, one question to two lines:

> Wilt thou forgive that sin by which I have won
> Others to sin? and made my sin their door?
> Wilt thou forgive that sin which I did shun
> A year or two, but wallowed in a score?
>   When thou hast done, thou hast not done,
>   For I have more. (7–12)

These sins seem even worse than in the previous stanza, since they involve corrupting others, not just himself. In a simple but effective figure of speech, his own sin has acted as a door to lead others to sin. The speaker's second question involves sins he has fallen into after resisting them for a short time. In other words, he knew very well they were sins, and yet he could not refrain from indulging, even "wallowing in" them for many years. Again his knowledge of them as sins underscores his own sinfulness. The last two lines repeat those from the previous stanza, reemphasizing his hardened state of sin and confirming the use of his name in a pun. Apparently, Donne could play with his own name in all seriousness. Does he continue to do this in the last stanza?

Donne becomes even more specific about his sins in this last part, explaining what is perhaps his worst one:

> I have a sin of fear, that when I have spun
> My last thread, I shall perish on the shore;
> Swear by thy self, that at my death thy Son
> Shall shine as he shines now and heretofore;
>   And, having done that, thou hast done,
>   I fear no more. (13–18)

It is his fear of damnation that leads him to the brink of despair, to doubt of God's ultimate mercy for sinners. He employs both the classical image of one's life being spun like a thread by the three Fates (who spin it, twist it, and cut it) and the Christian image of the soul not being allowed to cross the water, a traditional image for one's final passage into heaven. His only hope is in Christ's redemptive power that may continue to shine for him and save him from such a terrible fate. Note that even at this point Donne uses a pun, when he has the "Son" shine to evoke his saving grace, a traditional play on words in Christian writers. The Son, after all, is the life-giving "sun," or medium of God's grace and mercy for humans.

The final two lines resolve the series of questions the poet has raised by affirming that God will continue to have Christ shine forth as Savior, that he (the poet) will be saved and end up with God in heaven, and that therefore he need fear no more. But one other possible pun must be mentioned. Donne's wife was Ann More, whose name he seems to evoke in the poem to suggest that his love for her might get in the way of his love for God until the last line, when he indicates that this human love should not keep him from salvation. It may seem extraordinary to us that he could play with names in this way in a poem that is about such a serious subject. But Donne enjoyed playing with language, like Shakespeare and other writers of this time, even in the most somber moments. Such cleverness surely does not cancel out the profound nature of the topic and its treatment.

Once again Donne reveals himself to be a poet deeply concerned with structure, language, and rhythm in developing his ideas in this poem. The six-line stanza provides a firm framework within which Donne treats his ideas and images with relative simplicity, yet still with originality, economy, and flair. We have seen that the last two lines make a kind of refrain, which he varies in the final stanza to close his poem on a positive note. The last line of each with its two stressed syllables in contrast to the four stresses in the preceding lines brings emphasis as well as closure. The rhyme scheme is extraordinary in having only two sounds used in alternating lines, yet it sounds natural, not strained. The whole poem is highly compact and unified in its theme, language, and imagery, revealing Donne at his skilled best.

Poetry at its most creative is craft as well as imagination, both of which Donne displays in these poems about love. He is at once original and traditional, using older forms and creating new ones, employing different voices over time with different tones and inflections, and displaying a mind that challenges, teases, surprises, and persuades us to various points of view and emotional responses. As we proceed through the other poets in this book, we will not encounter many who equal his ability in provoking and amusing us with a unique combination of wit, learning, insight, and depth of feeling. The others will have their own voices and themes, of course, but rarely will we find again the vigorous blend of intellect, passion, and poetic power that we see in John Donne.

CHAPTER 3

Ben Jonson (1572–1637): Elegist, Satirist, and Moralist

Donne's contemporary, Ben Jonson, was a product of Westminster, a city near London that was home to Parliament and the Court, as well as the famous abbey. Jonson's father, who died about a month before his birth, was a clergyman, but his mother married again, this time to a bricklayer. Jonson went to Westminster School, probably the best school in the country at the time, where he received an excellent classical education of which he was quite proud. He studied under the eminent scholar William Camden, to whom he later wrote a fine poetic tribute. Since his family was not well off, Jonson did not go on to university but was apprenticed to his step-father, in order to learn a skill and so provide for himself. Such training did not please Jonson for long; he soon left his apprenticeship to pursue a military career. In the early 1590s he fought with English troops in Flanders, where, according to his own account, he killed a man in single combat in front of both armies.

When Jonson returned to England, he married Anne Lewis and started a family, then joined the vibrant London theater scene as a journeyman actor. Shakespeare was, of course, the leading London playwright at the time, and, after attempting to act in a play or so, Jonson decided to try his hand at writing them. One of his first plays, *The Isle of Dogs* (now lost), caused him to be thrown in prison in 1595, apparently because of its possibly dangerous implications for the queen. In 1598 Jonson barely escaped hanging after he killed a fellow actor in a duel. Throughout his life he could be proud and quarrelsome, and often found himself in conflict with the authorities or other eminent people. Despite these difficulties Jonson persisted in composing plays and soon achieved his first dramatic success with an amusing satire called *Every Man in His Humor* (1598), which mocks various human eccentricities and foibles. It was put on by Shakespeare's company, the Lord Chamberlain's Men, with Shakespeare himself taking a role in it. Though Jonson never became a serious rival to Shakespeare as a popular playwright, he did write several highly successful comedies, including *Volpone* (1606) and *The Alchemist* (1610), which are still performed today. He also wrote masques for the Court and for wealthy noblemen, often in conjunction with Inigo Jones, a prominent architect and set designer. (Masques were dramatic spectacles with elaborate costumes, sets, music, and dancing for the private entertainment of the Court and nobility.)

In 1616 Jonson brashly published his *Works* in a large, carefully edited volume, something no poet had done before and considered by many as ridiculously pretentious. The volume included many poems as well as most of his plays, and implicitly laid a claim for Jonson as a writer of permanent literature. As a result, Jonson became the most celebrated literary figure in England at the time, its unofficial poet laureate and a pensioner of the king. Soon after, he became the center of a group of younger men and poets called the "Tribe of Ben," who met at the Devil's Tavern to discuss literature and other topics. Jonson continued to write poetry and produce plays, but his career gradually faded into obscurity. In 1628 he suffered a paralytic stroke that all but ended his physical activity, though he still wrote a few plays and poems that failed, however, to add much to his reputation or fortune. At his death in 1637 Jonson was poor, little regarded, and almost forgotten, having been confined to his house for nine years, while the country moved inexorably toward civil war. Jonson's few remaining friends, however, arranged to have him buried in Westminster Abbey and the next year brought out a volume of poetic tributes to him.

Given Jonson's deep involvement with the theater, it seems appropriate to look briefly at an example of the poetry in one of his plays. Like Shakespeare, Jonson composed much of his dramatic writing in blank verse, or unrhymed iambic pentameter. It was a flexible medium that he could adapt to different kinds of character and scene, and is the closest of any poetic form to normal speech, yet still retains lines with, generally, ten syllables in each along with the iambic pattern of stresses. *Volpone*, a satiric comedy that is one of his best plays, was performed with great success at the Globe by the King's Men, Shakespeare's company at the time (King James had officially adopted them on his succession to the throne). In it Jonson ridicules the power of greed to subvert goodness and innocence, using a kind of beast fable, where the characters are animals, or at least have the names and moral attributes of animals. The two central figures, Volpone (Italian for old fox), a wealthy

Venetian, and his servant Mosca (Italian for fly) dupe three greedy men, each of whom hopes to inherit Volpone's wealth through the good offices of Mosca, an exceptionally clever and unscrupulous rascal. In the first two acts the three dupes keep visiting Volpone, who pretends to be on his deathbed, to see how he is, bringing gifts for Mosca to ingratiate themselves with Volpone's servant. By the beginning of the third act Mosca has set up the three men to think they will gain great riches through him, but he reveals his true feelings in a soliloquy that is a classic example of hubris, or excessive pride. Here he speaks aloud to himself, so the audience can share his exultation over his apparent success:

> I fear I shall begin to grow in love
> With my dear self and my most prosperous <u>parts</u>,   *mental faculties*
> They do so spring and burgeon; I can feel
> A whimsy in my blood: I know not how,
> Success hath made me wanton. I could skip
> Out of my skin, now, like a subtle snake,
> I am so limber. O! your parasite
> Is a most precious thing, dropped from above,
> Not bred 'mongst clods and <u>clodpoles</u> here on earth.   *thick heads*
> I muse the mystery was not made a <u>science</u>,   *any academic discipline*
> It is so liberally professed! Almost
> All the wise world is little else, in nature,
> But parasites or sub-parasites.   (3.1.1–13)

Mosca's cynicism is evident in his low evaluation of human nature, but he believes he is at the top of the rank, for no one can outsmart him. The images he uses to express his pride and contempt for others reveal his sublime exultation: he feels his powers are growing and blossoming and that he is so protean in nature, so changeable and many-sided, that no one can detect or thwart him. For Jonson, of course, Mosca's chameleon nature in which he glories, is not a compliment. The run-on sentence extending from line 5 to line 7 with the brief pause at "now," suggests the rapidity with which Mosca can alter his nature to seem someone different in a moment, depending on whom he wishes to please. The image of the "subtle snake" would have suggested Satan to an Elizabethan audience, while Mosca absurdly exalts parasites to divine origins and parasitism to the ranks of the arts and sciences. His inflated self-image is ripe for a fall, as we sense, and it eventually occurs, though not without a significant struggle in which the good and the innocent are nearly overthrown by the greedy and selfish opportunists who populate the play. Jonson's ability to capture Mosca in blank verse at this moment of self-revelation shows how the poet could shape this verse form into a passage of relatively natural colloquial speech (heightened for effect), and represents an excellent example of his poetic craftsmanship.

Turning from the drama to individual poems, we will see that throughout his career Jonson wrote in a great variety of forms, with many different themes and voices. Perhaps his favorite genre early on was the epigram, a brief, often witty type of poem, of which he wrote quite a few. They could be sharp and satiric like many of his plays, or laudatory, praising someone like an eminent nobleman. "On Something, That Walks Somewhere" is a good example of the satiric variety, for it is relatively short (eight lines), clever, and biting:

> At court I met it, in clothes <u>brave</u> enough   *fine, splendid*
>   To be a courtier, and looks grave enough
> To seem a statesman: as I near it came,
>   It made me a great face. I asked the name.
> "A lord," it cried, "buried in flesh and blood,
>   And such from whom let no man hope least good,
> For I will do none; and as little ill,
>   For I will dare none." Good lord, walk dead still.   (1–8)

Here Jonson turns his spotlight on the pretensions of one who, on the surface, seems to be a courtier and a statesman, who dresses the part, but who is neither good nor wise. Notice how Jonson diminishes him by using the neutral pronoun "it" rather than the masculine "he," thus echoing the title that characterizes him as a "thing" and that corresponds to the poet's use of "the name" instead of "his." In the first two lines Jonson parallels some phrases to bring out the hypocrisy of the man, such as "grave enough" and "brave enough" (with its internal rhyme and puns), and "to be" and "to seem." In this encounter Jonson creates a little scene as in a play as he lets the man speak, though "its" words seem rather imagined than realistic. That is, the "thing's" words are designed to reflect his attitude of superiority rather than what he might have actually said. The man's appearance asserts his proud title to nobility, but also his smug dedication to his own well being, especially the physical aspect. The words "flesh and blood" also suggest that his chief concern is only with his own family and his own safety. Moreover, "it" proclaims his refusal to care about others, as well as his fear of taking any risk even to do something wrong. He is a kind of "dead man walking," as Jonson's last dismissive words make clear, a nonentity who prides himself on external show without the moral courage to distinguish between good and evil. Jonson's use of the heroic couplet (iambic pentameter lines that rhyme) for both statements and dialogue is varied at the end with three heavy stresses in the final words to underscore his sarcastic comment. Satire at this time was generally harsh and judgmental, not gentle and humorous. It was meant to correct faults and expose unconscionable or absurd behavior that deserved lashing. Jonson succeeds admirably in laying bare the pretense of this insufferable human being in just a few lines of trenchant verse.

In another mood Jonson proves he can be sober, affectionate, and compassionate. Among his best poems are several epitaphs, including ones for two of his children. "On My First Son" concerns his son Benjamin (which in Hebrew means "child of my right hand"), who died in 1603 on his seventh birthday. Jonson links his son to his own career as poet, and admits that he cared and hoped too much for him:

> Farewell, thou child of my right hand, and joy;
> My sin was too much hope of thee, loved boy:
> Seven years thou wert lent to me, and I thee pay,
> Exacted by thy fate, on the just day.
> O could I lose all father now! For why
> Will man lament the state he should envy,
> To have so soon 'scaped world's and flesh's rage,
> And, if no other misery, yet age?
> Rest in soft peace, and asked, say, "Here doth lie
> Ben Jonson his best piece of poetry."
> For whose sake henceforth all his vows be such
> As what he loves may never like too much.   (1–12)

A part of himself has died, the poet suggests, his own right hand has been cut off and returned to his Maker, which clearly Jonson did not expect. It seems much too soon to lose his son for whom he had such high hopes, so Jonson exclaims that he should "lose all father now," an ambiguous phrase that suggests he is ready to give up all chance of being a father or that he feels somewhat guilty for his son's death. The poet knows that he should rejoice that his son has returned to his eternal home, so that the child will not have to experience all the misery and suffering and pain of growing up and living out a normal life, but that is clearly little consolation. It hurts too much for him to remain detached and objective. So he concludes with the conventional "rest in peace" phrase found in the epitaph, with the added sympathetic "soft" to suggest his deep affection and sorrow.

Jonson then imagines his son responding to a question someone might ask about who he is, saying he is his father's "best piece of poetry," because a poet is a "maker" or creator who brings to life a world of his own. Life is greater than poetry, Jonson seems to suggest, but he must not forget that all life ultimately belongs to God. This is why he vows never to place too much hope or expectation in the things of this world. Jonson's sorrow is deep and tinged with bitterness, but also restrained, and disciplined in part by the verse form he has chosen, the heroic couplet with a slow rhythm that is often interrupted by pauses from the frequent commas in many of the lines. It is a solemn, affectionate, well-crafted lament with no overt self-pitying or other display of violent emotion. The poet's grief is personal and deeply felt, never outrageous or false. He never bemoans his son's lost potential or imagines him with God. Nor does he share his grief with his wife, from whom he had been estranged when the boy died, apparently of the plague. This poem acts as Jonson's formal relinquishing of his son, a valediction that he had apparently not been able to effect in person.

In a lighter vein, Jonson displayed his ability to write smooth and tender songs in his plays as well as separately. The following poem, "Song: To Celia," became a "barroom favorite" many years later with music composed for it in the eighteenth century, though it celebrates love over drink. Oddly enough, Jonson blended several prose passages from an ancient Greek philosopher to create this popular love lyric:

> Drink to me only with thine eyes,
>   And I will pledge with mine;
> Or leave a kiss but in the cup,
>   And I'll not look for wine.
> The thirst that from the soul doth rise
>   Doth ask a drink divine:
> But might I of Jove's nectar sup,
>   I would not change for thine.
> I sent thee late a rosy wreath,   *recently*
>   Not so much honoring thee,
> As giving it a hope that there
>   It could not withered be.
> But thou thereon didst only breathe,
>   And sent'st it back to me;
> Since when it grows and smells, I swear,
>   Not of itself, but thee.   (1–16)

The poet seems to be celebrating a Neoplatonic kind of love that will be satisfied with a look, an imprinted kiss on the cup, and a drink of the gods' nectar. The poet takes the conventional stand that his beloved is a goddess whom he worships even more than the traditional gods. In a pleasing burst of hyperbole, the poet suggests that her presence can give the hope of eternal life to a bouquet of roses that otherwise must obey the law of nature and wither. But what has she done? Returned the roses. Is the poet dismayed? Not enough to stifle his imagination since he suggests that the flowers are flourishing from the life she breathed into them.

Jonson has fashioned a delightful song about unrequited love with two eight-line stanzas organized into alternating four and three stress lines having a complex alternating rhyme scheme. The language is simple, the images are traditional but not banal, and the rhythm flows evenly with few caesuras. It is a triumph of classic song making that shows how appealing simplicity can be, given the right context. We need not apologize for enjoying such a poem (probably even more so with the music), which can be admired on its own terms without overvaluing it.

On a more serious note, Jonson also wrote a few religious poems, though he never became a devotional poet or a clergyman like Donne. Still, Jonson can be serious about his spiritual feelings as he shows in "To Heaven," which was the final poem in his first collection. Here he reveals a surprisingly strong sense of his own sinfulness:

> Good and great God, can I not think of thee
>   But it must straight my melancholy be?
> Is it interpreted in me disease
>   That, laden with my sins, I seek for ease?
> Oh, be thou witness, that the <u>reins</u> dost know   *kidneys, seat of the feelings*
>   And hearts of all, if I be sad for show,
> And judge me after, if I dare pretend
>   To aught but grace, or aim at other end.   (1–8)

Typical of Jonson, he addresses God directly and forthrightly, pleading for understanding and forgiveness for himself. He knows he has not been as good as he should have been, that he is "laden with" sins, but he throws himself on God's mercy as he vouches for his genuine penitence.

As Jonson continues, he admits that he has been alienated from God, but calls on Him to be with him now in his need:

> Dwell, dwell here still: Oh, being everywhere,
>   How can I doubt to find thee ever here?
> I know my state, both full of shame and scorn,

Conceived in sin and unto labor born,
Standing with fear, and must with horror fall,
And destined unto judgment after all. (15–20)

It is a cry of desperation, a reaching out for a sign of saving grace in a time of deep need. At the end Jonson urges himself to quieter statements lest his poem "be thought the breath / Of discontent," which could be taken as a serious expression of despair, a dangerous sin in Christian terms. Jonson again employs the heroic couplet, this time with a good many medial caesuras to suggest his broken spirit and fragmented feelings. There are here no elaborate images or extended conceits as in Donne's poetry, but rather a series of straightforward declarations of great intensity about his many shortcomings.

Jonson's sense of his sinfulness and yet his desire to affirm his penitence and find reconciliation with God creates a tension and ambiguity that are not finally resolved in the somewhat pat ending of this poem:

I feel my griefs too, and there scarce is ground
Upon my flesh to inflict another wound.
Yet dare I not complain or wish for death
With holy Paul, lest it be thought the breath
Of discontent; or that these prayers be
For weariness of life, not love of thee. (21–26)

Jonson comes close to self-pity here when he suggests that his flesh has been covered by so many wounds that there is no room for more, but he restrains himself when he realizes this may sound like whining to God. He goes on to claim the apostle Paul as a model for distinguishing between the acceptable reason to long for death (to join Christ in heaven) and the unacceptable reason (to escape his trials on earth), though this claim may not appear very convincing to the reader. Jonson seems quite human and vulnerable in such a passage as this.

Perhaps Jonson's most admired poetry is in his ethical mode, in praise of such ideals as friendship or the good life. "To Penshurst" is undoubtedly the best known of these poems, one that is written for, and about, the Sidney family, prominent in the time as writers and patrons who inhabited Penshurst. But note that it is directed, ostensibly, to the manor itself, not the family, and praises the life of the country house as it traditionally existed, at least in ideal form. It is a poem too long to quote in its entirety (102 lines), but a few passages can give the reader a good idea of its contents. Jonson begins

by addressing the house by name and by focusing on an external view of it
and its grounds:

> Thou art not, Penshurst, built to envious show,
>   Of <u>touch</u> or marble; nor canst boast a row   *a fine black stone*
> Of polished pillars, or a roof of gold;
>   Thou hast no <u>lantern</u> whereof tales are told,   *cupola*
> Or stair, or courts; but stand'st an ancient pile,
>   And, these grudged at, art reverenced the while.
> Thou joy'st in better marks, of soil, of air,
>   Of wood, of water; therein thou art fair.   (1–8)

Jonson treats the estate as if it were human and capable of understanding his
speech, commending its solid plainness over the showy construction of more
ornate houses. It is not made of the fine stone or the gold of some manors. Its
appearance is not meant to draw envious looks from its neighbors. Rather, it
is venerated for an older style of architecture that is unpretentious but enduring. The house itself seems to take pride in its pleasant surroundings of
forest, water, and soil, natural resources that will provide the basic human
needs of the inhabitants. Thus, the exterior of the estate reflects the values
and ideals of the people inside, their concern with usefulness, moderation,
and modest appearances.

Jonson continues by describing the vitality and abundance in some of the
specific features of the estate, from its walks to its tall trees, as well as its fish,
fruit, and flowers. It seems to have everything one could want in animal life,
space, and natural beauty:

> Thy copse too, named of Gamage, thou hast there,
>   That never fails to serve thee seasoned deer
> When thou wouldst feast or exercise thy friends.
>   The lower land, that to the river bends,
> Thy sheep, thy bullocks, <u>kine</u>, and calves do feed;   *cattle*
>   The middle grounds thy mares and horses breed.   (19–24)

Barbara Gamage Sidney was the lady of the manor, the wife of Sir Robert
Sidney, who was the younger brother of Sir Philip Sidney, the great poet and
writer who died young. The way Jonson weaves the family into the description of the estate shows how much a part of it they were; it was not just
a random collection of trees and fields, but formed an integral part of their
family history and tradition. As if it were human, the manor provides food
and exercise for its family and their guests. Moreover, the fish on the estate

like the "Fat agèd carps that run into thy net" (line 33) are eager to fulfill their duty in life, which is to serve their human masters as food. The apricots and peaches hang low on the branches so "that every child may reach" (line 44) them. It is an ideal life, of course, a form of hyperbole to suggest the plentiful life on the estate that makes it into a kind of Eden.

But Jonson is not primarily concerned with the beautiful scenery or the animal life at Penshurst. As an ethical poet he is more interested in the quality of life created by the humans who inhabit the house. The estate, he avers, is not based on exploitation but on fostering a community spirit in the neighborhood. The owners seem to have succeeded admirably in this, according to Jonson's account:

> And though thy walls be of the country stone,
> They're reared with no man's ruin, no man's groan;
> There's none that dwell about them wish them down;
> But all come in, the farmer and the <u>clown</u>,   *peasant*
> And no one empty-handed, to salute
> Thy lord and lady, though they have no <u>suit</u>.   *a request or complaint*
> (45–50)

Clearly, the Sidneys have retained the love and respect of their tenants and nearby farmers, who do not envy them, but rather bring them gifts without expecting a favorable judgment or any other special treatment in return. This is the way the patriarchal society should work, with the lord and lady providing for, and looking after, their dependents, who in turn are happy to work for them.

Jonson, who knew the difficulties of dependence firsthand, underscores the liberality of the Sidneys' table in describing his own experience there:

> Here no man <u>tells</u> my cups; nor, standing by,   *counts*
> A waiter doth my gluttony envy,
> But gives me what I call, and lets me eat;
> He knows <u>below</u> he shall find plenty of meat.   *in the servants' quarters*
> (67–70)

By personalizing life at Penshurst, Jonson provides further evidence for the Sidneys' goodness and liberal spirit. They clearly honor the poet by treating him with courtesy and generosity, thus upholding the basic tenets of a civilized society. Apparently such cultivated behavior and social harmony were not common at the time, especially toward one's servants, but this remained the ideal for a country gentleman and his estate. It is an ideal that requires the nobility to foster a spirit of community and social well-being among all their connections.

Finally, Jonson praises the lady of the manor for her running of the household as well as for her virtuous conduct. Despite her absence when King James and Prince Henry (along with others in the royal entourage) happened to visit while they were out hunting, her organization was such that everything could be supplied the eminent visitors without her immediate presence. But her "high housewifery" is surpassed even by her integrity, another rarity in the time according to the poet:

> These, Penshurst, are thy praise, and yet not all.
> Thy lady's noble, fruitful, chaste withal.
> His children thy great lord may call his own,
> A fortune in this age but rarely known.
> They are, and have been, taught religion; thence
> Their gentler spirits have sucked innocence.

❧

> Now, Penshurst, they that will proportion thee
> With other edifices, when they see
> Those proud, ambitious heaps, and nothing else,
> May say, their lords have built, but thy lord dwells.   (89–94; 99–102)

Thus, Jonson concludes that this manor house may enjoy its preeminence for the true nobility of its owners' character. They have built not just a building but a home and a community based on moral and spiritual values of the highest order. In concise, authoritative couplets Jonson celebrates the achievements of a couple and family that have created a harmonious, unified neighborhood that flourishes under its direction. His tone is serious, elevated, and stately; his verse is, like the estate, unostentatious and noble. He indulges in no extravagant images or figures of speech, yet he manages to convey his great admiration for the life of this house and its superior (but not snobbish) owners. Jonson's praise of their principles and his own noble voice keep it from being mere flattery of potential patrons.

In the next-to-last poem of Jonson's that we will consider, "To the Immortal Memory [of] . . . Sir Lucius Cary and Sir H. Morison," he shows, late in his career (1629), that he is still capable of original and imaginative verse. In this ode, one of the first to imitate in English the ancient Greek poet Pindar's celebration of Olympic victors, Jonson offers Lucius Cary, a young man of noble family, a poetic consolation for the early death of Cary's dear friend, Henry Morison. Morison died of smallpox at the age of 20 in 1629, devastating Cary by the loss of one who was not only his friend but also a fellow poet. In his tribute to Morison, Jonson employs the same three-part stanzaic structure Pindar used, where the Greek chorus chanted different parts of the poem as they moved in one direction for the strophe (*The Turn*), turned in the opposite direction for the antistrophe (*The Counter-Turn*), and stood still for the epode (*The Stand*). In a somewhat more formal and elevated style than "To Penshurst," Jonson wishes to celebrate the nobility of this young man and to recommend a restrained and stoic sorrow appropriate to Morison's unfortunate death. In the first part of the poem Jonson emphasizes how life presents untold tribulations for everyone, and how difficult it is to maintain one's virtue and hope in the face of all its stresses and sufferings. He first notes two examples of misguided reactions to the difficulties of life: the baby who at birth returns to the womb to escape life's misery and the old man whose life is long but empty of any goodness. Morison, however, had scarcely begun his adult life when he died, yet he fulfilled the highest expectations, "A perfect patriot and a noble friend, / But most a virtuous son" (lines 46–47). In *The Turn* stanza of the third set of three parts, Jonson portrays him in figures of speech that evoke his central theme:

> It is not growing like a tree
> In bulk, doth make man better be,
> Or standing long an oak, three hundred year,
> To fall a log at last, dry, bald, and sere:
> A lily of a day
> Is fairer far in May,
> Although it fall and die that night;
> It was the plant and flower of light.
> In small proportions we just beauties see,
> And in short measures life may perfect be.   (65–74)

The concrete natural images of tree and flower, oak and lily, perfectly capture the visual contrast between an increasingly ugly long life and the inherent beauty possible in a short one. Note how Jonson underscores the withering of the tree trunk by using three stressed monosyllabic words out of four in "dry, bald, and sere." Then he switches in the next two lines to a much shorter, more swiftly flowing movement with the lily to imitate its brief but beautiful life. In the couplet that concludes the stanza Jonson returns to the iambic pentameter line to sum up his point with an abstract statement about beauty and life with the word "just" introducing a moral dimension into beauty and the word "measures" suggesting a careful and moderate amount of life. Jonson's clear, realistic declaration neatly caps this short little stanza. Morison's life is appropriately and artistically celebrated.

In *The Counter-Turn* Jonson offers the traditional consolation that Morison lives on in a better life, as well as in the memories of men on earth. He also introduces himself as one who commemorates the young man and indulges in a radical enjambment between this stanza and the next that is surely partly humorous:

> He leaped the present age,
> Possessed with holy rage,
> To see that bright eternal day,
> Of which we priests and poets say
> Such truths as we expect for happy men,
> And there he lives with memory: and Ben
>
> > *The Stand*
>
> Jonson, who sung this of him ere he went
> Himself to rest,
> Or taste a part of that full joy he meant
> To have expressed
> In this bright <u>asterism</u>. . . .   *constellation*
>   (79–89)

Even in a serious, elevated poem such as this there is room for a wry smile at the expense of the poet himself when he splits his name between the two parts of this section. We note also how Jonson links "priests and poets," a traditional correspondence exalting the prophetic powers and divine insight of the latter, but here no doubt somewhat tongue in cheek. Their names, then, Morison and Cary together, will live forever as the symbol of friendship based on the "simple love of greatness and of good / That knits brave minds and manners, more than blood" (lines 105–106). Jonson thus glorifies the ethical ideal of a bond between two young men that transcends family or any idea of personal gain to celebrate the noble idea of true communion shared with another. Occasionally, Jonson indulges in his extensive classical knowledge by comparing these young men to the mythical Greek twins Castor and Pollux, who form part of the constellation Gemini. But we must remember that such knowledge was an integral part of the classical education of the time, not an excuse to parade his learning before the dazzled reader. Jonson was certainly proud of his extensive knowledge, but here he is writing directly for an educated audience who would share the same background and no doubt recognize the allusion.

Finally, I must mention Jonson's poem in honor of Shakespeare, "To the Memory of . . . Mr. William Shakespeare." It was printed in the First Folio of the playwright's works in 1623. Jonson had nothing to gain by praising this poet who had been dead for seven years, yet his commendation is grand and generous, especially coming from a rival dramatist. Jonson calls Shakespeare the "Sweet swan of Avon" (line 71) and the

> Soul of the age!
> The applause! delight! the wonder of our stage!
> My Shakespeare, rise; I will not lodge thee by
>   Chaucer or Spenser, or bid Beaumont lie
> A little further to make thee a room:
>   Thou art a monument without a tomb,
> And art alive still while thy book doth live,
>   And we have wits to read and praise to give.   (17–24)

Shakespeare stands alone in English poetry, Jonson proclaims, and on a par with the great classical dramatists like Aeschylus and Sophocles. This was, for Jonson, the highest honor he could extend to an English writer. The classical writers were, for him and many others, the supreme models of literary greatness. As he says, Shakespeare "was not of an age, but for all time" (line 43), even though he had, as Jonson rather condescendingly puts it, "small Latin and less Greek" (line 31). Jonson claims that Nature must have been very pleased with Shakespeare's "designs" and "joyed to wear the dressing of his lines" (line 48), indicating that he was a natural genius. But Jonson also gives special praise to Shakespeare's "Art," which as he says, "must enjoy a part" (line 56) of his commendation:

> For though the poet's <u>matter</u> Nature be   *subject matter*
>   His Art doth give the <u>fashion</u>; and that he   *form, style*
> Who <u>casts</u> to write a living line must sweat   *undertakes*
>   (Such as thine are) and strike the second heat
> Upon the Muses' anvil; turn the same,
>   And himself with it, that he thinks to frame,
> Or for the laurel he may gain a scorn;
>   For a good poet's made as well as born.
> And such wert thou! . . .   (57–65)

Shakespeare thus displays, Jonson suggests, the powers of the greatest writers of all time, who have employed their imaginations and reason to select, organize, and articulate different facets of human nature and experience that everyone can understand and appreciate. Art is not easy to create, in Jonson's view, nor is it the product of simple inspiration; rather, it is hard work that requires careful observation, knowledge, and deliberate, focused thought. Jonson concludes by seeing the image of Shakespeare in the form of a constellation in the sky, as in the previous poem on the two friends, to suggest that he will last forever as an example of the great writer for future ages, but particularly in his book just published. A higher tribute to a contemporary writer can hardly be imagined.

Once again in this poem Jonson employs the heroic couplet with force and conviction, using a combination of metaphor, classical allusion, and direct statement of his ideas to carry his message. He did much to establish the heroic couplet as the standard poetic form in English. The poem is, as usual with Jonson, a balanced judgment on an artist of supreme powers spoken in clear, measured terms, with little in the way of extravagant or unusual imagery. It is, moreover, an important document in the contemporary testament to Shakespeare's existence and career as an important playwright, and shows that poetry may be plainspoken, reasonable, and unpretentious, despite Jonson's ostensible belief in the Renaissance doctrine that poetry is akin to prophecy.

Jonson's poetry may not generate the same kind of excitement as Donne's, but it represents a different approach to it, more of a public voice than Donne's or than we are used to today, in which ideas, craft, and a forthright manner are paramount. It is often meant to teach us not only about life in general, but also about poetry, both what it is and what it can do. Jonson's example shows us that poetry need not be limited to private confession or the exploration of deep, personal feeling, as it largely is today. It can handle quite successfully the discussion of ideas and values, even explicit moral judgments. Though Jonson was aware that he could not always follow or fulfill his own ethical teachings, his poetry typically asserts, in imaginative and appealing language, a passionate commitment to definite moral values based on clear insight into the complexities and difficulties of life.

CHAPTER 4

Robert Herrick (1591–1674): Poet of Time, Love, and Delight

Robert Herrick was perhaps the finest poet among the "sons" of Ben Jonson, one of several who claimed him as their mentor and friend. About Herrick's life we have only the barest of details. He was a London-born, Cambridge-educated son of a goldsmith who died when Robert was only a year old. Before going to the university, Herrick spent several years as an apprentice to his uncle Sir William Herrick, a wealthy London goldsmith. In 1623, after completing his education, Herrick took holy orders, but he remained in London for several years, acting as chaplain for different noblemen and enjoying the company of Ben's tribe in the Apollo Room at the Devil's Tavern. By 1625 Herrick had written enough good poetry to be ranked with Jonson himself by a contemporary observer. In 1627 he served the Duke of Buckingham as chaplain on the ill-fated expedition to aid French Protestants on the Isle of Ré, near La Rochelle. Three years later Herrick was installed as vicar of Dean Prior in Devonshire in the south of England. He remained there serving his local parish until 1647 when he was dismissed from his position by the Puritans for being a royalist supporter during the English Civil War. Herrick apparently then returned to London where he stayed until the Restoration in 1660, when he was again able to take up his clerical duties in Devonshire. While in London, Herrick published his only volume of poetry, *Hesperides*, in 1648. It attracted little notice at the time except perhaps among Royalists, in part because of the civil war, but a number of his poems were reprinted in various collections published in the seventeenth century, though often without his name attached. Herrick lived quietly in Dean Prior until his death in 1674 at the age of 83, apparently without writing any more poetry.

It should be helpful at this point to explain some of the historical developments of the time, since Herrick's own life and poetry were significantly affected by them. After James I died in 1625, his son Charles became the new monarch (as Charles I) and began to reform the royal court in order to rein in its lavish expenses and immoral lifestyle. At the same time he supported Bishop Laud's program to reorganize the Anglican Church along more formal, ceremonial lines, to the great dismay of the Puritans. In fact, this effort led to more and more emigration from England to the New World by those who felt oppressed in the Anglican Church, especially after the appointment of Laud as archbishop in 1632. Besides their doctrinal differences with the Anglicans, the Puritans wanted less ceremony, less elaborate ritual, and fewer (or no) images in the Church, with more emphasis on the sermon and the devotional aspects of worship. Like his father, Charles soon was at odds with his Parliament and decided in 1629 to govern without one, since it kept attempting to restrict his powers. When Charles and Laud tried to impose Anglicanism on Scotland in the later 1630s, the Scots reacted fiercely by invading England in defense of their Presbyterian Church. This created a crisis for Charles, who was thus forced into calling Parliament to meet in order to fund the defense of the country. After growing dissension and intransigence on both sides, armed conflict broke out in 1642 between Parliament and the king, when some members of Parliament (M.P.'s) attacked Charles's ministers as well as his policies and refused to provide any money until Charles agreed to their demands. The war was fought sporadically but bitterly over the next six years before Parliament finally obtained a clear victory in 1648, captured the king, and decided to put him on trial, but only after many of the moderate M.P.'s had been forcibly excluded by the army. Showing great dignity on the scaffold, Charles was beheaded on January 30, 1649, to the horror of many people who believed their king was divinely blessed. Oliver Cromwell, a Puritan who had emerged as the most outstanding military commander in the civil war, then ruled the English Commonwealth with the backing of the army for the next nine years until his death in 1658. The monarchy was restored in 1660 much to the relief of many, after the political and military leaders of the nation failed to find an acceptable compromise for a new government. Charles I's son, the heir to the throne, returned from exile on the continent in May 1660 to a triumphant welcome as Charles II, but the monarchy was no longer the all-powerful institution it had been. At least temporarily, though, a balance was achieved between Parliament and the king, who proved to be an adept politician but not a very good man, infamous to many for his libertinism and his secret dealings with France.

As a clergyman, Robert Herrick upheld the traditional hierarchy of the Anglican Church and supported the monarchy. As a poet, he wrote in the classical tradition, as is evident in the title of his book of poems, *Hesperides*. In classical mythology the Hesperides were nymphs who, with the help of a dragon, watched over a garden of apple trees with golden fruit situated at the farthest limits of the earth. These special apples, apparently given to Hera by the earth goddess, were said to confer immortality on anyone who ate them. As one of his twelve labors, Hercules had to go to the garden, kill the dragon, and take the apples back to Greece. Thus, Herrick suggests that his collection of poems may be viewed as his own fruit, which may confer immortality on him and perhaps on anyone who partakes of them. The word also means little stars, which may add a further dimension to the meaning of the poetry for him. Here we see Herrick the classicist alluding to information that would have been generally familiar to most of his readers at the time. As with Donne and Jonson, many of his poems had circulated in manuscript in his lifetime and later, though it was only in the nineteenth century that his complete poetry was reprinted. Since then, his reputation has gradually increased until he is often considered today as one of our finest lyric poets. His great poems are few, but they generally delight with their wit, their handling of nuance, and their command over sound and rhythm. Herrick's poetic art is often more subtle than we at first perceive.

The first of Herrick's poems we shall take up is called "Delight in Disorder," a fourteen-line lyric that does not, however, take the usual sonnet form. It runs like this:

A sweet disorder in the dress	
Kindles in clothes a wantonness.	
A <u>lawn</u> about the shoulders thrown	*fine linen scarf*
Into a fine distraction;	
An erring lace, which here and there	
Enthralls the crimson <u>stomacher</u>;	*decorative bodice covering*
A cuff neglectful, and thereby	
Ribbons to flow confusedly;	
A winning wave, deserving note,	
In the tempestuous petticoat;	
A careless shoestring, in whose tie	
I see a wild civility:	
Do more bewitch me than when art	
Is too precise in every part.	(1–14)

In this poem Herrick addresses the subject of nature and art, pondering which is better. He uses clothing to focus his account, and thereby involves other subjects as well, including proper dress, the relations between men and women, and love. He also raises the problem of perception, its subjective nature and its objective existence. This is a good example of how a poet can suggest much through very little.

Herrick seems at first to praise "disorder," yet by the end of poem we come to understand that this is all relative, that complete chaos is not at all what he values. It is a special kind of disorder that he commends, one that is attractive and pleasing, not the messy kind involving anarchy and conflict. It does prompt, he says, a certain "wantonness" in the clothes, which is odd because objects are not usually given moral qualities. Of course the clothes characterize the one who is wearing them, but "wantonness" in the seventeenth century probably did not carry quite the same associations that it does today. It seems to have meant something closer to unrestrained gaiety than immorality or lewdness. The interesting point is that Herrick plays with all the connotations of this word, raising various possibilities for meaning. As the poem continues, we can begin to sort out the senses that seem most relevant. Clearly, these clothes are those of a well-dressed lady of the upper class, not the simpler ones of the middle or lower classes. But, in any event, dress in itself is not his only, or even his main concern.

As we continue through the poem, we become acquainted with the effects of different pieces of this lady's clothing, mostly suggesting some degree of passion or irrationality. The lady's scarf gives the effect of a "fine distraction," that is, it can be a diversion or it can be an obsession, a light interest or a passionate one. The lace is said to be "erring," that is, wandering (morally?) or casually placed on the body, while it bewitches the bright red bodice covering it at least "here and there." All these terms are suggestive of much more than simple description, implying moral qualities or valuations. The flow of the ribbons confuses us for the moment, while the "tempestuous" petticoat, an undergarment that peeks out from beneath the dress, deservedly attracts us by its "wave," or undulating movement. Even the shoestring is "careless," though its bow implies to the speaker a paradoxical impression of disorderly order. Here we perceive the subjective nature of this whole picture, how the observer is responding to what he sees in the beauty of this young lady's dress. The conclusion emphasizes that this is a value judgment on the part of the poet, who is attracted and delighted by the artistic casualness of the lady's dress and who makes a firm statement in favor of a natural order that is not too obviously designed for its effect. For Herrick, art and nature are best combined to produce the most attractive object, which neither could do alone.

This is, it seems, a simple poem, written in iambic tetrameter (four stressed syllables) couplets, some run-on lines, and a rhythm that varies with the sense. When the scarf is "thrown" about the shoulders, the sense does not stop at the end of the line, but flows on to the next. The "here and there" slows down the movement to imitate the desultory nature of the lace and echoes the sound of "erring" that comes before, providing some significant internal rhyme. The phrase "deserving note," set off with commas, breaks up the regular flow of the line to highlight its meaning. All of these details add up to a portrait that captures some of the indefinable ingredients in the beauty of a carefully dressed, well-to-do lady of the time. The word "precise" was a recognizable code word at that time for "Puritan," thus suggesting that the poet rejects the excessive rigidity and austerity commonly ascribed to that religious group. The poet clearly charges his poem with multiple levels of association, connotation, and meaning that create a complex but coherent whole. It is altogether a delightful work, charged with feeling and radiating significance.

To follow up this poem with another on a similar subject, we will look at one of several Herrick wrote for his Julia, a name he used for an apparently fictional beloved. Poets from ancient times had traditionally done this, talking about their loves using assumed names like Catullus's Lesbia and Petrarch's Laura. In "Upon Julia's Clothes" Herrick focuses on the attraction generated by his beloved as she passes him dressed to kill (or at least to wound). This is no doubt a slighter poem than "Delight in Disorder," but it nevertheless shows what he can do in just a few lines of description. The poem is only six lines long, divided into two brief stanzas:

> Whenas in silks my Julia goes,
> Then, then, methinks, how sweetly flows
> That liquefaction of her clothes.
>
> Next, when I cast mine eyes and see
> That <u>brave</u> vibration each way free,   *fine, splendid*
> Oh, how that glittering taketh me!   (1–6)

Julia has put on her best, and it is sufficient. This does not happen all the time, but when it does, the poet savors it, repeating "then" for emphasis and slowing down the flow. It is a "sweet" movement that he captures with a long, abstract word that one would not expect to carry much sensual connotation. "Liquefaction" means literally the process of liquefying, but it also has a figurative sense referring to the "melting of the soul by the ardor of devotion"

(*Oxford English Dictionary*). In this case the liquid movement of Julia's clothes certainly melts the observer's heart and causes him to worship her.

In the second half of the poem the poet's appreciation for his beloved's appearance is enhanced by her walking movement within the fancy dress. He "casts" his eyes to follow her, emphasizing that this is his perception of her, not just anyone's. What he sees is a wonderful back-and-forth motion of the clothes, and the body within, that projects a sense of freedom; it is not restricted or limited in any rigid or artificial way. In the last line he exclaims how much this sight enthralls him, the "glittering" probably being the silk fabric that reflects the surrounding light and the motion of her body. It is a celebration of the power of the sight of his beloved, well-dressed and moving with grace, beauty, and ease. It is a sensual power, no doubt, but it completely entrances and delights him.

Yet he is able to write about this power with careful artistry, using iambic tetrameter that is varied at emphatic points such as in line 2 with the repetition of "then," when he stresses the first two syllables of the line (a spondee) instead of alternating the stress as he does in most of the poem. Another suggestive variation occurs when the meaning of this line continues on to the next, so that its "flow" echoes the sense, being the only run-on line in the poem. Note, too, that the poem has only two rhyme sounds, since each brief stanza of three lines has but one. It is not easy to compose such a seemingly simple poem with its perfect polish and delightful picture.

Herrick addresses more significant themes in other poems, such as the importance of time in human life and how suddenly it can end. The brevity of life is of course an old subject for poets, going back to ancient times, but Herrick is able to make his own mark in this long tradition. His "Corinna's Going A-Maying" is one of his most famous and one of his most classical poems. It is too long to quote all of it here, but we can look at several passages that reveal how Herrick develops his theme, which may surprise us with its depth of feeling and insight. It is a longer, more elaborate poem than the others we have discussed by him, comprising five stanzas of fourteen lines in iambic pentameter. Here is the first stanza:

Get up! get up for shame! the blooming morn
Upon her wings presents the god unshorn.
  See how <u>Aurora</u> throws her fair   *goddess of the dawn*
  Fresh-quilted colors through the air:
  Get up, sweet slug-a-bed, and see
  The dew bespangling herb and tree.
Each flower has wept and bowed toward the east

Above an hour since, yet you not dressed;
   Nay, not so much as out of bed?
   When all the birds have <u>matins</u> said,   *morning prayers*
   And sung their thankful hymns, 'tis sin,
   Nay, profanation to keep in,
Whenas a thousand virgins on this day
Spring, sooner than the lark, to fetch in May.   (1–14)

The poet speaks directly and emphatically to this young woman, Corinna, a name probably taken from the classical poet Ovid, to urge her in no uncertain terms to rise from her bed and go outside to celebrate the first of May, a traditional holiday in England. Aurora is the classical goddess of the dawn, and Apollo is the sun god, with his beams being portrayed like his hair in flowing locks, a sign of his virility. All of nature, the speaker notes, is already responding to the coming of this beautiful morning, except the young girl. The air is filled with the "fresh-quilted colors," the flowers have "bowed" toward the sun, the birds have already sung their prayers ("matins") and their hymns of thanksgiving, but she has done nothing at all to worship this force of nature that calls all life back into growth and vitality. Note how Herrick employs original, concrete images to convey this feeling, like the "dew bespangling herb and tree," which makes them glisten and sparkle in the sunlight. It is a religious observance that Corinna should join, the speaker implies, for it is sinful to stay inside and not worship, as nature and "a thousand virgins" are doing. Herrick thus combines the Christian sense of sin with the classical sense of delight in life to create a tension that is a blend of the smoothly flowing lines and the speaker's urgency.

In the second stanza the speaker urges Corinna to "put on her foliage" (line 15) like the rest of nature, not fancy jewelry, for the "leaves will strew / Gems in abundance upon you" (lines 19–20). He mentions the pagan gods Flora (flowers) and Titan (the sun), but also the idea of praying, though he says it should be brief. In the third stanza he wants her to notice how the people in the houses display their devotion with the whitethorn branches placed above each door, how everyone is out in the fields to celebrate the coming of spring as the "proclamation" of the king (Charles I) has ordained, in opposition to the Puritan desire to suppress all the old holidays that may be tainted with pagan origins. Like his father, Charles supported and encouraged the continuance of England's traditional folk customs with official government decrees in the *Book of Sports* (1618; 1633). Thus does Herrick incorporate controversial topics in a poem that, on the surface, seems to be innocent of any connection to contemporary history. He says, ironically, it is a sin *not* to celebrate life as the English had done for many centuries. It is, the poet suggests, proper "Devotion [that] gives each house a bough" (line 32) of whitethorn, the customary flower used to trim the doorways.

Moreover, as the speaker says, the rites of love associated with May Day have already been celebrated by many young people:

> And some have wept, and wooed, and <u>plighted troth</u>   *become engaged*
> And chose their priest, ere we can cast off sloth.
>   Many a <u>green-gown</u> has been given,   *grass stained*
>   Many a kiss, both <u>odd and even</u>;   *as in a kissing game*
>   Many a glance, too, has been sent
>   From out the eye, love's firmament....   (49–54)

The amatory games have progressed nearly to marriage at least for some, but Corinna is late for all this, when she should be actively involved in them, given her age and condition, for this is to behave in a way that is natural and normal for young people. Herrick seems to imply that such a celebration was an appropriate response to God's gift of life, though he does not expressly say so in the poem. That would make it much too heavy, in contrast to the spirit of life and joy that prevails in the poem as in the morning.

Herrick does incorporate some darker elements into the final stanza, giving his poem a deeper, broader, and somewhat more somber tone. Notice how the speaker now clearly involves himself in the scene, and by extension all of us:

> Come, let us go while we are in our prime,
> And take the harmless folly of the time.
>   We shall grow old apace, and die
>   Before we know our liberty.
>   Our life is short, and our days run
>   As fast away as does the sun;
> And, as a vapor or a drop of rain,
> Once lost, can ne'er be found again,
>   So when or you or I are made
>   A fable, song, or fleeting shade,
>   All love, all liking, all delight
>   Lies drowned with us in endless night.
> Then while time serves, and we are but decaying,
> Come, my Corinna, come, let's go a-Maying.   (57–70)

The active images of the days running away and the dew evaporating, with the vapor and the drop of rain are all commonplace to be sure, but Herrick does not dwell on them, emphasizing their rapidity and brevity. The images for us after death as "fable, song, or fleeting shade" also evoke our transitory, and possibly even questionable, existence. We conclude our lives "drowned ... in endless night," and though time seems to serve us while young, even then "we are but decaying." It is a vision some would call terribly pessimistic or melancholy, but it is nevertheless most definitely true about human life, that it will end in death and that our prime is very short, considering the grand scheme of life on earth. This is, of course, the traditional *carpe diem* (seize the day) theme in poetry, the call to enjoy ourselves while we have life, energy, and mind to do so.

Herrick's originality in the poem is to set it within the context of the May Day holiday, a celebration of life and love, and to make it an indirect refutation of all those (like the Puritans) who would like to get rid of such festivals by showing them what these moments of joy represent for human lives. Done as it is in a formal, complex structure with each stanza having six lines of iambic pentameter couplets, two at the beginning, two in the middle, and two at the end, with the other eight lines in iambic tetrameter couplets, indicates that Herrick felt he was making an important statement that required careful elaboration. Herrick does not offer the Christian consolation of a return to God after death perhaps because that would dilute the impact of his argument against the Puritans. For the strict Calvinists among them, only a few "elect" would, in any event, ever benefit from such a hope. We should also recall that in the early seventeenth century life expectancy was much shorter than in our own time. Without modern medicines and health care, a seemingly robust person could sicken and die very quickly. Life is transient and may end suddenly at any moment, a traditional theme that Herrick effectively dramatizes by imagining a scene associated with a special English holiday.

Another poem on the same general theme is "To the Virgins, to Make Much of Time." It begins with some familiar lines, but continues in a vein that may surprise us. Since it is relatively short, we can look at all of it here:

Gather ye rosebuds while ye may,
    Old time is still a-flying;
And this same flower that smiles today,
    Tomorrow will be dying.

The glorious lamp of heaven, the sun,
    The higher he's a-getting,
The sooner will his race be run,
    And nearer he's to setting.

That age is best which is the first,
   When youth and blood are warmer;
But being spent, the worse, and worst
   Times still succeed the former.

Then be not coy, but use your time,
   And while ye may, go marry;
For having lost but once your prime,
   You may forever tarry.   (1–16)

This time Herrick does not address any specific young woman, as in the last poem, but only the category of "virgins" to whom he makes some general remarks about how to live their lives to the fullest. The first line is famous, with its image of the rosebud, young and ripe with promise, standing for the love, beauty, and pleasure in life that we should enjoy while we can. The second line personifies the idea of time, as in Father Time, and suggests that he is, as he always has been, running rapidly away. More personification occurs in line 3 with the smile of the flower (it is blooming, to suggest the flourishing of life), while the "tomorrow" in line 4 is figurative, reinforcing the sense of death possibly coming at any moment.

In the next stanza Herrick turns to nature and its cycle of life, with the sun moving ever higher during the day only to drop from sight all the more quickly with the coming of the night. He may be "glorious" and associated with heaven, but he is not immortal as the pagans represented him. In the next stanza the poet affirms that youth is the best time of our lives, since that is when life is most intense and full, but our prime lasts only a short while and is soon exhausted. The image of the warmth of the blood that is quickly used up makes this graphically clear.

Finally, in the last stanza the poet concludes that young girls should not be too teasingly flirtatious, but that they should "go marry" and fulfill themselves in their time, for their chances may be lost forever if they do not. It is moral advice that may sound somewhat hackneyed to our ears, but it is validated by the context in which it is given, that of the cycle of time forever fleeting and from which we cannot escape, so we should use it to our advantage when we can. "To the Virgins . . ." is a relatively simple poem with traditional images and ideas set in a structure that is also fairly straightforward, though we should not miss the variation in the meter and the rhyme. Its lines alternate from four stressed syllables in lines 1 and 3 to three in lines 2 and 4 (tetrameter to trimeter). Its rhyme alternates as well, and there is an extra unstressed syllable at the end of each second and fourth line, giving a forward movement to the verse despite the predominance of end-stopped lines. The poem overall has a satisfying unity with an accessible, flowing surface that forms a polished and coherent message. This is not a simple accomplishment and can give us a good deal of pleasure in its handling of the brevity-of-life theme.

Two other poems will be examined briefly, for the additional dimensions they reveal in Herrick's verse. The first is "The Hock Cart, or Harvest Home," which is a poem about the end of the harvest when the final cart comes home decorated and followed by all the young harvesters. Like "Corinna Goes A-Maying" this too concerns a traditional festival in rural England, the time to celebrate the gathering of the crops to prepare for the long winter. In the seventeenth century England was still an agricultural country with the industrial revolution over a century away. Herrick dedicated the poem to Mildmay Fane, Earl of Westmoreland, one of his patrons who was also a poet (he published a book of poems in the same year as Herrick). Herrick focuses on the young people who do the celebrating as well as the work of the farm, recognizing their special contribution. This is how the poem begins:

> Come, sons of summer, by whose toil
> We are the lords of wine and <u>oil</u>;   *olive oil*
> By whose tough labors and rough hands
> We rip up first, then reap our lands.
> Crowned with the ears of <u>corn</u>, now come   *wheat*
> And, to the pipe, sing harvest home.
> Come forth, my Lord, and see the cart
> Dressed up with all the country art.   (1–8)

Note how Herrick begins by addressing himself to the young workers, bidding them come celebrate the end of their labors and acknowledging their crucial roles in producing the basic crops necessary for sustaining life. Though the earl probably had neither grapes nor olive trees on his land, these are symbols of the crops that provide the basic foodstuffs for everyone. They grow and are harvested through the hard labor of the peasants and tenant farmers. Herrick celebrates their work, urging them to eat and drink heartily at their lord's table, since the hard work is not over for good, just temporarily suspended; indeed, it will continue forever in the endless seasonal cycle of plowing, planting, and harvesting. The sanctity of the harvest is probably also hinted at in the bread and wine that can be made from the crops, to create a religious celebration in the form of Communion. But this is only discreetly suggested.

Moreover, the feast is a communal event in which everyone can participate, not just the workers. Herrick describes some of the amusements the young people engage in as they accompany the cart to its home, thus giving us some interesting historical information about these celebrations. It is a picture that combines Christian and pagan elements:

> About the cart, hear how the rout
> Of rural younglings raise the shout,
> Pressing before, some coming after,
> Those with a shout and these with laughter.
> Some bless the cart, some kiss the sheaves,
> Some prank them up with oaken leaves;
> Some cross the <u>fill-horse</u>, some with great   *shaft horse (for a cart)*
> Devotion stroke the home-borne wheat;
> While other rustics, less attent
> To prayers than to merriment,
> Run after with their breeches rent.   (15–25)

Herrick presents an effective, dynamic picture of the young people hurrying about the cart as it proceeds home, with some of them more serious than others, but all joining the merriment in their own way. He is particularly concrete in his description of their activities, with their shouting and laughter, along with their kissing, decorating, crossing (making the sign of the cross), and stroking. Herrick varies the rhythm of the lines, generally with a pause in the middle or none at the end, to suggest their different movements. Even the clownish behavior of a few boys with torn pants is incorporated into this comprehensive look at a village holiday. There is something quite appealing in this account of the innocent fun of rural youth, who enjoy the time of plenty before the coming of a long, cold winter. They are, it seems, seizing their day while it still exists.

In the final section the poet does not romanticize their work of cultivation or underestimate its value; he accepts the way things are and acknowledges the reciprocal relationship between lord and dependents bound together in ties of mutual obligation. Enjoy life when you can, he advises, for

> all go back unto the plow
> And harrow, though they're hanged up now.
> And you must know, your Lord's word's true,
> Feed him ye must whose food fills you,
> And that this pleasure is like rain,
> Not sent ye for to drown your pain
> But for to make it spring again.   (49–55)

Life and growth will return to the land, Herrick suggests, though it will do so at some cost, like the serious labor necessary to cultivate it. This is the eternal round of life, to which all must submit, so it is better to make the best of one's lot and be content with the scheme of things. As Americans, we may find it difficult to accept such fatalism, since our country is built upon a commitment to better one's life with a strong spirit of independence, but this was not true at that time for most people in England, many of whom were still tied to the land by ancient feudal relations. Herrick employs an iambic tetrameter couplet with the occasional triplet thrown in, as in the last three lines. There is little in the way of ornament or elaborate image making, which is appropriate to the plain, rough nature of his subject. It is a more earth-bound poem than the others we have discussed, less precious perhaps, but marked by greater realism.

The final poem by Herrick that we will consider is taken from the second part of his book titled *Noble Numbers*, published with the *Hesperides*. This part contains all his religious poems, of which there are 272, mostly brief lyrics or epigrams. "To His Conscience" presents a kind of dialogue between the poet and his conscience, as he tries to bargain with it to be less strict and more forgiving. He begins by questioning his conscience about overlooking some of his minor faults:

> Can I not sin, but thou wilt be
> My private <u>protonotary</u>?   *recording clerk in a court*
> Can I not woo thee to pass by
> A short and sweet iniquity?
> I'll cast a mist and cloud upon
> My delicate transgression
> So utter dark as that no eye
> Shall see the <u>hugged</u> impiety.   *warmly embraced, cherished*
>   (1–8)

Herrick imagines his conscience as his judge in a private court of law where he is charged with sinning. Why are you bothering me about these little faults, he wheedles, hoping to persuade his conscience to forgive him for these. He even hopes to gloss over these sins and make them seem better than they really are, because he loves them and finds it hard to let them go. He feels he can hide their true nature by refusing to allow any light to shine upon them. It is a typical stance of someone who has committed sins for which he has not repented. Herrick goes on to quote the Bible in his own defense:

> Gifts blind the wise, and bribes do please
> And <u>wind</u> all other witnesses: *corrupt*

And wilt not thou with gold be tied
To lay thy pen and ink aside?
That in the <u>mirk</u> and tongueless night   *murky, dark*
Wanton I may, and thou not write?   (9–14)

The first line derives from Deuteronomy (16:19), as editors have noted, and the answer to his query is clearly no, conscience is not about to wink at his serious failings. The power of gifts is great to corrupt justice and win favor, but not enough, as he expresses it in images, to make his conscience put down his pen and not write his name in the book of sinners (continuing the personification). It is, of course, wrong of him even to consider trying to bribe his conscience, so that, as he says, he may "wanton" in the silent night without consequences. But, he finally concludes, this is neither possible nor right:

It will not be; and therefore now
For times to come I'll make this vow,
From aberrations to live free,
So I'll not fear the Judge, or thee.   (15–18)

There is no sense of difficulty or ambivalence about this decision. Herrick simply realizes that he cannot sway his moral guide or his Maker, and therefore he will forget about the sinful pleasures he would like to enjoy and will live a good and righteous life instead. We have none of the agonizing of Donne or even the ambivalent struggle of Jonson. The poet's own desires are easily resolved, it seems, so his poem is less intense and afflicted than theirs. His religious devotion is clearly not of the same degree as his predecessors, nor does it compare with George Herbert's, whom we shall consider next. Yet it still appears genuine, even if not deeply distressed or conflicted. The form of the poem is simple with couplets in iambic tetrameter, but Herrick does employ several polysyllabic words mostly in rhyming positions, one of his favorite practices. He manages to incorporate some of the most unlikely long, abstract words into his verse smoothly and effectively. I suspect he took a wry pleasure in doing so.

All in all, Herrick's verse, at its best, is polished, memorable, and serious, and can give us much pleasure in reading and rereading it. He takes delight in much of this world and conveys his response with subtlety and art. He also sees life realistically and does not shrink from its grimmer aspects. It is the kind of poetry we may wish to memorize simply because of the pleasure it affords in remembering it and hearing its music occasionally resonate in our minds. From Herrick's bright lyrics we move on to the deeper, more sober, and sometimes more dramatic music of Herbert.

CHAPTER 5

George Herbert (1593–1633): Poet and Priest

Our next poet is generally considered to be one of the finest religious poets in the English language. George Herbert was born into a prominent Welsh family whose service to English royalty dated back to the Middle Ages. His father Richard died when George was only 4 years old, but his mother, Magdalen Newport, raised their ten children (seven sons, three daughters) in stalwart fashion, practically every one of them achieving notable status in their lives. George was the fifth of the seven sons, educated first at home by tutors, then at Westminster School, and finally at Trinity College, Cambridge University, where he distinguished himself as a Latin and Greek scholar. He became a fellow of Trinity, then a Reader in Rhetoric; in 1620 he was elected Public Orator of the University, a prominent position for a young man. Although he had long been interested in serving God in his life, at this point in his career he turned more toward public service instead of the Church. He was elected to Parliament first in 1624, and then again in 1625, but after the death of King James in that year, along with that of several of his friends and his mother in 1627, Herbert returned to his original idea and accepted ordination first as a deacon and in 1630 as a priest in the Church of England. He had married Jane Danvers in the preceding year and was given a small parish in Wiltshire, near Salisbury and its striking cathedral, where he would occasionally walk to play his lute with clerical friends and enjoy the beautiful church music. In the short time he had to live, Herbert cared for his flock, composed poetry, and wrote a book about the duties of a country priest. He appears to have found his calling in serving the humble people of his parish.

Not long before he died he gave his manuscript of poems to his good friend Nicholas Ferrar, who had established a private religious community nearby called Little Gidding. (T. S. Eliot later used this name for the title of one of the sections of his religious poem, *Four Quartets*.) Ferrar had the manuscript published with great care in the same year, and Herbert soon became one of the most admired and cited religious poets in English. His reputation faded somewhat during the eighteenth century, but since then he has never ceased to attract readers. His poetry appeals to people of various faiths because it dramatizes and details the search for a meaningful spiritual existence and the struggle to maintain it. As we will see, this is not an easy journey, for many pitfalls lie along the way, yet it also has many blessings. Herbert lived at a time when serious questions were being raised about the doctrine and practices of the Church of England, but he never gave up on his moderately reformed religion, though he engaged in some serious self-examination about it.

Herbert gave his book of poems the title of *The Temple* and divided it into three sections, the first of which is called "The Church Porch," to indicate its introductory status. In it Herbert presents a series of poems filled with moral and spiritual advice to guide the wavering or uncertain person to the central experience of faith, with its times of struggle, devotion, and praise. The first poem in the main section, called "The Church," from which all the following poems come, is "The Altar," a pattern or shaped poem whose lines form the structure of its subject. Such poems were popular in Herbert's time, but he wrote only two of them, both quite effective (the other is "Easter Wings"). More important than its shape is the theme of "The Altar," which introduces this section of the book by emphasizing the need for humility and personal sacrifice before the Lord. Here is the whole poem:

> A broken A L T A R, Lord, thy servant rears,
> Made of a heart, and cemented with tears:
>   Whose parts are as thy hand did frame;
>   No workman's tool hath touched the same.
>   A   HEART   alone
>   Is   such   a   stone,
>   As   nothing   but
>   Thy power doth cut.
>   Wherefore each part
>   Of my hard heart
>   Meets in this frame,
>   To praise thy Name:
>   That, if I chance to hold my peace,
>   These stones to praise thee may not cease.
> Oh let thy blessed S A C R I F I C E be mine,
> And sanctify this A L T A R to be thine.   (1–16)

This altar is based on the kind of stone structure found in the Old Testament, but here it is not for animal sacrifice but self-sacrifice, as one submits to the discipline and guidance of God's Word. In the Old Testament the Lord told Moses to build an altar from uncut stones, for to cut them would be to "pollute" them (Ex. 20:25). Herbert transforms this into a more personal and New Testament kind of construction.

The first requirement before entering the church is to have a penitent heart and to acknowledge God's unique power to pierce the sinner's defenses against admitting guilt. The sinner must then offer himself (or specifically his heart) on the altar as the only proper sacrifice to God. Only this self-abasement and dedication will enable one to approach God with the proper attitude. The imagery is simple and ordinary, based on the Bible and stressing the need to have a deep sense of one's sinful nature, as opposed to strictly following certain laws or rules. The individual speaks directly to God without the intervention of a priest or other intermediary. The poet offers his heart up to God on this altar of contrition. At the end he prays that Christ's sacrifice may atone for his own sins and serve for his salvation, though this is by no means inevitable. The short lines in the middle of the poem seem to underscore the hardness of his heart with their sharp consonants that echo rapidly with the repeated rhymes. The poem's seriousness of theme and its effective construction may mitigate any negative reaction that we might have at first to its shape on the page.

Throughout this middle section of *The Temple*, Herbert explores different aspects of the Christian faith within the structure of the Church, including its holy days, its doctrines such as "Redemption," and its emotional trials like "Affliction" (of which there are three different poems). "Easter" is one that comes early in this section of the book and commemorates the most important day of the year for Christians. Here Herbert engages in a dialogue with himself over what he should do on this day to celebrate its transcendent significance for him:

> Rise, heart, thy lord is risen. Sing his praise
>   Without delays,
> Who takes thee by the hand, that thou likewise
>   With him may'st rise;
> That, as his death <u>calcined</u> thee to dust,   *burned to powder*
> His life may make thee gold, and, much more, just.   (1–6)

He calls on his heart to rejoice in song, for Christ has died for him and been resurrected, so that he may find salvation. Christ's death has purified him of sin, as the alchemical process purified a mineral and, supposedly, reduced it to gold. As Herbert adds, it may make him "just," that is, good, or perhaps one of the elect. Herbert was, of course, no alchemist, but he uses the terms to suggest the transformation of the natural being through Christ's sacrifice for all of humanity.

In the next stanza Herbert calls on his musical instrument to take its part in this celebration:

> Awake, my lute, and struggle for thy part
> > With all thy art.
> The cross taught all wood to resound his name
> > Who bore the same.
> His stretched sinews taught all strings what key
> Is best to celebrate this most high day. (7–12)

Herbert personifies the lute, suggesting it will need to work hard to produce sounds worthy of this day. Of course, he is addressing himself indirectly in this passage, drawing upon his own love of music and his skill on the lute and the viol. Music provides a constant motif throughout *The Temple*. The wooden cross has taught all wood to resonate with Christ's message, while "His stretched sinews," like the cat gut of the lute strings, play in the right key for humanity. Christ is the ultimate musical instrument, furnishing the perfect melody and harmony for this celebration. Here Herbert approaches Donne in his use of extreme parallels.

Finally, both Herbert and his instrument must act together to compose a proper song for this day:

> Consort, both heart and lute, and twist a song   *harmonize / weave*
> > Pleasant and long;
> Or, since all music is but three parts vied   *increased by additions*
> > And multiplied,
> Oh let thy blessed spirit bear a part,
> And make up our defects with his sweet art. (13–18)

With the heart and the lute working together beautiful music can be made, using several melodic lines that are woven together as in the polyphony of the time. But it can be even better with the help of the Holy Spirit, which will perfect the whole through divine inspiration. Only this combination of elements would create praise worthy of Christ's blessed sacrifice. Herbert admits his own inadequacy, but believes it can be overcome with God's help.

The song that follows is a separate poem with its own structure and story, though a part of the whole poem about Easter. It is called simply "The Song" and is in three quatrains:

I got me flowers to <u>straw</u> thy way,   *strew*
I got me boughs off many a tree;
But thou wast up by break of day
And brought'st thy sweets along with thee.

The sun arising in the east,
Though he give light and th'east perfume,
If they should offer to contest
With thy arising, they presume.

Can there be any day but this,
Though many suns to shine endeavor?
We count three hundred, but we <u>miss</u>:   *misunderstand*
There is but one, and that one ever.   (19–30)

We know that Herbert occasionally set verses to music, but we do not have any of his musical settings, so we cannot interpret the song as it might have been heard. But we can say that it is a fairly simple song with Christ at its center, as the poet celebrates His extraordinary sacrifice that is beyond the capacity of anything human or natural to equal. Christ does not need the poet's offering in the way of palm branches and flowers, for he has brought all the "sweets" needed with him. Moreover, Christ has given far more light and lovely fragrances to the world than the sun, and his one day is eternally precious, not just good for the moment. Our human nature is too feeble to comprehend the magnitude or meaning of this event or even to give it adequate praise. The human cannot measure the divine. This is the meaning of Easter, and a lesson that humans in general, Herbert suggests, find it difficult to accept.

Sometimes Herbert reflects more directly on the power of language to encompass the truth of Christ and his sacrifice. In "Jordan (1)" he suggests that the artifice of poetry is not necessary or especially helpful in communicating such truth. The river Jordan, marking the beginning of the Promised Land for the Israelites, also came to symbolize the cleansing power of baptism. Dressing up the verse in fancy images, allegories, or symbols, Herbert suggests, does not enhance the truth but may hide it in veils or riddles:

Who says that fictions only and false hair
Become a verse? Is there in truth no beauty?

Is all good structure in a winding stair?
May no lines pass, except they <u>do their duty</u>　　　　　　*pay reverence to*
　　Not to a true, but painted chair?　　　　　　　　　　　*(1–5)*

It is, of course, ironic that the poet uses metaphors to denigrate figurative language, as in "false hair" and a "winding stair." These are concrete images that represent the pretended attractions in characters and a story set in a complex structure. The "painted chair" also suggests the fancy, highly decorated throne of a king or bishop. Yet Herbert seems to reject the very idea of using figurative language to convey the truth.

In the second stanza he strikes particularly at the hackneyed images of the pastoral and romance traditions, when he speaks of the "enchanted groves" and "purling streams" of many contemporary poems:

Is it no verse, except enchanted groves
And sudden arbors shadow coarse-spun lines?
Must <u>purling</u> streams refresh a lover's loves?　　　　　　　*rippling*
Must all be veiled, while he that reads, <u>divines</u>,　　　　　　*guesses*
　　Catching the sense at two removes?　　　　　　　　　　*(6–10)*

Such pretentious and commonplace artifice obviously will not do. The truth is better expressed directly and openly, not in the complicated, symbolic way of allegory. If the sense of the poem is only grasped "at two removes," it will not be found by many.

In the last stanza the poet confirms his point by praising those who speak or sing their faith clearly and affirmatively:

Shepherds are honest people: let them sing;
Riddle who <u>list</u>, for me, and <u>pull for prime</u>:　　　　　*wish / draw a lucky card*
I envy no man's nightingale or spring;
Nor let them punish me with loss of rhyme,
　　Who plainly say, *My God, My King.*　　　　　　　　　*(11–15)*

Herbert is talking about declaring one's faith, believing it is better to be open about it than concealing it beneath a mask or a pose. Those who use complex metaphors may seem only to mystify the reader and perhaps need the help of chance (as in drawing the right card, a metaphor itself and not a very clear one to us today) to make them comprehensible. Yet Herbert loves figures of speech as well as any poet, and can often seem to enjoy making his meaning more esoteric than he would need; plainness, after all, can only go so far. Herbert was, no doubt, conscious that he was defending the idea of plainness using metaphors throughout, so that the irony is clear. Perhaps he is suggesting that extravagant figures of speech are like sin and need to be purged away by the water of baptism. The Jordan, after all, was the symbol of cleansing to the Israelites, who needed to cross over it to enter the Promised Land. The river was also the location of Christ's baptism by John. The second "Jordan" poem makes Herbert's self-criticism clearer by describing how he began by thinking up all sorts of ways to express his faith, but then realized later that such fine words are not necessary and really derive from pride and vanity. The best devotional verse is that which expresses one's faith most directly and naturally.

"Virtue" is one of Herbert's most appealing poems, a brief one that employs several figures of speech to describe rather than define the nature, or rather the outcome, of this concept. His stanza is a simple quatrain with alternating rhyme, a refrain, and a good deal of repetition. The poem moves from the specific to the general, from the natural to the supernatural. Here is the whole poem:

> Sweet day, so cool, so calm, so bright,
> The bridal of the earth and sky:
> The dew shall weep thy fall tonight,
>   For thou must die.
>
> Sweet rose, whose hue, <u>angry</u> and <u>brave</u>   *red-hued / fine, splendid*
> Bids the rash gazer wipe his eye:
> Thy root is ever in its grave,
>   And thou must die.
>
> Sweet spring, full of sweet days and roses,
> A box where <u>sweets</u> compacted lie;   *perfumes, candy*
> My music shows ye have your <u>closes</u>,   *final musical cadence*
>   And all must die.
>
> Only a sweet and virtuous soul,
> Like seasoned timber, never gives;
> But though the whole world turn to coal,
>   Then chiefly lives.   (1–16)

The poet addresses the day in the first stanza, describing it as perfect, sunny but cool and serene, with the earth and sky in perfect harmony. The rhythm itself is slow and deliberate, restrained by the several pauses and intensified by the repetition of "so." Yet the day itself must die and be mourned by the weeping of dew, for it cannot last. The dew is personified and symbolizes the sorrow of the day's fate, but there is no escape for it: it is mortal like everything else in nature. This realization is absolute; there is no qualification to it, no hope for anything on earth, even for that which seems perfect.

The second stanza is addressed to the perfect rose, the symbol of all beauty and love, with its brilliant red and pleasing shape. It seems to embody in itself all the loveliness of the world, which can cause the observer to weep with the extraordinary power of its sight if he gazes too directly at it. Perhaps the tears are as much because the observer also realizes that it, like the day, cannot last, that it is a natural object that will die as soon as the day is over. Its root itself is in its grave, so that death is present in all life and beauty, though it may be hidden from the observer. The same iron law of natural decay applies to the rose, as the poet recognizes.

The third stanza is addressed to the spring, which, according to the poet, is even greater than the other two, the day and the rose, because it includes them both. It is the distillation of all delight on earth, the embodiment of joy in the renewal of nature that is beyond any other pleasure. Spring has its own music, Herbert suggests, but like music it too must end. This time the refrain is not addressed to spring only, but asserts that "all must die." Is there, then, no hope at all?

The fourth stanza offers some consolation, the only way to escape this iron law. It is the "virtuous soul" that contains the eternal sweetness of existence. The poet compares it to something in nature that seems to last forever, the "seasoned timber" which will never bend or break. This is the true strength that will endure while everything else around it decays and dies. Even if the world burns up, as in the final conflagration suggested in the Bible, the virtuous soul will live, since it has accepted God's principles, which transcend the material existence of human life. In fact, it is only in the spiritual realm that the soul truly lives. The change in the refrain in line 4 of each stanza from the emphasis on dying to an affirmation of life asserts this idea. Thus does this relatively simple poem express Herbert's deepest faith in the salvation of human beings if they live for and through God rather than simply in nature.

"The Collar" offers a more dramatic opening in the style of Donne, but Herbert uses it to lead the reader toward a more humble spiritual life. The title alludes to the clerical collar worn by priests as well as to the band or strap of restraint for dogs and horses and even, occasionally, prisoners. The voice in the poem speaks with a vehemence not often found in Herbert's poetry. The first sixteen lines set the scene and the main themes:

> I struck the board and cried, "No more;
>   I will abroad!
> What? shall I ever sigh and pine?
> My lines and life are free, free as the road,
>   Loose as the wind, as large as <u>store</u>.   *abundance*
>   Shall I be still in <u>suit</u>?   *attendance, waiting on someone*
>   Have I no harvest but a thorn
>   To let me blood, and not restore
> What I have lost with <u>cordial fruit</u>?   *restorative to the heart*
>   Sure there was wine
>   Before my sighs did dry it; there was <u>corn</u>   *grain, wheat*
>   Before my tears did drown it.
>   Is the year only lost to me?
>   Have I no <u>bays</u> to crown it,   *laurel wreath*
> No flowers, no garlands gay? all blasted?
>   All wasted?"   (1–16)

In this dramatic monologue the speaker reveals his deepest feelings about his life. He is exasperated by the restraint and moderation he has been living under, and wants desperately to assert his freedom to show that he, too, can go wherever and do whatever he wants. His emotional rejection of a past dominated by self-control and discipline is particularly evident in his striking the table, which may be any table or possibly a Communion table. The latter possibility becomes increasingly relevant as we move through the poem and discover more allusions to Christian elements of worship that may not be consciously apparent to the speaker, but are to the reader. In this dialogue with himself, the speaker wonders why he should not indulge himself in the pleasures of life, in eating and drinking since there is plenty of wine and bread to be had if only he would "seize the day." Again, the allusion to the elements of the Communion service remind us of the Christian terms of his outlook, as does the thorn that reflects not only his own sense of the pain of life, but also suggests Christ's crown of thorns. Note that the lines are irregular in length and rhyme, with no fixed pattern or regular stanzaic form in them, suggesting his desire for freedom and his sense of a fragmented existence. Is his life a waste so far? This is what he seems to think. It is a powerful, almost modern cry of desperation.

But the rebellion does not end here. It gathers strength as he reflects on what he still can do with his life despite what he has done so far. His own answer to the last question he raised gives him some hope for the future:

> "Not so, my heart; but there is fruit,
> And thou hast hands.
> Recover all thy sigh-blown age
> On double pleasures: leave thy cold dispute
> Of what is fit or not. Forsake thy cage,
> Thy rope of sands,
> Which petty thoughts have made, and made to thee
> Good cable, to enforce and draw,
> And be thy law,
> While thou didst wink and wouldst not see.
> Away! take heed;
> I will abroad.
> Call in thy death's-head there; tie up thy fears.
> He that forbears
> To suit and serve his need,
> Deserves his load."   (17–32)

In these lines the speaker tries to convince himself that there is plenty he can do now to redress the situation. The fruit of life is there for the plucking to give himself "double pleasures"; he must simply abandon his endless concern for what is right and wrong and throw off the restraints that are in fact self-imposed, not enforced from above. He reaffirms his plan to go abroad and calls for his "heart," the other voice in this dialogue, to take away the "death's-head," the symbol of human mortality. It was not uncommon for monks to have a skull in their room or cell to remind themselves of the possibility of their own imminent death and thus their need to live according to God's laws. Anyone who does not take his life in his own hands, then, deserves his misery. The speaker's will appears to have won the debate at this point, for the heart has nothing more to say.

The resolution, however, comes suddenly and succinctly. It could scarcely be more humiliating for the speaker. It takes just a few lines:

> But as I raved and grew more fierce and wild
> At every word,
> Methoughts I heard one calling, *Child!*
> And I replied, *My Lord.*   (33–36)

As the speaker rants and raves in his wilful rebellion, he suddenly hears a
voice that reminds him of who he is, and whose he is. This is all it takes to
make him realize that he is throwing a childish tantrum and to call him back
from rebellion to obedience and calm. In a flash he sees how absurd he has
been and how he must acknowledge his dependent role in God's universe.
All this bluster has been so much pent-up hot air that evaporates when he is
reminded of his true identity. In these final lines Herbert makes sure that the
iambic pattern is definite and the rhymes are good to reinforce the sense that
harmony and order have been restored. It is a dramatic turnaround after all
that defiant outpouring. This is generally considered one of the most powerful of Herbert's poems.

The final poem in "The Church" section of Herbert's volume is "Love (3),"
the third poem in the collection with this title. Once again the poet does not
try to define this concept, but rather dramatizes a brief encounter between
the poet and Love, who greets him kindly and offers him a meal. The scene is
only vaguely described, with the speaker arriving somewhere feeling rather
dirty after his voyage and reluctant because of this to enter the place to which
he has come and partake of some food. It is a brief, simple encounter between
these characters, composed in three stanzas of six lines each with alternating
long and short lines, yet it is one of the most spiritually powerful of Herbert's
poems. We know from the first word, however, that it is a kind of allegory.
The first stanza runs as follows:

> Love bade me welcome: yet my soul drew back,
>   Guilty of dust and sin.
> But quick-eyed Love, observing me grow slack
>   From my first entrance in,
> Drew nearer to me, sweetly questioning
>   If I lacked anything.   (1–6)

We see immediately that this "Love" is not Venus as we might expect, and the
place is not simply a kind of inn. Perhaps it is heaven where the "soul" has
arrived, feeling guilty from the sins of his life and troubled to be so warmly
welcomed. But that does not deter Love from urging him to enter and asking
if there is anything he needs. Love is clearly caring and sensitive toward him,
far beyond what the speaker feels he deserves. Note that the run-on lines (3
and 5) by going on to the next lines diminish the effect of the rhyme, which
otherwise would be much more prominent in the short lines. The unstressed
rhyme in lines 5 and 6 has the same effect.

The dialogue between the two figures carries much of the rest of the poem. The second stanza begins with the poet's response to Love's query at the end of the first stanza:

> "A guest," I answered, "worthy to be here":
>   Love said, "You shall be he."
> "I, the unkind, ungrateful? Ah, my dear,
>   I cannot look on thee."
> Love took my hand, and smiling did reply,
>   "Who made the eyes but I?"   (7–12)

The speaker, feeling deeply uncomfortable, says that the only thing he lacks is worthiness, that he has been far too neglectful of the many blessings he has received to warrant such a welcome. He even goes so far as to suggest that he should not turn his eyes on Love because of his strong sense of being undeserving, even after Love has suggested that he is worthy. In order to underscore this invitation to his reluctant guest, Love gently grasps the speaker's hand and points out that he is the creator of the eyes, after all, implying that he knows all about their use and misuse, and that the speaker should not worry. The play in the last two lines on the long *I* sound reinforces the rhyme and the sense that the speaker belongs to God.

The third stanza reaffirms the point that the speaker is acceptable to God no matter how he feels:

> "Truth, Lord; but I have marred them; let my shame
>   Go where it doth deserve."
> "And know you not," says Love, "who bore the blame?"
>   "My dear, then I will serve."
> "You must sit down," says Love, "and taste my meat."
>   So I did sit and eat.   (13–18)

The speaker's strong sense of guilt prompts him to ask for his due punishment, in order to satisfy justice in his case. Love, or Christ, as this figure has clearly become by now, confirms that he has taken the speaker's sins away, so there is nothing more for him to worry about. The speaker then must further learn that he will feast at the banquet where Christ himself will serve, that he is not to be God's servant. This passage echoes Luke's version of Christ telling his disciples that they must be prepared "to sit down to meat" when he returns, and he "will come forth and serve them" (Luke 12:37). The speaker finally realizes that his salvation will be complete through Christ's extraordinary sacrifice and humbling of himself for all humanity.

This quiet act of sitting down to a meal embodies, in simple allegorical terms, his final reconciliation with God through His son. It is a kind of Communion celebrating Christ's victory over sin combined with the banquet that awaits the believer in heaven. The strict stanzaic form with its alternating iambic pentameter and iambic trimeter (three stressed syllables) lines and an alternating rhyme scheme in the quatrain with couplets in the concluding lines is handled with remarkable colloquial fluency. The dialogue between Love and the speaker is simple and natural, despite the complicated poetic form, and strikingly understated for the soul's entrance into heaven. There are no trumpets blowing or angels singing. It is a remarkably quiet, personal scene for such a momentous event. This poem is a fitting end for the many highs and lows, the foolishness and the errors dramatized in the rest of the poems in this second section of Herbert's book. The speaker, despite his initial hesitation, has finally found the peace and reconciliation he both desires and needs.

George Herbert remains today a much-loved religious poet because of his exceptional talent for giving voice to common feelings of doubt and inadequacy in one's faith, along with a deep, abiding joy in it. There are no easy triumphs for the believer, Herbert implies, but there can be sudden revelations and hard-won recognitions. Though Herbert occasionally sounds like John Donne, most of the time his voice is distinctively his own as he explores the many pains and perils of his spiritual journey, together with some of the satisfactions in it, all in dense, often haunting language, imagery, and figures of speech. The seeming simplicity of his poetry, with its concise and disciplined form, belies its great and powerful artistry.

CHAPTER 6

John Milton (1608–1674): Poet of English Puritanism

John Milton is generally considered the greatest English poet after Shakespeare, though he is probably less read today than a good many others. Milton's writing career is unusual in that he composed not only several exceptional poems, but also a number of important prose works that arose from his close involvement in the turbulent political life of his country. In fact, he became a revolutionary writer, who worked closely with the Cromwellian government and strongly defended the beheading of the king and the creation of a republic to replace the long-established monarchy. At the restoration of the monarchy in 1660, Milton barely escaped being put on trial for his role in the rebellion. Fortunately, with the aid of some important friends, Milton survived to compose some of his greatest poetry, including *Paradise Lost*.

Like many of the other poets we have met, Milton was born and raised in London, the son of a scrivener, whose money lending and other successful business interests enabled him to provide an excellent education for his son. After being tutored at home, Milton went first to St. Paul's School in London (associated with the famous cathedral) and then to Cambridge University (Christ's College), where he stayed for seven years, earning his B.A. and M.A. (1625–1632). He then returned home for six years, engaging in a systematic program of reading and writing before going off on a tour of the continent, where he spent most of his time in Italy. After learning of the deepening conflict between Parliament and the king, Milton cut short his tour to return to England in 1639. Once at home he joined with those who opposed the attempt by King Charles I and Archbishop Laud to impose a strong Anglican

Church, with its hierarchy of bishops and extensive ritual, not only on England but also on Scotland. Milton began his attack on the Church of England and its bishops with a tract called *Of Reformation* (1641) and continued writing controversial tracts on a variety of subjects (including several in support of divorce), throughout Cromwell's rule (1648–1658). Even at the very moment of the Restoration, just three months before Charles returned to England, he published *The Ready and Easy Way to Establish a Free Commonwealth* (1660). Milton had served in an official capacity as Secretary for Foreign Tongues in Cromwell's government from 1649 to 1659, writing letters and other documents in Latin for it. Afterwards, he was seriously compromised by this work, as well as by his defiant attitude toward the restored monarchy.

During this time of public involvement, Milton's personal life was filled with stress and difficulty. He became completely blind by 1652, having gradually lost his sight over several years, so that he had to work closely with readers and amanuenses. He had married Mary Powell in 1642, though she left him shortly afterwards (for reasons not fully understood) and spent three years away from him until she returned to live with him in 1645. This experience certainly prompted his writing in favor of divorce for reasons of incompatibility. Once she came back, however, they had several children together. After Mary died in 1652 giving birth to their daughter Deborah, Milton married a second time (in 1656) to Katherine Woodcock, who lived only until early in 1658 when she died from complications resulting from childbirth. In 1663 Milton married for a third time, to Elizabeth Minshull, the daughter of a friend. He spent his remaining years with her, apparently in relative happiness. Though he had gone into hiding at the Restoration and was very briefly imprisoned in the fall of 1660, Milton was never prosecuted for his association with the Cromwellian government and was allowed to resume his life as a private citizen, though under a cloud of suspicion and resentment.

The last part of his life was lived in quiet and isolation as he worked on much of the great poetry for which he is now known. *Paradise Lost*, an epic about the biblical history of Adam and Eve, was completed by 1665 and first published in 1667 in ten books. For it he received only five pounds and no royalties, since authors at the time sold the copyright to the publisher. He brought out a second edition in 1674, this time in twelve books, to reflect more closely the structure of previous epics like Virgil's *Aeneid*. In 1671 he published *Paradise Regained*, a mini-epic in four books about Christ's temptation by Satan, and *Samson Agonistes*, a kind of Greek tragedy about the biblical Samson. It was only after his death in 1674 that Milton came to be regarded as one of the greatest poets in English, especially with the lavish subscription edition of *Paradise Lost* (1688) with its beautiful illustrations.

Because of his controversial opinions on a variety of public issues, it took years for Milton's literary work to be accepted by many of his countrymen. Even toward the end of the eighteenth century, over one hundred years later, Samuel Johnson still had harsh words for Milton's politics in *Lives of the Poets*, though he also recognized Milton's greatness as a poet. Johnson thought that Milton's republicanism was "founded in an envious hatred of greatness, and a sullen desire of independence," but he also declared that *Paradise Lost*, "considered with respect to design, may claim the first place, and with respect to performance the second, among the productions of the human mind" (*Lives of the Poets* 1: 109, 117). This was an extraordinary tribute from a man who was a vehement opponent of Milton's revolutionary ideas, but indicative of the high regard for Milton the poet prevalent at the time (Milton's influence on the Romantic poets in the next generation is well known). Perhaps the main difficulty modern readers of Milton's poetry experience arises from his exceptional knowledge of classical literature and mythology, together with his knowledge of, and devotion to, Christian doctrine and history. Some of these references will require explanation, but once readers become familiar with this material, they will be better able to understand and appreciate Milton's remarkable poetic accomplishments.

We will begin by looking at one of Milton's sonnets, which shows him responding to the personal tragedy of his blindness. It is clearly a deeply felt poem that reveals something of his own reaction to serious adversity. Here is the full sonnet, written about 1652:

> When I consider how my light is spent,
>   Ere half my days, in this dark world and wide,
>   And that one talent which is death to hide
>   Lodged with me useless, though my soul more bent
> To serve therewith my Maker, and present
>   My true account, lest he returning chide;
>   "Doth God exact day-labor, light denied?"
>   I <u>fondly</u> ask; but Patience to prevent   *foolishly*
> That murmur, soon replies, "God doth not need
>   Either man's work or his own gifts; who best
>   Bear his mild yoke, they serve him best. His state
> Is kingly. Thousands at his bidding speed
>   And post o'er land and ocean without rest:
>   They also serve who only stand and wait."   (1–14)

Here Milton tries to come to terms with his new and severely limited physical condition, to justify how he can now fulfill his sense of mission on earth as he had understood it heretofore. It was unusual to use the sonnet form at this time for a private exploration of one's deepest feelings, having been previously employed mainly for love or religious themes. Milton depicts his inner struggle by describing his personal situation in the first few lines, questioning God's justice in the middle, and concluding with the reply from "Patience," a personified figure who speaks with clarity and authority to Milton's dilemma.

Self-pity and a sense of injustice dominate the octave, with the voice of the poet complaining about the impossibility of his newfound situation. In developing his response Milton alludes to the parable of the talents (Matt. 25:14–30) to heighten the irony of his new condition, punning on the meaning of the word talent, which in the Bible refers to a unit of money. In that story Jesus praises those who put their master's money to work and condemns the one who buried the talent he had been given. In fact, Jesus says that the one who hoarded his money should have it taken away and then be thrown "into [the] outer darkness" for his failure to serve his master while he was away. For a Puritan like Milton, the threat of damnation was always lurking around the corner, if one should fail to respond to God's call made to each human being to serve His cause. The problem is that God seems to be asking the impossible of him, since his one talent is to write and act in support of the Word, which he no longer feels able to do. In quoting his own words in line 7, Milton again echoes the Bible in the parable of the vineyard keeper (Matt. 20:1–16), who pays the same amount to the worker who works only a short time as to those who worked all day, and also to John 9:1–5, where Jesus explains that the man blind from birth did not sin, but that God's work is to be made manifest in him through Jesus: "I must work the works of him that sent me, while it is day: the night cometh, when no man can work" (John 9:4). Thus, in alluding to these biblical texts, Milton poses some crucial questions for his own life and faith, as he continues his way on a path where there seems to be no more light. He desperately needs some spiritual illumination. What is he to do?

Patience has the answer for him. This figure, a combination of the conscience and the Holy Spirit, provides the light that he lacks. It speaks the rest of the poem, putting Milton's feelings into a divine perspective. It is a Protestant point of view in that it emphasizes that human works cannot please God, who prefers that we put our faith and trust in His love. God has many creatures who serve Him, such as the angels who do his bidding, but human beings can also serve even though they may "only stand and wait."

The debate over which was more important, faith or works, had been one of the central points in the conflict during the Reformation, with the Protestant side, led by Luther and Calvin, arguing vigorously in favor of faith. Man cannot earn his salvation by what he does, they argued, but only by what he believes, specifically, by believing in Christ as savior. Milton here accepts, though not without some deep personal struggle, the idea that he must resign himself to God's will for him in this life and accept his fate with all its limitations, however severe. As it turned out, his blindness did not constrain him very much, for he was able to continue his reading and writing through help provided by others. Some of Milton's greatest works were yet to come.

This sonnet is in the Italian form with its two-part structure consisting of an octave containing two quatrains rhyming *abba abba*, and a sestet rhyming *cdecde*. Milton preferred this form, as opposed to the Shakespearean form (organized with three quatrains and a couplet), probably because he knew Italian literature quite well and had written several sonnets in Italian using this form years before. Though the rhyme scheme is intricate, we hardly notice it because of all the run-on lines in the poem. They de-emphasize the rhyme by leading the reader on to the following line rather than underscoring it through syllabic stress. At least half the lines are run-on, a high proportion for such a short poem. This is part of Milton's craft, to understate the sound effects in order to stress the substance and feeling of his poem, as he works to make it sound like a speaking voice rather than a strictly patterned work. Later on, Milton dismissed rhyme as a "troublesome and modern bondage" (in his preface to *Paradise Lost*), but here he shows he can still use it effectively as he had in earlier poems.

To go back a little in time to some years before England's Civil War began and before Milton's blindness, we may look briefly at another poem generally considered one of his finest compositions. "Lycidas" was originally written for a volume of poems published in memory of a promising young scholar and poet, Edward King, who was a fellow at Cambridge and who drowned in a shipwreck as he traveled to Ireland in August 1637. King was only 25 at the time, so Milton clearly felt some deep affinity for this man whom he knew and who was just a few years younger than himself. Milton had been engaged in his reading program for several years and was considering a possible continental tour. He probably took the name Lycidas from Virgil's ninth eclogue (or pastoral poem), where the name is used for a poet-shepherd who speaks with another poet about the brutal effect of the Roman civil wars on the state of poetry (and poets). Milton may be anticipating the effect of the growing conflict in his own country on the fine arts (and other peaceful pursuits), as several passages in his poem suggest. The poem, in fact, seems as much about Milton and his views on current social issues as it is about Edward King. The first few lines establish the poet's personal involvement with the fate of this other young man and his poetic career:

Yet once more, O ye laurels, and once more	
Ye myrtles brown, with ivy never sere,	
I come to pluck your berries harsh and <u>crude</u>,	*unripe*
And with forced fingers <u>rude</u>,	*unskilled*
Shatter your leaves before the mellowing year.	
Bitter constraint, and sad occasion dear,	
Compels me to disturb your season due;	
For Lycidas is dead, dead ere his prime,	
Young Lycidas, and hath not left his peer.	
Who would not sing for Lycidas? He knew	
Himself to sing, and build the lofty rhyme.	
He must not float upon his watery bier	
Unwept, and <u>welter</u> to the parching wind,	*be tossed about*
Without the <u>meed</u> of some melodious tear.	*reward*
	(1–14)

The poet in these lines seems more aggrieved by being forced to write a poem before he was ready than by King's death. Milton's classical culture is evident in the references to the laurel leaves that were traditionally associated with Apollo, god of poetry, the myrtles with Venus and love, and ivy with Bacchus and his wild parties; all were evergreen and symbolic of the immortality of poetry. But can poetry be forced from a reluctant poet? Apparently so, for the poet continues and reviews the reasons to lament the fate of this unfortunate young man. We must not forget, he declares, this noble, learned fellow singer, who was lost at sea and now could use a sympathetic lyric voice. We might note that Milton composed his poem mainly in iambic pentameter lines with an irregular rhyme scheme, apparently imitating the freedom of the Italian canzone (Hughes, p. xlix). Such a form gave him great flexibility to arrange his lines according to his meaning and emphasis.

After this opening, the poet continues in the classical vein by invoking the Muses to inspire his singing, so some future poet may sing a lament for him after he has died. He stresses the finality of Lycidas's death, noting that no one could have saved King even if he had been nearby. The speaker further notes parallels from classical poetry to indicate how other poets have suffered a similar fate, and he is led to wonder what is the point of all this hard work on poetry, if death can intervene at any moment:

Alas! What <u>boots</u> it with incessant care   *profits*
To tend the homely slighted shepherd's trade,
And strictly meditate the thankless Muse?
Were it not better done as others use,
To sport with Amaryllis in the shade,
Or with the tangles of Neaera's hair?
Fame is the spur that the clear spirit doth raise
(That last infirmity of noble mind)
To scorn delights, and live laborious days;
But the fair <u>guerdon</u> when we hope to find,   *reward*
And think to burst out into sudden blaze,
Comes the blind Fury with th'abhorrèd shears,
And slits the thin-spun life.   (64–76)

The poet clearly is led to question his own devotion to the life of the mind, especially given the difficulties in writing highly wrought poems, even with the potential for great fame. Would it not, he wonders, be better to enjoy life and love than to dedicate himself to a lonely, austere existence, toiling over words and paper? Instead of fame, the result could be nothing but oblivion, which Milton images forth as a "blind Fury," not the usual Fate who cuts the thread of life, but one of the three Furies who pursue those who commit crimes on earth. Milton's sense of the possibility that all this work could come to nothing through the precarious nature of life emerges from his verse with great power, being especially prominent in the sound and emphasis of the last line. King's tragic fate could well be his own, it would seem.

After this emotional passage, the mood turns quieter as various classical figures proceed to try to account for the tragic accident. Triton, Neptune's herald, Aeolus, the god of the winds, and Camus, the god of the river Cam that flows through the Cambridge University campus, all wonder what happened and who is responsible. The last figure to speak is, however, an important Christian saint, Peter, the founder of the Church. Peter does not explain the sad event, but bemoans the loss to the Church of this young man, who would presumably have made a fine addition to the clergy (as university graduates often became and as Milton had thought seriously about becoming). His words reveal some strong thoughts about the nature of the contemporary Anglican clergy, according to Milton's increasingly critical point of view. In a striking metaphor he calls them

"Blind mouths! That scarce themselves know how to hold
A sheep-hook, or have learned aught else the least
That to the faithful herdsman's art belongs!

> What <u>recks</u> it them? What need they? They are <u>sped</u>;   *matters / provided for*
> And when they <u>list</u>, their lean and flashy songs   *wish*
> Grate on their <u>scrannel</u> pipes of wretched straw.   *thin, harsh*
> The hungry sheep look up, and are not fed,
> But swoln with wind, and the rank mist they <u>draw</u>,   *inhale*
> Rot inwardly, and foul contagion spread,
> Besides what the grim wolf with privy paw
> Daily devours apace, and nothing said.
> But that two-handed engine at the door
> Stands ready to smite once, and smite no more."   (119–131)

This is another passage in which Milton's passionate concern for his church and his country breaks through the otherwise somewhat artificial situation of the shepherd in the fields guarding his flocks. Here the bad shepherd is clearly a symbol for the corruption among the contemporary clergy, who, Milton believed, were concerned only with their own advancement and prosperity, not with the people who desperately needed their care. The disease (or sin) of sheep-rot is destroying the flock, along with the secret agents of the Roman Catholic Church (the wolf) that are flourishing within the Church at the expense of the poor, bewildered, and trusting English people. This is Milton's response to the growing effort of Archbishop Laud and Charles I to proceed with their efforts to expand the power of the bishops and to eliminate the Presbyterian Church in Scotland. Judgment awaits them, St. Peter declares, for God will not approve their divisive endeavors. The harsh images of disease, brutish violence, and "the two-handed engine" (a much-discussed image that suggests, among other things, an executioner's axe) combine to represent the growing conflict in the country that four years after the poem was published erupted into civil war.

After this dissonant passage Milton returns to the pastoral mood again with a catalogue of flowers that may be used to decorate Lycidas's bier, though the poet notes that his body has never been found and may be anywhere at sea or under it. He continues, however, to offer consolation to the shepherds with the news that Lycidas after all is alive in heaven through Christ's redemptive action. Lycidas, he suggests, is now enjoying the society of the saints, and may even serve as the local "genius of the shore" where he died, to protect others who may pass that way in the future. Milton concludes his poem by introducing another speaker, who describes the shepherd that had been "singing" the poem up to this point:

> Thus sang the <u>uncouth swain</u> to th'oaks and rills,   *rustic youth*
> While the still morn went out with sandals gray;

He touched the tender stops of various quills,
With eager thought warbling his <u>Doric lay</u>:   *pastoral song*
And now the sun had stretched out all the hills,
And now was dropped into the western bay;
At last he rose, and twitched his mantle blue:
Tomorrow to fresh woods, and pastures new.   (186–193)

Here we step outside the poet to observe him from a third-person perspective. We see the young pastoral poet completing his poem as the day
ends, taking up his blue cloak (the color of hope) and preparing to move on
to new challenges in the future. It is an image of closure with the sun falling
into the water and the evening spreading across the sky, as the poet puts the
tragedy of his friend behind him, but also one of renewed expectation for
what is to come. The last eight lines form a perfect stanza of ottava rima, an
Italian form used by poets such as Tasso (*Jerusalem Delivered*) and Ariosto
(*Orlando Furioso*), with its end-stopped lines, alternating rhyme, and a couplet at the end, reinforcing the sense of completion. All in all, it is a quiet
close to a poem that alternates between a conventional pastoralism and a passionate personal statement on the part of the poet, with the tensions resolved
and the emotions subdued. It is clearly a skilled performance that promises
much for the future of poetry.

It was a promise, however, that took a long time to be fulfilled, for Milton
wrote little poetry that we know of through the 1640s and 1650s (except for
some sonnets), involved as he was in the Puritan cause and later in the
operation of the government. *Paradise Lost* is his great achievement, but it
was only published much later, in 1667, though he may have worked on it
through these years of service. Milton had long thought of writing an epic that
would celebrate his country, but that goal changed over the years to focus
more on the story of the creation from the Bible, including the fall of the
angels and, especially, the fall of human beings from God's grace. For the
Renaissance, the epic was the supreme form of poetry, with Homer and Virgil
acknowledged as the greatest of all poets. Milton set out to match, and
transcend, these revered classical writers by detailing the biblical account and
dramatizing its cosmic implications. He believed that the Christian story far
outweighed the classical actions involving Troy and Rome, being more universal and ultimately more true. His main purpose, as he states at the outset of
his poem, is to "assert Eternal Providence, / And justify the ways of God to
men" (1: 25–26). Milton adapts the epic form, then, to his Christian message.

It will obviously be impossible to cover the whole of the poem, since *Paradise Lost* runs to more than 10,500 lines in all. We will examine only a few

representative passages that illustrate some of the most important aspects of Milton's art in the poem. From these, however, readers should be able to follow on their own the complicated developments of the action and the various interrelations of the characters and their deeds. Milton assumes a modest knowledge of Christian history on the part of the reader as well as some knowledge of classical epics, which I will discuss at certain points to help elucidate what is going on. A good example is the first verse paragraph in the poem, which contains not only the poet's statement of purpose, but also an invocation to the gods as was commonly found in an epic poem. Here are the first ten lines:

> Of man's first disobedience, and the fruit
> Of that forbidden tree, whose mortal taste
> Brought death into the world, and all our woe,
> With loss of Eden, till one greater Man
> Restore us, and regain the blissful seat,
> Sing Heav'nly Muse, that on the secret top
> Of Oreb, or of Sinai, didst inspire
> That shepherd, who first taught the chosen seed,   *Moses*
> In the beginning how the heav'ns and earth
> Rose out of Chaos. . . .   (1–10)

Here Milton, like previous epic writers, introduces us to the subject of his story, starting with the biblical account of original sin and the redemption provided by the incarnate Christ. Notice that the poet inverts the normal order of an English sentence by beginning with the object rather than the subject, reaching the verb ("Sing") only in line 6. This is typical of an epic, which often employs less common grammatical and linguistic forms because the subject and treatment are more elevated and significant than usual. Moreover, Milton calls upon the "Heav'nly Muse" to aid him in this task, signaling that it is the divine spirit that inspired Moses to write the Pentateuch he is invoking, not the usual classical god. Muses were necessary inspiration for epic poets because they needed special help to compose their long, complicated stories, but Milton calls upon a particularly holy muse for his sacred epic. He must be raised up by this muse "to the height of this great argument" (l: 24) as he says, in order to retell a story that is normally beyond human capacity. Thus does Milton establish from the start of his epic tale that he is writing in the classical mode, but with some significant differences based on its Christian content, more of which will be noted as we proceed. His choice of blank verse for his poetic medium enables him to use paragraphs of varying length to break up the narrative flow, instead of stanzas, and not to have to worry about rhyme.

The main characters in Milton's poem are, of course, Adam and Eve, but there are also supernatural figures such as Satan, Christ, and God the Father, together with important angels like Michael and Raphael, and various devils. Satan occupies our attention in the first part of the story because Milton begins with his rebellion and journey to the earth. This is the middle of the story (the technical term is from the Latin phrase *in medias res*), which forces the poet to go back in time later on to fill in some of the background of the action. Satan and his fallen angels find themselves in Hell after being "Hurled headlong flaming from th'ethereal sky" (line 45) by God when they began their rebellion against Him. Satan must find a way to regroup his troops in order to gain revenge against God, though he knows it will not be easy. He calls an assembly of the fallen angels and has a capitol erected whose construction is impressively rapid, but whose solidity is doubtful: "out of the earth a fabric huge / Rose like an exhalation" (1: 710–711) in the shape of a temple. This is called "Pandemonium" (a Miltonic coinage meaning "all demons"), where all the leaders of the various groups of fallen angels are to meet and discuss the recent events to see what might be done. As they gather, Milton employs a traditional epic simile of a swarm of bees to describe their coming together:

As bees

In springtime, when the sun with <u>Taurus</u> rides,   *a zodiac sign*
Pour forth their populous youth about the hive
In clusters; they among fresh dews and flowers
Fly to and fro, or on the smoothèd plank,
The suburb of their straw-built citadel
New rubbed with balm, expatiate and confer
Their state affairs. So thick the aery crowd
Swarmed and were straitened; till the signal giv'n,
Behold a wonder! They but now who seemed
In bigness to surpass Earth's giant sons
Now less than smallest dwarfs, in narrow room
Throng numberless, like that Pygmean race
Beyond the Indian mount, or fairy elves,
Whose midnight revels, by a forest side
Or fountain some belated peasant sees,
Or dreams he sees. . . .   (1: 768–784)

At first this may sound like a positive comparison between the fallen angels and the busy bees of spring working among the flowers and bushes, but the irony emerges more clearly when they are compared to dwarfs and pygmies, and even to fairies, which may in fact be illusions. The irony is even greater when we recall the purpose of the fallen angels' actions: they are considering how to gain their revenge against God. Physically, these angels have reduced themselves to the condition of insects; morally and spiritually, their condition is equally diminished, as they prepare to make war on their Creator. Their marvelous sudden diminution illustrates the supernatural powers they have and that they misuse. Their "straw-built citadel" is hardly a solid foundation to build on, and they discuss their "state affairs" as if they were political leaders of an important country. Meanwhile, most of them swarm together in groups, acting like conventional people who have no independent thoughts. Milton's poem contains humor that is often sardonic, if not actually satiric. Without stating his point, Milton expresses it obliquely, yet with clarity and incisiveness.

In Book 2 Satan opens up the discussion of their present situation by allowing some of his closest associates to present their advice. He presides like a eastern potentate sitting "High on a throne of royal state, which far / Outshone the wealth of Ormus [modern Hormuz on the Persian Gulf] and of Ind" [India] (2: 1–2). This strongly suggests Satan's pride and pretense, since he is ironically described as having been "by merit raised / To that bad eminence" (2: 5–6). It soon will be obvious that Satan is concerned primarily with his own power and prestige, and hopes to regain at least something of his lost stature by leading the attack on God in revenge for their defeat. It is a foolish and futile hope, of course, but he is able to accomplish more than we might expect because of the weakness and sinfulness of human beings. After allowing several other speakers to suggest possible ways of responding to God's punishment, Satan volunteers for the heroic task of venturing forth from Hell to explore the universe to see if there is any means to escape from their present condition. He plays the role of the epic hero here, bent on challenging God's order in whatever way he can; no one else is to share this task with him. As he leaves Hell, Satan meets two allegorical monsters: Sin, who is part woman and part serpent, but also his daughter whom he does not at first recognize, and Death, a fierce shadow who challenges Satan's desire to leave, and who, it turns out, is his son by Sin. Their incestuous relationships illustrate their immoral past, while the interaction among the three of them at this point is amusingly grim. After their initial hostility to one another, they come to form a kind of Infernal Trinity, bound together in hatred, malice, and vindictiveness. Sin eventually opens the gate of Hell for Satan, but cannot shut it. Satan then flies out into the chaos of space that tosses him about, but he gains encouragement from old Night (chaos) to spread "havoc and spoil and ruin" (2: 1009) where he can, especially in the newly created earth. It is an ominous beginning for Satan's journey, as he wends his way toward the new planet that is connected to heaven by a golden chain. The first act in the battle has begun.

At the beginning of Book 3 the narrator again invokes the "Holy Light" of the "Heav'nly Muse" to celebrate, in a sense, his own escape from Hell to the regions nearer the light of God, mourning his limitation as a blind bard, who has, he feels, only a weakened physical and spiritual condition to recount this powerful story. It is a poignant moment as the poet considers his personal relation to the tragic tale he has been called to retell, wondering if he has lost divine favor. The narrator, nevertheless, does find the inner strength through God's grace to continue his active role throughout the epic as our guide to its meaning and significance. As he says to his special muse,

> thee I revisit safe,
> And feel thy sovran vital lamp; but thou
> Revisit'st not these eyes, that roll in vain
> To find thy piercing ray, and find no dawn;
> So thick a drop serene hath quenched their orbs,
> Or dim <u>suffusion</u> veiled. . . .   *cataracts*
>   (3: 21–26)

Milton feels the ray of light, but cannot see it because of the cataracts (it seems) that left his eyes in perfect external condition, but sightless. After comparing himself with Homer, Tiresias, and other blind figures of old, Milton describes his unfortunate condition in relation to nature and its meaning for him:

> Thus with the year
> Seasons return, but not to me returns
> Day, or the sweet approach of ev'n or morn,
> Or sight of vernal bloom, or summer's rose,
> Or flocks, or herds, or human face divine;
> But cloud instead, and ever-during dark
> Surrounds me, from the cheerful ways of men
> Cut off, and for the <u>book of knowledge</u> fair   *nature*
> Presented with a universal blank
> Of nature's works to me expunged and <u>razed</u>,   *erased*
> And wisdom at one entrance quite shut out.   (3: 40–50)

Although one whole avenue of knowledge about God (through nature and the human form) has been eliminated for him, the narrator realizes that he still has the inner light of the Holy Spirit available to him, on which he is now completely dependent. It is doubly distressing to him because he once had his sight, and clearly remembers the seasons and the other beauties of nature. Thus does Milton transform the conventional invocation into a beautifully sad personal lament that is also a reaffirmation of his theme, justifying God's ways to human beings.

The voice of the bard, in fact, helps to unify and direct this long, complex poem in ways that reflect Milton's purpose in it. Other invocations occur at the beginning of Book 7 and Book 9, where he declares that he "now must change / Those notes to tragic" (9: 5–6) and contrasts his poem with the epics of old that celebrated knights and battles. His own is about a "higher" subject, which seems to have divine support as he continues to be inspired by his "celestial patroness, who deigns / Her nightly visitation unimplored" (9: 21–22). The narrator also occasionally interrupts the action to comment on it, as he does when he appears to identify himself with the angelic choir that sings the praises of the Father and the Son, especially when Christ offers to sacrifice himself for human sin:

> O unexampled love,
> Love nowhere to be found less than divine!
> Hail Son of God, Saviour of men, thy name
> Shall be the copious matter of my song
> Henceforth, and never shall my harp thy praise
> Forget, nor from thy Father's praise disjoin.   (3: 410–415)

Moreover, the narrator's similes and metaphors often make clear where his sympathies lie, as when he compares Satan to a vulture after that rebellious angel has landed on the outermost sphere of the cosmos for the first time, to survey what damage he can do. Like a bird of prey, Satan is ready to "gorge" himself on "the flesh of lambs or yeanling [newborn] kids" (3: 434), though in his case it is less physical than moral feeding. At the beginning of Book 4 the narrator desires to have that "warning voice" heard by John (Rev. 12:3–12) to alert humans to the desperate danger that threatens them, though he knows it is utterly futile. The narrator is a partisan, though he knows his cause is lost, at least in the immediate context.

Milton's characterization of Satan is occasionally more complex than we might expect. He is evil embodied, of course, but he was an archangel before he fell and retains some of his old luster, even though his mind is deeply stained by his rebellion against God and his desire for revenge. Early in Book 4 the narrator describes him as being filled with "horror and doubt" (4: 18) as he considers what he hopes to do to get even, with his conscience moving him to distraction and despair. In a kind of dramatic soliloquy Satan speaks aloud to himself, revealing the depth of his inner turmoil. Here he is more honest with himself than he usually is when he talks to others, so this passage gives a good indication of his mental state. He even admits that it was his own "pride and worse ambition" that caused his fall and that "all [God's] good proved ill in me" (4: 40, 48). He also confesses that what he did was by his own choice, that his will was free, yet that is not enough to make him repent of his sin. Though he is tortured by his sin and admits his guilt, he will never submit to his Creator:

> "Me miserable! Which way shall I fly
> Infinite wrath, and infinite despair?
> Which way I fly is Hell; myself am Hell;
> And in the lowest deep a lower deep
> Still threat'ning to devour me opens wide,
> To which the Hell I suffer seems a Heav'n.
> O then at last relent! is there no place
> Left for repentance, none for pardon left?"   (4: 73–80)

Satan is fully conscious of his choices, but because he is driven by pride, rage, and ambition, he cannot choose remorse and submission as he should. He recognizes that he must give up all hope of mercy because Hell is within him, not a separate place, but he clings to a foolish belief in his own power to share sovereignty with "Heav'n's King":

> "Evil be thou my good; by thee at least
> Divided empire with Heav'n's King I hold
> By thee, and more than half perhaps will reign;
> As man ere long, and this new world shall know."   (4: 110–113)

It is a dramatic moment as we watch Satan deliberately opt for evil, knowing full well what this means. The human passions that beset him are surely ones we can also recognize in ourselves or in others around us, and help make him a more human figure than we have seen heretofore.

From Satan we shall skip over a large part of the middle section of the poem in order to focus more in detail on the climax of the action. We thus miss much of the background of the story, recounted by the archangel Raphael to Adam and Eve, including Satan's mutiny against God, the war in heaven, and the creation of the earth and its inhabitants to replace the fallen angels. The picture of God in these passages is perhaps the least-admired part of the poem, because He seems (to some at least) to talk like an arrogant tyrant or a grumpy old schoolmaster. Adam also tells Raphael about his and Eve's creation, since the archangel is interested in learning about how humans came to be on earth; angels, clearly, are not omniscient like God. In describing Eve, Adam reveals how deep his feeling is for her beauty, suggesting a fatal weakness in his nature. Raphael in fact warns him about his susceptibility to her charms before he leaves them, and admonishes them to be sure to obey God's rules. In any event, the "happy pair" are now fully instructed in God's rules for the garden. Ignorance can never be their excuse. They have complete freedom there, except for the prohibition on eating the fruit of the Tree of Knowledge. That is the one requirement. Both know it and gladly obey it, at first. Satan, meanwhile, is lurking about the garden. The stage is set for their ultimate trial.

Satan's first entrance into Paradise is stopped by the angel Gabriel after he is caught whispering in Eve's ear and causing a disturbing dream to trouble her thoughts. He returns to Paradise, however, in disguise, first as a mist and then as a serpent, the "subtlest beast of all the field" (9: 86). Deceit is the only way to fulfill his goal of revenge, since the angels are carefully guarding Eden, having been warned of his presence. Fortunately for him, Eve suggests to Adam that they would be more productive in their work of pruning and cultivating if they separate, instead of working together. Although Adam objects to this idea, he eventually allows her to work away from him because he thinks she will be unhappy with him otherwise. It is a fateful decision, to say the least. From it stems "all our woe," for Eve is not meant to stand alone in confronting evil. When Satan finds her by herself, he rejoices, but he also, ironically, delights in seeing her "heav'nly form" (9: 457); in fact, her beauty momentarily stuns him until, through an act of will, he deliberately dismisses such feelings in order to carry out "her ruin" as he has planned. Even Satan, Milton suggests, could still have been saved had he allowed his natural feelings their proper expression. But he is too committed to revenge and malice to change.

The temptation scene is a masterpiece of deception and self-deception. Satan, in the serpent's shape, engages Eve's attention by addressing her in highly flattering terms as a "goddess among gods," who should be attended by "angels numberless" (9: 547, 548). She is naturally astonished that this snake can speak, which gives him an opening to claim he has been transformed by eating the fruit of a certain tree in the garden nearby, making him a reasonable creature with the gift of language, unlike all the other animals. Eve's curiosity is piqued, though she also notices that he is "overpraising" her in his speech, which raises questions about his truthfulness. Nevertheless, she asks to be taken to see the fruit, so Satan is able to play the role of a miraculously enlightened serpent, who wants to help her become a better, more knowledgeable person. When Eve sees the tree, she realizes that God has expressly forbidden her to taste its fruit, and tells Satan this. He is incredulous (or poses at being), and draws himself up like a classical orator of old, who believes that he must defend human liberty against the restrictions of the "Threatener" (9: 687), the enemy of human freedom and growth:

> Queen of this universe, do not believe
> Those rigid threats of death; Ye shall not die:
> How should ye? By the fruit? It gives you life
> To knowledge. By the Threatener? Look on me,
> Me who have touched and tasted, yet both live,
> And life more perfect have attained than fate
> Meant me, by vent'ring higher than my lot.   (9: 684–690)

Satan claims that he himself is living proof that eating the fruit will not cause death, and he suggests that God is a tyrant who wants to keep Adam and Eve "low and ignorant" (9: 704), without the sublime knowledge of divine beings. How can God be just and deny wisdom to them? It is a superb speech, filled with lies and half-truths, innuendo and rhetorical questions, made plausible by his wit and his overwhelming desire for revenge.

Eve is impressed with his arguments, and adds her own to make her eating of the fruit irresistible. She wonders how God can justify his rule against eating it since it brings knowledge and wisdom. As she exclaims,

> what forbids he but to know,
> Forbids us good, forbids us to be wise?
> Such prohibitions bind not. But if death
> Bind us with <u>after-bands</u>, what profits then   *later bonds*
> Our inward freedom? In the day we eat
> Of this fair fruit, our doom is, we shall die.
> How dies the serpent? He hath eat'n and lives,
> And knows, and speaks, and reasons, and discerns,
> Irrational till then. For us alone
> Was death invented?   (9: 758–767)

Eve is incredulous about God's rules, claiming they are not truly binding, but she does waver a bit when she thinks of the punishment for disobedience, though she does not know yet what death is. Certainly the serpent has not died after eating it; in fact, he has been transformed by the fruit into a rational creature, or so it seems. The empirical evidence supporting the snake is strong, and, after all, why would death be just for humans? It makes no sense to her, and so she eats, impulsively and without further ado. The earth shudders, but she does not notice, wrapped up as she is in the delightful taste of the fruit. As she savors the luscious bite, Eve experiences a kind of ecstasy and revels in her newfound knowledge, but she also wonders if the "great Forbidder" (9: 815) has seen her and considers how best to approach Adam with her discovery. Should she share her secret with him or keep it to herself, so she can have an advantage over him? That will not do, however, if she is going to die, and Adam is not. What if he finds another Eve to keep him company? "A death to think" (9: 830), she declares, and goes to share her fate with him. Her own reasoning has betrayed her and soon will betray her mate.

When she finds Adam, Eve exults in her new condition, claiming that the forbidden fruit has caused her eyes to be opened, among other effects:

> Dim erst, [now] dilated spirits, ampler heart,   *before*
> And growing up to godhead; which for thee
> Chiefly I sought, without thee can despise.   (9: 876–878)

Her claim to divinity is false, of course, as is her claim to have done it for him. The lies begin, and nothing can stop the downward spiral of their relationship. But how does Adam respond to this sudden, unthinkable development? He is horrified and knows she is lost. What should he do? It is a momentous decision he must make now, but it does not take him long.

Adam makes, naturally, the wrong decision. He opts to share Eve's fate because he cannot imagine life without her, so dear to him has she become since her creation. As he says,

> "Should God create another Eve, and I
> Another rib afford, yet loss of thee
> Would never from my heart; no no, I feel
> The link of nature draw me: flesh of flesh,
> Bone of my bone thou art, and from thy state
> Mine never shall be parted, bliss or woe."   (9: 911–916)

He tells her, quite calmly, how wrong she has been to disobey God, but maybe, he rationalizes, God will not do what He said He would, and allow Satan to claim victory over Him. In any event, Adam proclaims, "to lose thee were to lose myself" (9: 959), so he feels, tragically, that he has no choice but to follow her example. The images of flesh and bone are not metaphors for Adam, but actual physical ties that bind him irrevocably to her. Eve is naturally ecstatic, and believes they will experience "life / Augmented," with "opened eyes, new hopes, new joys" (9: 985–986). So Adam eats, and nature groans again, though he too does not notice. The first effect of the Fall is that Adam and Eve become inflamed with lust and take "their fill of love" (9: 1042), but their innocence is gone. When Adam awakes from this "amorous play," he proceeds to condemn Eve for giving in to "that false worm" and advises that they cover themselves to conceal those parts of their bodies that are most shameful, a feeling they never had before. From this point, they fall to mutual recrimination over their sin until it seems it will never end. They sound very much like a modern couple on the brink of separation and divorce, though their language is somewhat more formal. It is now a portrait of a marriage in serious trouble. Their innocence is gone, and tragedy has struck.

Book 10 is filled with the inevitable consequences of the Fall. God sends Christ to pronounce judgment upon the guilty pair, who at first blame each other or Satan, but not themselves. We also see Sin and Death, Satan's offspring, speeding toward the earth over a new bridge that crosses chaos now that they have been given dominion there. Satan returns to Hell to proclaim his great victory before the assembled multitude of fallen angels, but when he finishes his victory speech, as he and all the rest begin to celebrate, they suddenly fall to the ground hissing like snakes as God carries out his judgment against them. They, too, are fooled by the appearance of the Tree of Knowledge, and as they partake of the delicious-looking fruit, find that it is only dust and ashes in their mouths. Meanwhile, Adam and Eve debate how to react to God's judgment, finally deciding, after considering all their options (including suicide), to seek His forgiveness through repentance and submission. Eve is the first to urge contrition after Adam harshly rejects her for causing him to fall. Throwing herself at his feet, she begs him to be merciful and kind toward her, and offers to go back "to the place of judgment" where she will, as she puts it,

> with my cries importune Heaven, that all
> The sentence from thy head removed may light
> On me, sole cause to thee of all this woe,
> Me me only just object of his ire.   (10: 933–936)

The pathos in Eve's voice shows how Milton can vary his poetic voice according to the context. His manner is not only the "grand style" of the epic, but incorporates a vast range of tone, nuance, and feeling. Eve's offer to accept all the punishment on her own head, even for him, teaches Adam the true meaning of sacrificial love. As a result, he relents and offers to do the same for her, saying that God has not been so harsh with them but that some good will come out of their sin. Her seed, after all, will "bruise / The serpent's head," and God will teach them how to adapt to their new way of life if they submit to His judgment with humility and sorrow. They are beginning to understand and accept the serious nature of their sin and their need to repent.

Books 11 and 12 continue their education. After Christ pleads for mercy for them, the archangel Michael is sent to announce their exile from Paradise and to instruct them in the future of their race. Both are much dismayed by the need to leave their home. Adam alone is given a vision of what is to come, and it is not a pretty picture. Rather, it is an endless succession of conflict and degradation, weakness and violence, as humans fail to follow God's laws or His prophets. Adam is seriously depressed by what he witnesses. Occasionally, God's grace enters history, often in the life of an individual like Noah or Abraham, to alleviate, at least temporarily, the otherwise endless suffering and evil. Such sights make Adam rejoice, but these are only brief moments of respite until the coming of Christ, the Messiah, who offers his life for all of humanity and their sins. Adam has learned that to love and obey God is what he most needs to do, in order to retain that "paradise within" that Michael says can be preserved, despite the evil of the world. The Holy Spirit will provide guidance and comfort for humans in the world, but corruption will enter even the church where "Wolves shall succeed for teachers" (12: 508), concerned only for their own gain. Life will not be easy, but Adam says he is ready for whatever might come. Eve too is ready, having been instructed through dreams about their future life in the fallen world. As Michael leads them by the hand east out of Eden, "Our lingering parents" naturally turn back to look at their "happy seat" with both resignation and regret:

> Some natural tears they dropped, but wiped them soon;
> The world was all before them, where to choose
> Their place of rest, and Providence their guide:
> They hand in hand with wand'ring steps and slow,
> Through Eden took their solitary way.   (12: 645–649)

It is a perfect closing for Adam and Eve with their full knowledge of the life to come and of their guilt, chastened and subdued but not desperate, for they have "Providence" to lead them on. The image of them holding hands as they slowly proceed to exit Paradise suggests they accept the mutual dependence they now must practice in order to live in the fallen world. Milton ends not with a bang or a whimper, but on a note of tempered pathos, a mixture of realistic expectations for a difficult future with the hope of God's continuing guidance for them.

We have only touched the surface of this great poem. It is a magnificent achievement that will hold its own against the other great epics in literature, a human drama to which, I think, we all can relate, no matter what our beliefs. As with Shakespeare, the more one reads Milton's poem, the more it will reveal of depth and insight into the human condition.

One final work by Milton is worth our consideration. He took the familiar biblical story of Samson and Delilah (or Dalila, as Milton spells her name) and cast it in the form of a Greek tragedy called *Samson Agonistes*, again adapting a classical form to serve a Christian purpose. It was, however, never intended to be performed on stage (and as such is called a "closet drama"), being more an exercise in literary construction than part of a theatrical tradition (the Puritans being very suspicious of the theater). It is, nevertheless, a highly successful dramatic poem. The title refers to the struggle Samson undergoes as he wrestles with his unexpected fate: he had thought he was intended by God to become a hero to his people, but his enemies, the Philistines, have captured and enslaved him. The struggle is thus primarily an inner one that is carried on at several levels: physical, moral, and spiritual. Milton employs some of the standard features of the Greek tragedy, including a chorus representing a group of ordinary Hebrews, a series of encounters between the hero and several other characters, and a climax that is violent but not pictured directly, only reported by a messenger who has witnessed the scene. The story was no doubt especially meaningful for Milton, who must have been attracted by this heroic figure who becomes a savior of his people, though blind and surrounded by his enemies.

The scene opens near the end of the biblical narrative of Samson with him as a miserable prisoner of the Philistines, reflecting on his wretched existence while taking a break from his forced labor of grinding grain for them. They have blinded him and now are celebrating a holiday honoring their god Dagon for delivering their great enemy, Samson, to them, despite his enormous physical strength. Samson can only wonder at his humiliating condition ("Eyeless in Gaza at the mill with slaves" [line 41], as he puts it) and reproach himself with his weakness, having revealed the secret of his strength to his wife. It is his blindness of which he most complains, when he describes his condition in graphic and pathetic terms:

O dark, dark, dark, amid the blaze of noon,
Irrecoverably dark, total Eclipse
Without all hope of day!
O first created Beam, and thou great Word,
"Let there be light, and light was over all";
Why am I thus bereav'd thy prime decree?   (80–85)

Samson has lost all hope, not only physically but also spiritually. God is completely missing from his life, the light of day having been totally eliminated. God is light and formed his world from it, so Samson can only lament his apparent alienation from his Maker as he wallows in self-pity and despair. It is a sad sight to see this powerful man brought to such a low condition.

As the Chorus discreetly approaches him wondering at this terrible fate, Samson seems ready for death. But in talking with them he "revives" a little as he considers his situation. He now claims that his blindness is the least of his worries, since he could not bear to see himself in such a condition, and he blames others, from Dalila to the Hebrew leaders and even God, for betraying him. He also occasionally blames himself (though not for long) as he struggles to make sense of his fate. When his father, Manoa, comes to see him, he too laments his son's miserable condition and announces that he intends to ransom Samson and take him home to live quietly in obscurity. Samson declares, however, that he is responsible for what has happened to him, for a "foul effeminacy held me yok't," as he puts it, Dalila's "Bondslave" (lines 410–411). He is weary of life, he says, tormented by a sense of abject failure, and all he wants now is to die as soon as possible, an early death being his last hope. In the kind of choral ode typically found in a Greek tragedy, the Chorus sums up their view that Samson should be patient and resigned, since it is impossible to fathom the reason for his fall and suffering, God's providence being ultimately mysterious. They agree that from their view it appears that the "Just or unjust alike, seem miserable" (line 703), so there is little reason to hope for Samson. No one can understand why he must suffer like this, but such is life.

Samson's next visitor, his wife Dalila, provokes him more than his father. As she approaches, the Chorus describes her in memorable terms:

But who is this, what thing of Sea or Land?
Female of sex it seems,
That, so bedeckt, ornate, and gay,
Comes this way sailing

Like a stately ship
Of _Tarsus_, bound for th'Isles   *in Turkey*
Of _Javan_ or _Gadire_,   *Greece / Cadiz*
With all her bravery on, and tackle trim,
Sails fill'd, and streamers waving,
Courted by all the winds that hold them play,
An Amber scent of odorous perfume
Her harbinger, a damsel train behind. . . .   (710–721)

Dalila is clearly a flashy, fragrant woman who is out to attract attention to herself, hoping especially, as we will see, to allure her alienated husband. The image that Milton employs of the sailing ship decorated for entry into a harbor clearly suggests her pride and concern with outward appearance. She is a dangerous kind of femme fatale that Samson has succumbed to before. This time she is not successful, however, as he sternly rebukes her, even though she pleads for him to forgive her and admits her guilt. He treats her as a traitor and refuses to have anything to do with her, despite her promises to love and serve him at home for the rest of his days. He will pardon her, he says, but only at a distance, since otherwise he might be prompted to violence by her nearness. As she leaves disappointed, the Chorus comments with some sardonic humor, calling her a "manifest Serpent by her sting / Discover'd in the end, till now conceal'd" (lines 997–998).

One more character comes to visit Samson, Harapha, the giant Philistine warrior who hopes to triumph over the fallen Hebrew hero. Milton has invented this character to offer a final challenge to Samson, perhaps as a further stimulant to rouse him from his despair. Harapha brags that he would easily have beaten the Hebrew warrior if they had ever met in hand-to-hand combat, and declares that he would have "left thy carcase where the ass lay thrown" (line 1097), as he puts it. Samson challenges him directly, but Harapha says he will not fight a blind man, as if that would be too easy. Of course, he makes sure he does not get too close to Samson, who treats him with contempt for his obvious cowardice. Out of this encounter Samson discovers a growing sense of faith and a renewed belief in his own special destiny. He accepts more fully than before his own responsibility for what has happened, and declares his absolute "trust . . . in the Living God" (line 1140):

All these indignities, for such they are
From <u>thine</u>, these evils I deserve and more,   *thy people*
Acknowledge them from God inflicted on me

Justly, yet despair not of his final pardon
Whose ear is ever open; and his eye
Gracious to re-admit the suppliant;
In confidence whereof I once again
Defy <u>thee</u> to the trial of mortal fight,   *Harapha*
By combat to decide whose god is God,
Thine or whom I with *Israel's* Sons adore.   (1168–1177)

Unwilling to fight, Harapha goes away, baffled by this defiant, imperious prisoner whom he had hoped to cow. Thus Samson's renewed spirit prepares him for the final scene when he must be ready for the ultimate sacrifice, confident in the support of his Lord. His despair is overcome, and his trust in the grace and forgiveness of his God has returned. Samson has been reborn.

Finally, when a Philistine officer comes to take Samson to the temple of Dagon to perform feats of strength for the crowd, the Israelite at first refuses to go with the officer for fear of dishonoring his God by serving His enemies. But before the officer returns to renew the order, Samson indicates to the Chorus that he could change his mind; he believes now that perhaps there is a good reason to go to the festival if he can do so without displeasing God. As he says to them,

Be of good courage; I begin to feel
Some rousing motions in me which dispose
To something extraordinary my thoughts.   (1381–1383)

We hear a new confidence in Samson as he encourages the Chorus not to give up hope, for a strange feeling appears to be leading him to change his mind to go to the temple, despite his qualms. This seems to be the Holy Spirit, guiding him to act without a clear idea what is to come. Even though Samson himself does not know what he will do there, he feels it still may present some opportunity for him. After he bids farewell to the Chorus and reassures them he will not do anything to dishonor his God or his people, the action moves swiftly to its close. Manoa comes to discuss with the Chorus his hope of ransoming Samson, but they are interrupted first by a great shout from the crowd as Samson performs something spectacular, and shortly after, an even greater shout and noise reaches them from the festival, which stuns and terrifies them. A witness soon arrives from the scene to report what has happened, though he delays revealing Samson's fate for some lines in order to break the news gently to Manoa. When he does tell them that Samson is dead, Manoa is ready to indulge his grief until he discovers the manner of his death. The messenger's full description of the incident reveals that Samson has heroically destroyed all the Philistine leaders and priests who had gathered there, thus consoling Manoa for his son's death. As a result, Manoa can now celebrate Samson's noble action:

> Nothing is here for tears, nothing to wail
> Or knock the breast, no weakness, no contempt,
> Dispraise, or blame, nothing but well and fair,
> And what may quiet us in a death so noble.   (1721–1724)

Samson has turned the tables on the Philistines by using his extraordinary strength to destroy them and their temple. This is the typical reversal (or *peripeteia*) at the end of a Greek tragedy, which brings about a result opposite to that expected or intended. Manoa promises to build a monument to his son that will inspire young men of the future to serve God and their people. Even the Chorus is in awe of the power of God to bring good out of a seemingly impossible situation. It is a triumph for Samson, so the Chorus pays tribute to the "calm of mind, all passion spent" (line 1758) that they feel in the aftermath of the tragic event. This response is similar to the catharsis or purging of pity and fear that Aristotle believed was the effect of a typical tragedy, and which readers may feel as well in empathizing with Samson's fate.

Thus does Milton combine classical form with Christian themes in many of his works to present a cogent account of human weakness and evil, together with a suggestion of human potential for good if one will only act in accordance with God's will. Even without sharing Milton's faith, readers today can appreciate his vision of how human beings go astray, deluded by their own (or others') foolishness or malice, and how they can, perhaps, with help from a higher power, overcome their deficiencies and even triumph over great odds. Despite his strong beliefs, Milton was still able to project himself into many different minds and give voice to their thoughts as well as imagine a variety of situations that dramatize his vision with artistic grace and power. His own voice is no doubt that of seventeenth-century English Puritanism, but in many ways it is still relevant and meaningful today.

CHAPTER 7

Andrew Marvell (1621–1678): Pastoral Poet of Time and History

Our next poet, Andrew Marvell, was a friend and associate of Milton, but his life and poetry are less well documented than Milton's. We know only the broad outlines of Marvell's life, even though he served as a member of Parliament (M.P.) from 1659 to his death. We also are uncertain about the exact circumstances of some of his poems, such as when they were written, which ones are actually his, and, in a few cases, what words were his final choice for them. Most of Marvell's poems were never published in his lifetime, but were printed only after his death by his housekeeper, who claimed to have been his wife. The poems were largely ignored until the nineteenth century, gradually gaining in appreciation and reputation over the years. Since the early part of the twentieth century, they have been widely accepted as among the best lyric poems written in the seventeenth century.

Marvell spent his childhood in Hull (Yorkshire), the son of a clergyman who preached at Holy Trinity Church and his wife, Anne Pease, about whom little is known. He went to Trinity College, Cambridge University, where he stayed for two years after receiving his B.A. From 1642 to 1647 Marvell traveled on the continent, polishing his knowledge of modern languages and avoiding the bloody conflict of the English Civil War. In the 1650s he tutored children associated with the Cromwellian regime and eventually became (in 1657) Milton's assistant as Latin Secretary for the Commonwealth. In 1659 he was elected M.P. for Hull and served his constituents faithfully for nineteen years, regularly writing informative letters to them about the state of the kingdom. In his later years Marvell, drawing on his involvement in the political issues of his time, wrote several satires in prose and verse, attacking abuses in the government, especially the corruption in the court of Charles II. Satire was a newly popular form of poetry at this time, but Marvell's are so dense with topical allusion and contemporary references that they are difficult for the ordinary reader to appreciate. It is Marvell's fine wit, resonant ideas, haunting images, and rhythmic verse that attract most readers today.

Marvell's poem "To His Coy Mistress" is undoubtedly his best-known work, and deservedly so. He transforms the *carpe diem* (literally "seize the day") tradition in this poem with original imagery and powerful arguments. The poem consists of three verse paragraphs with the speaker addressing his beloved throughout, trying to convince her to be less "coy." In contrast to Donne's love poetry, there is here no strong sense of an immediate situation or a distinct personality who is speaking. In the first paragraph the speaker imagines what he would do if they had an infinite amount of space and time to pursue their love:

> Had we but world enough, and time,
> This coyness, lady, were no crime.
> We would sit down, and think which way
> To walk, and pass our long love's day.
> Thou by the Indian Ganges' side
> Shouldst rubies find; I by the tide
> Of <u>Humber</u> would complain. I would   *a river near Hull*
> Love you ten years before the Flood,
> And you should, if you please, refuse
> Till the <u>conversion of the Jews</u>.   *just before the Last Judgment*
> My vegetable love should grow
> Vaster than empires, and more slow;
> An hundred years should go to praise
> Thine eyes, and on thy forehead gaze;
> Two hundred to adore each breast,
> But thirty thousand to the rest:
> An age at least to every part,
> And the last age should show your heart.
> For, lady, you deserve this state,
> Nor would I love at lower rate.   (1–20)

If they had time, the poet proclaims, they could savor their love in anticipation at great distances, from the exotic Orient with its lovely precious stones to the prosaic English river, and over many centuries from "before the

Flood" (an impossibility, of course) to the end of time. It is, clearly, an elaborate compliment to the lady, who is worthy of the most extended courtship, even worship, as is suggested by the biblical images. The images are extravagant, even absurd, with the speaker's "vegetable love"growing in scope and time to cover the globe and the whole of human history. The poet focuses on the number of years he could devote to adoring her beauty, not on describing it (unlike many such poems), with the final act being the revelation of her love for him. All of this is in good fun, of course, self-consciously witty and imaginative on the part of the speaker as he develops his attack on a conventionally modest and reluctant beloved, who remains a shadowy figure in the poem.

The second paragraph introduces a realistic note in the courtship. We cannot afford to indulge our wishes in this process, the poet declares, because time is passing quickly and death is ever near. Once dead, our love will be lost, so we must act now:

> But at my back I always hear
> Time's winged chariot hurrying near;
> And yonder all before us lie
> Deserts of vast eternity.
> Thy beauty shall no more be found,
> Nor, in thy marble vault, shall sound
> My echoing sound; then worms shall try
> That long-preserved virginity,
> And your quaint honor turn to dust,
> And into ashes all my lust:
> The grave's a fine and private place,
> But none, I think, do there embrace. (21–32)

The urgency is vivid and powerful, as the imagery becomes threatening and bleak. Time's flight is embodied in the "winged chariot," which suggests a warrior of old speeding through the air ready to cut them down. Eternity is a desert, huge and desolate (in contrast to his "vegetable love" that is green and growing). The only active force left will be the worms that destroy her beauty in the grave, and make a mockery of her "quaint honor," which has kept her pure and unsullied. "Quaint" is finely dismissive and superior. The poet's praise of the grave is highly ironic, and its lack of love finely understated, especially with the interrupting phrase, "I think." Through these images Marvell brings the dangers that surround them and threaten their love down to concrete terms that graphically portray their vulnerability.

In the final paragraph the poet concludes that, in order to meet this threat, they must act on their feelings now. Otherwise, they will be subject to time's inexorable climax, to death and the end of all possible enjoyment, which may come at any moment. It is the old argument of the libertine and hedonist that immediate pleasure should never be deferred because it may be lost forever:

> Now therefore, while the youthful hue
> Sits on thy skin like morning dew,
> And while thy willing soul transpires
> At every pore with instant fires,
> Now let us sport us while we may,
> And now, like amorous birds of prey,
> Rather at once our time devour
> Than languish in his slow-<u>chapped</u> power.   *jawed*
> Let us roll all our strength and all
> Our sweetness up into one ball,
> And tear our pleasures with rough strife
> <u>Thorough</u> the iron gates of life: *through*
> Thus, though we cannot make our sun
> Stand still, yet we will make him run.   (33–46)

The imagery here becomes even more powerful and violent. The poet describes his beloved as both moist and burning, ready for the final consummation of their love. This is his reading of her, of course, but it is part of his persuasive argument. They must act "now" (note the insistent repetition of this word) and slay time or he will slay them, inevitably and inexorably. The speaker concedes that time is ultimately all-powerful, a beast that is ready to devour them, but for a moment, he declares, they can seize the opportunity to enjoy life even in his very shadow, by giving free rein to their feelings and concentrating them into this brief, furious experience of physical passion. The sweet ball of their love suggests unity, strength, and the sphere of perfection, but it also involves fierce physical action that may include breaking through "the iron gates of life" (a much-discussed image) into another realm. The sun represents their time of life, the daytime of their love. It is a sexual experience he is describing, certainly, but also one involving other ideas, such as time, death, and love. Marvell has the gift for evoking broad implications of meaning that go beyond the literal and the physical.

Not only are the images vividly concrete and highly suggestive on several levels, metaphorical as well as literal, they make the poet's case for their pursuit of pleasure in the context of human mortality. It is an argument of images and feelings rather than of ideas or propositions. The whole poem takes the form of a hypothetical syllogism, which was a logical formula for condensing an argument into a simple three-part statement: If such and such were true, then we could do thus and so, but it is not true, so we must do something else. No doubt Marvell drew on his extensive training in logic and rhetoric, central elements in the education of the time, to create this poem. The octosyllabic couplets in iambic meter underscore the poet's meaning with their regularly returning rhyme (as "youthful hue" is linked to "morning dew"), adding an echoing sound to the other pleasures of the verse. The last couplet in this passage is rhythmically effective as it runs on from the next-to-last line to the final one, suggesting through its continuing flow the difficulty in making time stop for themselves, and then confidently asserting in the last few words the couple's ability to delay time's power, if not to defeat it. In sum, this is an almost perfect example of its kind, though the genre itself may not be everyone's favorite. Some readers may object to the intent of the poet as immoral, but still one must admit that he has carried out his purpose with clarity, unity, imagination, and expressive force. Oddly, this is Marvell's only real love poem.

Other poems by Marvell give quite a different picture of him and his interests. He wrote several religious poems, as well as others that are clearly philosophical in import. In "The Coronet" Marvell raises serious Christian themes with a directness not found elsewhere in his poetry. The title refers to a floral wreath (it can be a collection of praise poems as well) that he wishes to offer Christ to replace the crown of thorns put on Him in mockery on Calvary. He gathers all the flowers he can find, including ones from his shepherdess's head, but his coronet is not as beautiful as he had hoped:

> And now, when I have summed up all my store,
>   Thinking (so I myself deceive)
>   So rich a <u>chaplet</u> thence to weave   *a wreath for the head*
> As never yet the King of Glory wore,
>   Alas! I find the serpent old,
>   That, <u>twining</u> in his speckled breast,   *entwining*
> About the flowers disguised does fold
> With <u>wreaths</u> of fame and interest.   *coils or garlands*
> (9–16)

Instead of the pure beauty of the flowers, the poet discovers a snake hidden in the bouquet, or sin in the form of his ambition, his self-interest, and his pride in his creation. The poet finds his motives for weaving his poems like the flowers to be mixed at best, certainly not as pure as he had thought. This is, of course, a general statement about how sin can creep into even the most seemingly innocent of human acts. It also implies that Christ's sacrifice is necessary and cannot be replaced by human effort or beauty. Christ must be humiliated, suffer greatly, and die before we can be saved. The poet concludes that only Christ has the power to break the reign of sin over us, to pierce the layers of deceit and self-delusion to which we are subject in this fallen world. So, the coronet perhaps,

> while thou [Christ] on both their spoils dost tread,
> May crown thy feet, that could not crown thy head.   (26–27)

It is a humbling conclusion, but at least, the poet thinks, his flowers might serve to decorate and honor Christ's feet. This is a good example of the Protestant emphasis on the prevalence of human sin, which permeates even the seemingly perfect world of the pastoral. Marvell, too, was not averse to puns, and may be thinking of his poetry again, with their feet of verse. The regular iambic lines in the last ten verses, after the irregularity of the first part, confirm the steadiness and stable order of Christ's victory over Satan.

A second religious poem, "Bermudas," takes an actual place for its subject. Although the Bermuda Islands had been discovered by a Spaniard early in the sixteenth century, the English had only recently taken an interest in them, as a haven from the religious conflict in their own country. Marvell lived for a few years with a Puritan clergyman by the name of John Oxenford, who had visited these islands when escaping the persecution of Archbishop Laud at home. The poet begins with the arrival of a "small boat" in the Bermudas with the travelers singing a hymn to the "listening winds" as they row along. The islands seem to rest comfortably and secretly in the safety of the maternal sea:

> Where the remote Bermudas ride
> In the ocean's bosom unespied,
> From a small boat that rowed along,
> The listening winds received this song:
>   "What should we do but sing his praise
> That led us through the wat'ry maze
> Unto an isle so long <u>unknown</u>,   *discovered only in 1515*
> And yet far kinder than our own?
> Where he the huge sea monsters <u>wracks</u>,   *destroys, wrecks*
> That lift the deep upon their backs;
> He lands us on a grassy stage,
> Safe from the storms, and prelate's rage.   (1–12)

Marvell suggests the fragility of these people as they sail along at the mercy of a powerful nature, but thankful for God's special grace to them. This was the time when the Puritans were leaving England in large numbers to settle in the New World, notably in Massachusetts. It has a definite historical basis, but Marvell treats it more as a symbolic voyage of some Puritans to escape from a harsh world to the relative security of a pristine island far from their old home. The "grassy stage" suggests the self-conscious, almost theatrical role the Puritans considered everyone played in acting out their divinely appointed mission on earth.

Bermuda offers them a haven that is not only safe from persecution but seems to be a kind of paradise on earth. The weather is temperate, and food grows naturally and abundantly there. It is an ideal refuge for God's people:

> He gave us this eternal spring
> Which here enamels everything,
> And sends the fowls to us in care,
> On daily visits through the air;
> He hangs in shades the orange bright,
> Like golden lamps in a green night,
> And does in the pomegranates close
> Jewels more rich than Ormus shows;   *Hormuz, in the Persian Gulf*
> He makes the figs our mouths to meet,
> And throws the melons at our feet;
> But apples plants of such a price,   *probably pineapples*
> No tree could ever bear them twice. . . .   (13–24)

Springtime seems to last forever here and beautifies the landscape with flowers and other plants. God also provides meat and fruit that seem intended expressly for the people's own use. It is a good example of personification too, as the fruit appears to have a will of its own, eagerly presenting itself to the new settlers to be eaten. The vivid colors of the oranges and pomegranates light up the night and seem to be precious jewels in their own right. The voyagers have everything they need to live there in safety and prosperity. God has taken good care of them.

Meanwhile, their spiritual life has been not been neglected. God has enabled the Gospel to flourish on their shores and has even provided a place of worship for the little band of faithful, but persecuted believers:

> "He cast (of which we rather boast)
> The Gospel's pearl upon our coast,
> And in these rocks for us did frame

A temple, where to sound his name.
O let our voice his praise exalt
Till it arrive at heaven's vault,
Which, thence (perhaps) rebounding, may
Echo beyond the <u>Mexique</u> Bay."

Gulf of Mexico
(29–36)

The good news of the Gospel is not lost on swine here, but cultivated and cherished. The people have discovered a natural site that seems designed for their worship and praise of Him. Perhaps, the poet suggests, their faith will spread beyond their little island to other parts of the New World, especially the Spanish (Catholic)-controlled western side. This ideal place may become, the poet suggests, the center of the New World's religious activity and the hope of many Puritans who come to this country.

The poet ends with a brief return to the scene of the boat moving on the surface of the ocean as the small band of faithful proceeds with their rowing and singing:

Thus sung they in the English boat
An holy and a cheerful note;
And all the way, to guide their chime,
With falling oars they kept the time.

(37–40)

We note that their attitude is both pious and "cheerful," not self-righteous or conquering. They are going to live in harmony with nature and look forward with joy to their freedom to worship. The octosyllabic couplets in iambic meter that was Marvell's favorite verse form become exceptionally regular in the final lines as he imitates their rowing in the rise and fall of the stress pattern. Here the pastoral mode combines with a brief narrative to create a historical portrait that may not be precisely accurate, but that surely conveys some of the feelings the Puritans must have had as they came to the New World in the seventeenth century. Marvell himself must have shared some of these feelings to put them into such effective poetic form.

Marvell also worked more fully in the pastoral mode in several other poems, most notably "The Garden," which is generally regarded as one of his finest. It is a poem of nine stanzas of eight lines each in octosyllabic couplets. His theme is the quiet joy and fulfillment one may find in the countryside far from urban life or the court. This is the conventional praise of retirement found in many pastoral poems of the Renaissance, but done in original terms. Like every great poet, Marvell transforms the genre he employs to convey new themes and ideas. Here the garden appears to give the poet the kind of contemplative space he needs to transcend earthly concerns and reach a paradise of the imagination.

Since it is a relatively long poem, we will look at only six of these stanzas in detail, with a brief summary of the others. Marvell opens by describing the usual life of man spent in the pursuit of worldly honors. It is a picture of frustration and limitation even when successful:

> How vainly men themselves amaze
> To win the <u>palm</u>, the <u>oak</u>, or <u>bays</u>, *for military, civic, and poetic honors*
> And their uncessant labors see
> Crowned from some single herb or tree,
> Whose short and narrow-<u>vergèd</u> shade *edged*
> Does prudently their toils upbraid;
> While all flowers and all trees do <u>close</u> *unite, agree*
> To weave the garlands of repose! (1–8)

Marvell suggests that such a life of constant striving for renown has little to recommend it, since it results only in a narrowly circumscribed recognition that mocks all the hard work. In contrast, the flowers and trees of the garden provide the kind of rest and nurturing that one really needs. Instead of stupefying and exhausting oneself in chasing earthly goods or worldly acclaim, one can turn to nature, which furnishes all that is necessary to a happy, fulfilled life. Marvell sounds these themes in the first line when he employs a couple of puns in "vainly" (meaning both "in vain" and "proudly") and "amaze" ("astonish" and "a bewildering maze"). A good pun, he knew, can condense and multiply the implications of his meaning.

In the second stanza the poet suggests he has discovered "Quiet" and her sister "Innocence" in the garden, after having mistakenly sought them in the world. Marvell often works with allegorical figures in his poetry to suggest a more general significance than a specific name could. In the third stanza he goes on to describe the garden in terms of color and activity, contrasting it to the normal life of action. Green is a lovelier color than the red and white associated with female beauty because it represents a love that is less possessive and frantic:

> No white nor red was ever seen
> So amorous as this lovely green.
> Fond lovers, cruel as their flame,
> Cut in these trees their mistress' name:
> Little, alas, they know or heed
> How far these beauties hers exceed!

Fair trees, wheresoe'er your barks I wound,
No name shall but your own be found.   (17–24)

The love of the garden, the poet implies, is deeper and higher than normal
human love, which leads to acts that deface nature in proclaiming one's love
by cutting the lady's name in the bark of the trees (a typical activity of lovers
in pastoral poems). The poet values the natural beauty of the garden too
much to commit such a misdeed, unless it would be the name of the tree that
he inscribes, to indicate his own love of the natural. He has learned to appreciate each kind of plant for what it is, a thing of beauty and an object of
adoration. The implication is that the pursuit of human love and beauty is
just as futile and destructive as the pursuit of worldly honors. Marvell's symbolic use of color compresses much meaning into a few lines.

In the fourth stanza the poet suggests that the garden provides a kind
refuge from the heat and strife of mortal love. The classical gods, he notes, in
their pursuit of mortal women, sometimes turned them into shrubs or trees
at the end their chase: Marvell wittily transforms the myths of Apollo and
Daphne, and Pan and Syrinx into stories that prove his point. In the next
stanza the poet describes the kind of life he leads in the garden. As in
"Bermudas," the fruit of the garden proves eager to be eaten by the speaker in
order to fulfill its destiny, reaching out to him in sensual pursuit:

> What wondrous life in this I lead!
> Ripe apples drop about my head;
> The luscious clusters of the vine
> Upon my mouth do crush their wine;
> The nectarine and <u>curious</u> peach   *exquisite*
> Into my hands themselves do reach;
> Stumbling on melons as I pass,
> Insnared with flowers, I fall on grass.   (33–40)

The speaker marvels at the way all the ripe fruits press themselves on him to
be eaten, though they also make him stumble and fall. Is this a tragic fall, like
the original one in Eden? In this case it does not seem so, since his fall is
softened by the grass and the flowers, hardly dangerous objects. They may
"crush their wine" on his mouth, but food and beauty are things that restore
him rather than destroy him.

In the next stanza Marvell moves to another level in the experience of the
garden. Beyond the physical paradise, the poet discovers a paradise of the

mind in the garden, where he can exercise his imagination to its fullest extent.
Here, I believe, is the heart of the matter:

> Meanwhile the mind, from pleasure less,
> Withdraws into its happiness;
> The mind, that ocean where each kind
> Does straight its own resemblance find;
> Yet it creates, transcending these,
> Far other worlds and other seas,
> Annihilating all that's made
> To a green thought in a green shade. (41–48)

The mind's ability to create "other worlds" is what constitutes its bliss, not
simply reproducing the known world. The mind is like the ocean in containing all kinds of objects and ideas, but it also has the power to form new
objects and original thoughts. Imaginative activity, in sum, far exceeds sensual pleasure as it transforms everything into the green innocence of the
garden. Here, finally, time, the great enemy of humanity, can be transcended.
This is a supremely evocative statement of the power of art, or the human
mind, to create.

In the seventh stanza Marvell imagines further how this artistic power
works in nature. He develops a kind of Metaphysical image that expresses the
imagination's working. It constitutes at first a complete identification between the poet and nature:

> Here at the fountain's sliding foot,
> Or at some fruit tree's mossy root,
> Casting the body's <u>vest</u> aside,   *garment*
> My soul into the boughs does glide:
> There like a bird it sits and sings,
> Then <u>whets</u> and combs its silver wings,   *preens*
> And, till prepared for longer flight,
> Waves in its plumes the various light. (49–56)

The mind seems to take power from fountain and tree to soar into the strato-
sphere of creativity. The body is transcended, yet the mind (or soul) is likened to
a bird that carefully prepares itself to take wing on an extended journey,
higher up and farther out. The "various light" is probably the different colors
of this world as opposed to the "white radiance of eternity" (*Norton Anthology*,
p. 1700, n. 8), which seems to be its ultimate goal. The mind does not reject

nature, but takes off from it to proceed into a higher realm. This is a kind of Neoplatonic vision that begins with the material world but soon outstrips it to reach heaven or the outer spheres of the imagination.

In the next stanza (no. 8) Marvell suggests that this garden is like Paradise without a woman, the helpmeet who helped undo man. It was not possible for him to remain alone in the garden forever, however, so Marvell concludes his poem by describing the sun dial that the gardener created out of the natural elements he had to work with, the flowers and herbs, to chart the sun's progress through the day:

> How well the skillful gardener drew
> Of flowers and herbs this dial new,
> Where from above the milder sun
> Does through a fragrant zodiac run;
> And as it works, th'industrious bee
> Computes its time as well as we!
> How could such sweet and wholesome hours
> Be reckoned but with herbs and flowers? (65–72)

We are not beyond time in the garden, but it and nature harmonize to create such a pleasant life there that it almost seems to be perfect. It is a mild sun that passes through "a fragrant zodiac" made up of herbs and flowers to make for "sweet and wholesome hours." What could be more desirable for us as for the hard-working bee that finds its time (and thyme, a common pun) well spent in such a garden? In this poem, then, Marvell explores how close one can approach heaven and yet remain on earth. With the proper setting, retirement from the world can become a rich blessing. The garden, the pastoral ideal, provides both the quiet and the inspiration necessary for the imagination to fulfill its potential.

Occasionally, poets will tackle historical subjects when events around them seem of particular significance. When they do, readers from later centuries will often need some extra help in reading such poems, though all the details of what actually happened are not necessarily relevant. In the last poem by Marvell we will discuss, "An Horatian Ode upon Cromwell's Return from Ireland," it will be helpful to know some background before looking at the poem. After the execution of Charles I in January 1649, Oliver Cromwell, leader of the Parliamentary forces, went to Ireland in August of that year in order to put down a rebellion by both English Protestant colonists and native Catholic troops. He scored crushing victories at Drogheda and Wexford, at the latter of which he permitted the brutal massacre of the civilian population as well as of the enemy forces. It took two more years of military action to subdue Ireland, but Cromwell returned to England in May 1650, having established the dominance of the English army there. Scotland was also in the process of rebelling, ignited by the presence of the young Charles II. Cromwell left for this northern hot spot at the end of July 1650 to suppress the royalist uprising there, which he did with little difficulty. The final defeat for Scottish troops was at Worcester, in England, in September 1651 after Charles led a desperate invasion of the southern kingdom, hoping to rouse the English royalists to action; the young king barely escaped capture. This battle, however, came more than a year after Marvell seems to have written the poem, in the summer of 1650. Because of the length of the poem, we will look at only a few of the stanzas in detail, with the rest being broadly paraphrased.

To open the poem, Marvell generalizes about the necessity for any young man who wants to distinguish himself to go out into the public world of action and leave behind the private world of thought and poetry. This represents the traditional life choice one must make between contemplation and action, since one cannot succeed in both at the same time. Clearly, Cromwell chose action, moved by the conflict between Parliament and the king:

> So restless Cromwell could not cease
> In the inglorious arts of peace,
> > But through adventurous war
> > Urgèd his active star;
>
> And, like the three-forked lightning, first
> Breaking the clouds where it was nursed,
> > Did thorough his own side   *through*
> > His fiery way divide. . . .   (9–16)

Here Marvell records the sudden emergence of Cromwell from relative obscurity to become the most powerful leader of Parliament's forces. At first, Cromwell had not been much involved in the conflict, but once the war began, he could no longer stay away and soon proved to be a remarkable military leader. The "lightning" simile suggests that Cromwell is an elemental and irresistible force of nature that may be associated with Zeus, who was often pictured with the lightning bolt in his hand ready to unleash it on the earth. Thus, Cromwell erupts onto the scene, even bursting through his own side's ranks with his passion and discipline.

Marvell describes Cromwell's destructive progess briefly, but vividly, carrying on the lightning image from the previous lines. Here the Parliamentary military commander becomes a divine force who is, nevertheless, responsible himself for much of what happened:

Then burning through the air he went,
And palaces and temples rent;
    And Caesar's head at last
    Did through his laurels blast.

'Tis madness to resist or blame
The force of angry heaven's flame;
    And if we would speak true,
    Much to the man is due....   (21–28)

It is absurd to try to change fate if it represents God's will, but still, Cromwell seems also to embody his own force and passion. Marvell balances the possibility that Cromwell is an overwhelming divine force with the sense that Cromwell is also acting to some degree on his own free will, fulfilling his character rather than God's will. Marvell's portrait of Cromwell thus combines both darker and lighter shades into a complex picture that is neither simple praise nor blame, but a mixture of both. This blend is continued in the rest of the poem, with further additions and enhancements.

Marvell proceeds to contrast Cromwell's previously peaceful life on his farm (or his "private gardens") to his violent, destructive effect on the country when he enters the conflict. From the pastoral world to war, his entry became revolutionary. Cromwell showed how one

Could by industrious valor climb
To ruin the great work of Time,
    And cast the kingdom old
    Into another mold;

Though Justice against Fate complain,
And plead the ancient rights in vain:
    But those do hold or break,
    As men are strong or weak.   (33–40)

Marvell seems to feel some nostalgia for the old way of life that has been completely changed by Cromwell, yet he also sees that justice and tradition cannot last unless they are defended with strength and resolution. Cromwell is fate, it seems, which again suggests that he is a divinely appointed leader sent to remake England's political order into a new "mold."

From Cromwell Marvell shifts to the king and a brief look at his execution, to broaden the historical perspective on England's new order. The contrast between the two men is striking. Charles I is portrayed with some sympathy as he is led to Whitehall and the block to be beheaded:

That thence the royal actor borne,
The tragic scaffold might adorn;
    While round the armèd bands
    Did clap their bloody hands.

He nothing common did or mean
Upon that memorable scene,
    But with his keener eye
    The ax's edge did try;

Nor called the gods with vulgar spite
To vindicate his helpless right;
    But bowed his comely head
    Down, as upon a bed.   (53–64)

In his final moments Charles acts nobly and courageously, though Marvell also calls him, with some ambiguity, a "royal actor." The king's performance is masterful and regained for him much of the lost respect he had suffered during the civil war. The Parliamentary soldiers clap, ironically, with their bloody hands, while the king's eye directly and unflinchingly surveys the ax that is about to chop off his head. It is a scene from a tragedy, Marvell suggests, with a clear hero who is about to suffer a martyr's death. The execution of Charles I was a traumatic event for the whole country, given the sanctity traditionally associated with the monarchy. The result was, of course, that the legitimacy of Parliamentary authority was thrown into question. As Marvell notes in the next stanza, Cromwell's rule is based on a "forcèd power" (line 66), yet such power, paradoxically, may lead to greater achievements like advances in civilization or empire. Clearly, in Marvell's view good and bad continue to be mixed in these historical events as in the people.

After this rather positive picture of Charles, Marvell concludes his poem with further praise of Cromwell and his effective use of power. He especially commends Cromwell's submission to Parliamentary authority, indicating that the commander is not winning battles for himself or his own glory, but for the cause embodied by Parliament. Cromwell, according to the poet, is a proper ruler because he willingly accepts higher civic authority. The image Marvell develops comes from falconry, a traditional form of hunting:

He to the Commons' feet presents
A kingdom for his first year's rents;
    And, what he may, forbears
    His fame to make it theirs;

And has his sword and spoils ungirt,
To lay them at the public's skirt:
    So, when the falcon high
    Falls heavy from the sky,

She, having killed, no more does search,
But on the next green bough to perch;
    Where, when he first does lure,
    The falconer has her sure.   (85–96)

Cromwell is like a trained bird of prey that does no more than his handler wants, but is ready for further action if asked, as he was for Scotland. Other countries, too, may have something to fear from this awesome warrior, who can strike terror into anyone nearby. Marvell compares Cromwell to Caesar and Hannibal, great generals in the past who conquered other lands for (or against) the Roman Empire. They were not particularly good men, but they were among the most powerful military leaders in history, so comparing Cromwell to them is high tribute indeed. The Englishman, however, never conquered for personal aggrandizement, implying his moral superiority.

Marvell ends on a note of political realism when he comments that Cromwell must now keep his sword ready in order to ensure the maintenance of order in the country. After all, he says, "The same arts that did gain / A power must it maintain" (lines 119–120). The poet has thus been led, by a relatively minor historical event (Cromwell's return from Ireland), to meditate on the new political order in England and to try to see it in a broad perspective. It is a balanced view that perceives both good and bad in the new leader and his organization, which is perhaps why Marvell calls his poem "An Horatian Ode." Horace, one of the great Roman poets, wrote odes in Latin using four-line stanzas and an informal approach to treat broad themes of love, friendship, and politics. Using the same stanza (with two octosyllabic lines and two six syllable lines), Marvell depicts Cromwell as the man of the hour for England now, no matter how much ruin he may have caused in the process. He has, after all, created a new order for the country, though it is one that may be based on his own will as much as on God's. Marvell thus shows in "An Horation Ode" how poetry can offer a highly nuanced view of contemporary history, without assuming too much knowledge on the part of the reader. The picture is not black and white, but various shades of gray, like human motives and actions.

This poem, then, provides further evidence of Marvell's ability to treat a wide variety of subjects in poetry with rare skill and power. He can, we see, explore love, religious feeling, historical events, and philosophical issues with exceptional suggestiveness and aplomb. Unusual for his time, Marvell seems often to capture something of the ambiguity of life in his poetry, using a broad allegorical approach that is, for the most part, not tied too closely to the contemporary scene. His terms and settings are often generalized, and his rhythm, in relatively short lines, subtly enhances the particular theme of each poem. Sometimes, no doubt, his symbolism can be difficult and his meaning elusive, but the more one rereads and reflects on his poetry, the more understanding and pleasure one will find in it.

CHAPTER 8

John Dryden (1631–1700): Poet of the Restoration

The history of the Restoration period in England is one of growing dissension and conflict in the country leading up to the Glorious Revolution in 1688–1689, when Parliament established a constitutional monarchy after the debacle of James II's brief attempt at ruling. After Cromwell's death in 1658 and his son's failure to establish an acceptable government, a group of leading noblemen, military officers, and clerics agreed to invite Charles Stuart to return to the throne as Charles II, which he did to much fanfare in May 1660. Charles proved to be an adept politician who kept the various religious and political factions of the time at bay (though barely) until his own death in 1685. The Anglican Church was reestablished as the national church at the Restoration, but a growing body of dissenters and nonconformists opposed the official religion with increasing vigor. There was also a flourishing body of democratic political thought that was sometimes allied with the religious dissenters. When Charles II's brother succeeded him as James II (Charles had no legitimate heirs) and began to promote Catholicism (his own religion), a fierce opposition arose throughout the country. This led a group of prominent noblemen and bishops to invite William of Orange (a Dutch Prince) and his wife Mary, James's daughter, to come to England to restore order. William led a small army across the English Channel in late 1688, James fled to the continent after briefly making a show of resistance, and Parliament declared William and Mary joint sovereigns once they had agreed to the Declaration of Rights, which provided for democratic reforms and prohibited a Roman Catholic from succeeding to the throne. In turn, though, this essentially bloodless revolution prompted further opposition, especially from those who believed the line of succession to the monarchy had been violated and thus refused to swear allegiance to the new rulers (they became known as "non-jurors"). Various attempts were made to restore James or his descendants by his supporters (called Jacobites after the Latin version of James's name, Jacobus) down to the invasion of Bonnie Prince Charlie (Charles Edward Stuart) in 1745 from Scotland, which was ended by the battle of Culloden in April 1746 with the defeat of the Jacobite troops.

John Dryden, our next poet of note, came into prominence after the Restoration when he established himself as one of the most important writers of the age, in drama and criticism as well as poetry. He was born and raised in Northamptonshire, the son of a country gentleman. After being sent to Westminster School to study under the renowned scholar Dr. Richard Busby, he went on to Trinity College, Cambridge, where he graduated in 1654. After spending some time in London, Dryden began to make a name for himself as a playwright once the theaters had been reopened following the Restoration. (They had been closed by the Puritans in 1642 since they were thought to represent an immoral element in public life.) He wrote both comedies and heroic tragedies with some success, along with occasional poetry and criticism, then became more involved in politics after he was appointed Historiographer Royal and Poet Laureate by Charles II. In the 1670s and 1680s Dryden wrote both satire and serious commentary on political and religious issues in verse, producing some of the finest work in English literature on such matters. After the Glorious Revolution, he lost his official government positions due to his conversion to Catholicism, but maintained his faith despite intense pressure to return to the Anglican fold. In the final decade of his life, Dryden returned first to the theater to seek a living and then turned to translating the classics (his version of the *Aeneid* is one of the best) as well as some later writers (including Chaucer and Boccaccio) for further income. He completed his final work, *Fables Ancient and Modern,* with an excellent introductory critical essay, shortly before his death in 1700. Dryden was the complete man of letters, a successful poet, playwright, critic, and translator, who enjoyed wide respect and admiration among his contemporaries. For the next generation, he was the model of the practicing writer who earned his living by his pen and achieved great distinction through diligence, determination, and a serious dedication to literature.

Although he had published a number of poems and plays in verse, Dryden came into his own as a poet later in his career with his turn to satire, a form or mode of literature that represents an imaginative attack on some person, institution, or idea. In "Mac Flecknoe" (written in 1678–1679), Dryden wittily and creatively ridicules Thomas Shadwell, a rival dramatist with whom he had a dispute, thus raising personal satire to high art. The title literally means "son of Flecknoe," referring to another, even more minor playwright of the time. In this poem Dryden imagines a coronation scene in which the current ruler of the land of Nonsense, Flecknoe, will pass on the symbolic scepter of rule to his hand-picked successor, Shadwell. (The succession to the throne of England was at this time a hot political issue that was about to burst into violence with the Exclusion Crisis, a conflict over the Duke of York's right to succeed to the English throne caused by his Catholicism.) Dryden opens his poem with a general statement about the law of life—the relentless rule of change in human affairs—setting the action in a kind of pseudo-philosophical frame:

> All human things are subject to decay,
> And when fate summons, monarchs must obey.
> This Flecknoe found, who, like Augustus, young
> Was called to empire, and had governed long;
> In prose and verse, was owned, without dispute,
> Through all the realms of Nonsense, absolute.   (1–6)

Even kings must accept this law, so Flecknoe, who has enjoyed a long and quiet reign (i.e., dull and insignificant) decides that now is the time to name his successor. Dryden compares Flecknoe to the great Caesar Augustus, the first Roman emperor who came to the throne at the age of 32 and ruled for forty-five years (31 B.C.E.–C.E. 14). Such a comparison is patently absurd, especially given the inferior quality of Flecknoe's literary work. Dryden thus mocks this man by relating his rule in literature to that of one of the greatest of all Roman emperors. This kind of satire has come to be called the mock heroic because of the use of exalted parallels to ridicule the pretensions and claims to greatness of some minor figure. Flecknoe's empire is, of course, the land of Nonsense, which makes him all that more absurd. Dryden will use other comparisons from classical history and literature to continue this mode of satire in the poem. Since it works by way of ironic contrast and assumes some knowledge on the part of the reader, it is a relatively sophisticated method that depends on wit and imagination, in contrast to simple name calling and in-sults. The epic was considered the highest of all poetic genres in the period, so to apply its conventions to a distinctly unheroic subject is to make that subject the lowest of all things.

Dryden continues his satire by dramatizing Flecknoe's formal speech ex-plaining the choice of his successor. Only Shadwell, Flecknoe claims, fulfills all the qualifications for this high position. Shadwell, after all, has the native intellect, the educational background, and the experience necessary to rule successfully in such a land. Flecknoe explains:

> " 'Tis resolved; for nature pleads that he
> Should only rule, who most resembles me.
> Sh------ [Shadwell] alone my perfect image bears,
> Mature in dullness from his tender years:
> Sh------ alone, of all my sons, is he
> Who stands confirmed in full stupidity.
> The rest to some faint meaning make pretense,
> But Sh------ never deviates into sense.
> Some beams of wit on other souls may fall,
> Strike through, and make a lucid interval;
> But Sh------'s genuine night admits no ray,
> His rising fogs prevail upon the day."   (13–24)

It is a portrait of marvelous wit and controlled irony, pretending to be a formal panegyric on his successor. Dryden speaks indirectly through Flecknoe's words to reduce his adversary to perfect inanity, just the opposite of what one would expect or wish in a real literary exemplar. Shadwell's maturity is in dullness, his sense is perfect nonsense, and his darkness is the triumph of night and fog over the sun and daylight. The images are traditional, to be sure, but used in an original way to suggest the contrary of the normal and desirable. Here, as the reader has probably noticed, Dryden employs the heroic couplet to underscore key words through the rhyme. When words like "pretense" are made to chime with "sense" and "ray" with "day," the poet heightens Shadwell's failings, in contrasting them to the ideal.

Sometimes Dryden uses biblical allusions to diminish his pseudo-hero. In the following passage he compares Shadwell to Christ, while Flecknoe assumes the role of John the Baptist, who has come to announce the arrival of the new Messiah:

> "Heywood and Shirley were but types of thee,   *popular earlier dramatists*
> Thou last great prophet of tautology.   *circular logic*
> Even I, a dunce of more renown than they,
> Was sent before but to prepare thy way;
> And, coarsely clad in Norwich drugget, came   *a coarse woolen cloth*
> To teach the nations in thy greater name."   (29–34)

To be a "type" was to foreshadow someone or something before the real thing arrived. It was used especially in theology to suggest that certain Old

Testament figures like Moses or Solomon were forerunners of Christ, lesser men but nevertheless with great powers who played important roles in guiding or recalling the ancient Israelites to their divine mission. Flecknoe even admits he is a "dunce" who has prepared audiences for Shadwell's triumphant rule over the contemporary stage. This may not be realistic, of course, but it is funny. His coarse clothing not only reflects John the Baptist's primitive garb, but also indicates an inferior class status that mocks those contemporary prophets from the lower classes who had been trying to preach radical religious and political doctrines (like the Levelers and the Quakers) to the upper classes. Here Dryden blends the literary with the sacred and the political with great skill.

The coronation scene, in an area of ill repute near the "Nursery" (a school for young actors—see Chapter 1, pp. 7–8), comes next to complete the absurd action with its heroic pretensions. Flecknoe appears as a wise and loving ruler, who imitates the real king's transfer of power with the proper rites of consecration and blessing. The description of him and Shadwell as they go through the motions of the coronation is a masterpiece of the mock heroic:

The hoary prince in majesty appeared,	
High on a throne of his own labors reared.	
At his right hand our young <u>Ascanius</u> sate,	*son of Aeneas*
Rome's other hope, and pillar of the state.	
His brows thick fogs, instead of glories, grace,	
And <u>lambent</u> dullness played around his face.	*flickering, luminous*
As <u>Hannibal</u> did to the altars come,	*great Carthaginian general*
Sworn by his sire a mortal foe to Rome,	
So Sh------ swore, nor should his vow be vain,	
That he till death true dullness would maintain....	(106–115)

Flecknoe's throne is made up of his works, not the usual elaborate seat, and Shadwell sits on the honored side, the right, as the heir, like Aeneas's son, "Rome's other hope," as Virgil described him in the *Aeneid*, around whose head plays a flickering flame to indicate his favor by the gods. Good notes to the poem will help us understand Dryden's classical allusions, since most readers today lack the detailed knowledge of the classics he assumed in his readers. Shadwell's solemn oath to carry on his "father's" role mimics the vow of a new king, while "thick fogs" play about his face, instead of the light of truth. Dryden's method is to treat the paltry as if it were something truly great, wittily creating an incongruity that renders his subject ridiculous.

In the last part of the poem Flecknoe pronounces his blessing on his heir, describing how closely Shadwell follows in his tradition. He contrasts Shadwell with other writers of the time, who are much wittier and more original. Whatever Shadwell tries in the way of specific dramatic or poetic effect, even when he tries to satirize someone, he is only able, in fact, to produce the opposite of his intentions:

> Like mine, thy gentle <u>numbers</u> feebly creep;   *verses*
> Thy tragic Muse gives smiles, thy comic sleep.
> With whate'er gall thou sett'st thyself to write,
> Thy inoffensive satires never bite.
> In thy felonious heart though venom lies,
> It does but touch thy Irish pen, and dies.   (197–202)

Thus Shadwell's artistic power, like Flecknoe's, is nonexistent, though he thinks it is great. Even before Flecknoe's speech is over, he suddenly disappears from the scene, still declaiming, through a trapdoor in the stage floor, like an actual scene from one of Shadwell's plays, leaving his robe behind, as Elijah left his mantle to the younger prophet Elisha when he was carried to heaven in a chariot of fire. It is a farcical conclusion to a sophisticated satire, done in the way it should be, which Dryden himself described, in his "Discourse on Satire," as quite different from "the slovenly butchering of a man" (with names and insults), but with, instead, "the fineness of a stroke that separates the head from the body, and leaves it standing in its place." Satire can be high art, if done with the proper imaginative effects. This period, from the Restoration to the mid-eighteenth century, indeed, will see some of the finest satires in English published in both verse and prose. Dryden is the poet who raises it to a new level of artistic excellence.

The next poem to consider, *Absalom and Achitophel*, is significantly longer and more complex than "Mac Flecknoe," but worth looking at in some of its parts because of the brilliance of the verse. It is a kind of political allegory with biblical characters used to comment on the contemporary scene. Like other writers before him, Dryden takes the well-known story from the Bible (in 2 Sam. 13–18) about Absalom's rebellion against his father, King David, to represent the contemporary attempt to replace James, Duke of York, as the successor to the throne with the king's illegitimate son, the Duke of Monmouth. In this allegory David is Charles II, Absalom is the Duke of Monmouth, Achitophel (or Ahitophel, one of David's counselors who became a supporter of Absalom) is the Earl of Shaftesbury, a prominent politician who, by 1673, had become a determined opponent of the king. The political crisis centered on the possible succession to the English throne of James, Duke of York, the King's brother and a Catholic, which to many Englishmen was unacceptable. In his poem Dryden dramatizes this narrative to defend the king who wanted his brother to succeed him, and does so with great power, especially in attacking Charles's bitter foes. His portrait of the English people is a good example of what he can do in summarizing the royal attitude toward rebellious citizens, who had in the English Civil War overthrown the monarchy and executed the king, and were now threatening to do something similar once again. The Jews in this allegory are the English, who have not only rebelled against their legitimate ruler, but have taken to various religious cults and sects during the reign of the Puritans:

> The Jews, a headstrong, moody, murmuring race,
> As ever tried the extent and stretch of grace;
> God's pampered people, whom, debauched with ease,
> No king could govern, nor no God could please
> (Gods they had tried of every shape and size
> That god-smiths could produce, or priests devise);
> These Adam-wits, too fortunately free,
> Began to dream they wanted liberty;
> And when no rule, no precedent was found,
> Of men by laws less circumscribed and bound,
> They led their wild desires to woods and caves,
> And thought that all but savages were slaves.   (45–56)

Dryden is clearly no democrat, but scornful of the behavior of the unreasonable, uneducated masses, who let their feelings and desires rule them. They act more like children than grown-ups, constantly testing God's forgiveness and creating new gods to worship. The terms "god-smiths" and "Adam-wits" are themselves witty characterizations of the people's abuse of free will. Their desperate search for the free expression of their wildest ideas has led to their exaltation of the natural man, or "noble savage" as it came to be known in the eighteenth century. Dryden employs the heroic couplet with ease and authority, as well as the allegorical parallels between the Israelites, who continually turned away from God's grace, and the English.

The most damning portrait in the poem is that of Achitophel (Shaftesbury), who becomes a kind of satanic figure tempting Absalom (Monmouth) to rebel against his father in order to replace Charles's brother, James, as the next heir to the throne. Achitophel, in Dryden's account, will stop at nothing in his attempt to persuade Absalom to curry favor with the public, of whom he was already a favorite, and expand his base of power. Here are a few lines from Dryden's portrait:

> Of these the false Achitophel was first;
> A name to all succeeding ages cursed:
> For close designs, and crooked counsels fit;
> Sagacious, bold, and turbulent of wit;
> Restless, unfixed in principles and place;
> In power unpleased, impatient of disgrace:
> A fiery soul, which, working out its way,
> Fretted the pygmy body to decay,
> And o'er-informed the tenement of clay.
> A daring pilot in extremity;
> Pleased with the danger, when the waves went high,
> He sought the storms; but, for a calm unfit,
> Would steer too nigh the sands, to boast his wit.   (150–162)

His chief trait, in Dryden's portrait, is lack of principle, thus suggesting he is an opportunist who will do anything to gain popular support for his cause, which is to undermine the monarchy. There is also a good side to Shaftesbury, however, which Dryden acknowledges when he mentions the integrity and wisdom Shaftesbury previously displayed as a judge (lines 187–191). But Shaftesbury's energy, intelligence, experience, and knowledge all make his shiftiness, boldness, and infidelity extremely dangerous. The imagery Dryden uses of the "fiery soul" that wears out the small, fragile body it inhabits (Shaftesbury at this time was short, infirm, and aging) brilliantly captures his power as an opponent. Then Dryden shifts his metaphor to describe him as a ship's captain who loves the storms at sea and would actually seek them out to show his seamanship. Such a man, Dryden implies, is hardly fit for piloting the ship of state, a common metaphor, through the turbulent sea of life.

Perhaps the most effective satire in the poem comes with Dryden's description of some of Shaftesbury's allies in the conflict against the king. They are political and religious leaders of importance, yet less dangerous than someone like Shaftesbury since they are more absurd than he is. Zimri was a biblical villain noted especially for his conspiracy against a King of Israel whom he murdered (see 1 Kings 16:9–20) and then replaced, briefly, as monarch. Here Dryden applies the name to the Duke of Buckingham, a notoriously dissolute and intriguing nobleman who had joined the opposition to Charles:

In the first rank of these did Zimri stand;
A man so various, that he seemed to be
Not one, but all mankind's epitome:
Stiff in opinions, always in the wrong;
Was everything by starts, and nothing long;
But, in the course of one revolving moon,
Was chemist, fiddler, statesman, and buffoon....

❧

Railing and praising were his usual themes;
And both (to show his judgment) in extremes:
So over-violent, or over-civil,
That every man, with him, was God or Devil.
In squandering wealth was his peculiar art:
Nothing went unrewarded but <u>desert</u>.   *merit*
Beggared by fools, whom still he found too late,
He had his jest, and they had his estate.   (544–550; 555–562)

Buckingham is, according to Dryden, unstable and lacking in moderation and clear judgment, but therefore not as dangerous as Shaftesbury. He is ready to try anything, such as the new science of chemistry, yet his interests constantly change, and he pursues nothing with rigor or discipline. The moon seems to govern his moods and was traditionally associated with madness, as embodied in our word lunatic (from Latin *luna*). He seems to have some native gifts, such as his energy and love of variety (Dryden calls him a "Blest madman" [line 553] at one point), but with a definite tendency to self-destruct. Buckingham was enormously wealthy, but wasted much of his fortune in various schemes and had eventually to be restrained by trustees appointed to control his expenses and pay off his debts. There is enough truth in Dryden's portrait to be effective satire, though there is clearly some exaggeration here. Dryden said in his "Discourse on Satire" that he thought this passage was "worth the whole poem," though we might find other passages that are equally worthy. In his use of the heroic couplet, note how variable is the placement of the caesura in each line, how it helps to keep the sense clear and compact with short phrases and clauses. In the last line, for example, its two parts highlight the ironic contrast between Buckingham, who has his joke, and the "fools" who take his estate.

In another of the satiric portraits of Achitophel's supporters, Shimei, also an opponent of David (see 2 Sam. 16:5–14), illustrates the hypocrisy often charged against the Puritans in Restoration literature. He represents Slingsby Bethel, one of the actual sheriffs of London who packed juries with royal enemies (coming to be known at the time as Whigs) whenever they were arrested and investigated for serious crimes against the state (like Shaftesbury):

> Shimei, whose youth did early promise bring
> Of zeal to God and hatred to his king,
> Did wisely from expensive sins refrain,
> And never broke the Sabbath, but for gain;
> Nor ever was he known an oath to vent,
> Or curse, unless against the government.

❧

> During his office, treason was no crime;
> The sons of Belial had a glorious time;
> For Shimei, though not prodigal of <u>pelf</u>,   *wealth*
> Yet loved his wicked neighbor as himself.

❧

> Chaste were his cellars, and his <u>shrieval board</u>   *the Sheriff's dinner table*
> The grossness of a city feast abhorred:
> His cooks, with long disuse, their trade forgot;
> Cool was his kitchen, though his brains were hot. . . .   (585–590; 597–600;
>   618–621)

Shimei's main interest in life is money, despite his profession of a strict Protestant code of ethics. His zeal against the king began early, like other notable figures whose childhood revealed special indications of their future greatness. He is frugal and seemingly temperate, except in his hatred of the monarchy and his greed. Ironically, during his time as magistrate only injustice and the worst crimes flourish, and his table reflects his stinginess and apparent ascetic morality, though in the meantime his mind is working to subvert the accepted government. Under Shimei's influence, everything good is turned upside down and either abused or refused, while the bad is accepted and encouraged. This is superb Juvenalian satire (named after the Latin poet, Juvenal), harsh and biting, but still witty and imaginative.

There is much, much more to this poem than these few passages, of course, but from them we can grasp something of Dryden's power as a satirist. There is a positive side to the poem as well, with favorable portraits of some of Charles's most important friends, and a statement from the king at the end about how he must now crack down on his enemies, though much to his regret. All in all, Dryden's poem is a complex treatment of a serious political conflict, one that could have led to civil war once again had Charles not managed to control the situation through clever manipulation of the political system. Shaftesbury was finally indicted (after the king was able to pack his own juries) and fled to the continent where he died, a broken and defeated man, in 1683.

Another side to Dryden's poetic achievement is evident in his *Religio Laici, or A Layman's Religion* (1682). This is his ability to compose poems in which the discussion of ideas is central to the poem's subject. Dryden wrote it to explain and justify his faith in the Anglican Church, the national religion, to the public at a time when the debate about such topics was extremely intense. Despite the emotional nature of the topic, Dryden manages to argue several of the critical issues with admirable clarity. Some readers may believe that poetry should not deal with ideas in any rational way, but Dryden, I think, is quite successful in explaining what his faith represents for him and how he sees its differences with other forms of religion, notably Deism and Catholicism. The first eleven lines of the poem set the tone by invoking the sun, moon, and stars in a poetic way to introduce one of the central themes of the poem:

> Dim as the borrowed beams of moon and stars
> To lonely, weary, wandering travelers,
> Is reason to the soul; and, as on high
> Those rolling fires discover but the sky,   *reveal*
> Not light us here, so reason's glimmering ray
> Was lent, not to assure our doubtful way,
> But guide us upward to a better day.
> And as those nightly tapers disappear,   *candles*
> When day's bright lord ascends our hemisphere;
> So pale grows reason at religion's sight;
> So dies, and so dissolves in supernatural light.   (1–11)

Human reason is compared to the reflected light of the moon and stars, a faint and uncertain guide to our feet along the dark and solitary path of life. In these similes Dryden suggests that reason's function is only to lead us to a higher and better light, that of the sun, the brilliant, overwhelming light of God. The limited, weak nature of human reason is beautifully evoked here, but in less rational terms than Dryden employs in the rest of the poem. Despite the constraints of rhyme and the heroic couplet, Dryden manages to compose these images into a smooth, natural, evocative descriptive vision of his main argument.

In two other passages from this poem Dryden summarizes the chief premises of his faith. The first occurs after he has rejected the Deist's notion that all people from birth have been given the idea of God as well as the responsibility of doing good and avoiding evil. If we commit some sin, according to this doctrine, we should repent and ask for God's mercy, and we are expected to worship God in praise and prayer. Deism was in the process of becoming a recognized religious philosophy to be taken up more extensively by the Enlightenment in the eighteenth century, but here Dryden offers traditional Christianity's response to such a "natural" religion:

> Thus man by his own strength to heaven would soar,
> And would not be obliged to God for more.
> Vain, wretched creature, how art thou misled
> To think thy wit these godlike notions bred!
> These truths are not the product of thy mind,
> But dropped from heaven, and of a nobler kind.
> Revealed religion first informed thy sight,
> And reason saw not, till faith sprung the light.
> Hence all thy natural worship takes the source:
> 'Tis revelation what thou think'st <u>discourse</u>.   *reason*
> (62–71)

Pride has led some to believe that humans are responsible for creating their own religious view of the universe. But, Dryden objects, reason alone would never have reached such conclusions if God had not first revealed these ideas to the human mind. Human beings are simply deluded to think they can determine God's will and role in the universe without His intervention. Dryden briefly alludes to the myth of Icarus, who soared too near the sun on wings made of wax which then melted, to suggest that humans are trying to transcend their proper limits and reach heaven itself on their own, but are doomed to fail. His tone of sarcasm and irony directed at human pretense is nevertheless based on clearly stated principles.

The other passage from *Religio Laici* to consider is near the end, after Dryden has reviewed various objections to Christianity, ranging from problems with the text of the Bible to the claim of exclusive truth for the Catholic Church. Dryden calls for moderation in examining religious issues, a trait he felt was seriously lacking in recent spiritual and political discourse. Without greater restraint, he believes that discussion cannot make progress:

> What then remains, but, waiving each extreme,
> The tides of ignorance and pride to stem?
> Neither so rich a treasure to forgo,
> Nor proudly seek beyond our power to know.

Faith is not built on disquisitions vain;
The things we must believe are few and plain:
But since men will believe more than they need,
And every man will make himself a creed,
In doubtful questions 'tis the safest way
To learn what <u>unsuspected</u> ancients say;   *trustworthy*
For 'tis not likely we should higher soar
In search of heaven, than all the church before;
Nor can we be deceived, unless we see
The scripture and the Fathers disagree.   (427–440)

Here Dryden argues that the basic ideas of Christianity are clear and straightforward; one does not have to be a theologian to comprehend them. Note how he characterizes the human propensity to err by comparing it to the sea's movement, the ebb and flow of the tide, about which we can do nothing. We can only "stem" it, that is, restrict or restrain our ignorance and pride rather than stop them altogether. In recognition of the importance of tradition and in humility toward the faithful fathers of the young church, we should examine what they have said about these issues, but when they disagree with Scripture or become too contentious in disputes over minor points, we may safely part company with them. Faith should not, according to Dryden, be a function of logic or intelligence; reason can only enhance or refine it, not prove it. Humility is the best attitude toward the mysteries of life and faith. All this Dryden argues in relatively informal, direct language that should appeal to the educated reader, though perhaps not to the philosopher or theologian. Such a poetry of ideas, couched in layman's terms, can sharpen and enhance our own thinking today about these important issues. It is a kind of poetry not much in fashion now, but not, I think, to be dismissed without serious consideration.

In 1687 Dryden was asked by the Musical Society of London to write a poem in honor of St. Cecilia, the patron saint of music and long associated with the development of the organ in early Christian times. It was to be set to music by a composer, and the work performed by chorus and orchestra at the celebration on her feast day, November 22. Dryden's poem, "A Song for St. Cecilia," is one of the finest public lyrics written in English. The musical setting by G. F. Handel (not the original one, which was done by G. B. Draghi) is a glorious example of baroque art. For this task Dryden wrote an irregular ode with various stanza lengths about the creation of the universe and the role music plays in the life of human beings on earth. His first stanza begins with an unusual account of the creation:

From harmony, from heavenly harmony
   This universal frame began:
   When Nature underneath a heap
      Of jarring atoms lay,
     And could not heave her head,
The tuneful voice was heard from high:
     "Arise, ye more than dead."
Then cold, and hot, and moist, and dry,
In order to their stations leap,
     And Music's power obey.
From harmony, from heavenly harmony
   This universal frame began:
   From harmony to harmony
Through all the compass of the notes it ran,
The <u>diapason</u> closing full in man.   *the entire range of notes*
                                                  (1–15)

God's creative word (the Logos) is sung, bringing together all the basic elements of the universe in harmonious order. The four elements, earth, air, fire, and water "leap" into their proper places in absolute obedience to His will from their chaotic natural state. In this process God runs through the whole scale of notes, the complete Chain of Being in the cosmos, culminating in the creation of human beings. It is a vision of the creation that combines divine goodness and omnipotence into a perfect universe, using rhyme, alliteration (note especially the *h*s), repetition, varied line lengths, and a final couplet to complete the process and form a fluent and mellifluous whole. The stanza itself blends into a harmonious unity, like God's perfect universe.

The earthly music that follows generally plays a less exalted role. Appropriate to its festival context, Dryden shows how powerfully music can affect human emotions. In the second stanza he dramatizes its introduction among human beings with a biblical story taken from Genesis:

What passion cannot Music raise and quell!
     When Jubal struck the <u>corded</u> shell,   *stringed*
   His listening brethren stood around,
   And, wondering, on their faces fell
    To worship that celestial sound.
Less than a god they thought there could not dwell
     Within the hollow of that shell
     That spoke so sweetly and so well.
What passion cannot Music raise and quell!   (16–24)

According to the Bible, Jubal invented both the lyre and the pipe, representing two different modes of music, the stringed instrument and the wind instrument. When he plays them for his brothers, they are so struck by the sounds that they immediately bow down in worship; only a god could create such loveliness and power. Thus Dryden shows how music stimulates sacred wonder in these early human beings. In this stanza he employs more end rhyme than in the first, using just two sounds through these lines as well as alliteration (note the ws and the ss), repetition, and consonance (especially the l sound). Nevertheless, the lines flow smoothly and naturally; there is no distortion of the syntax to meet the demands of the sound patterns. Dryden manages to create wonderful verbal music as he narrates the powerful impact of music's discovery on human feelings. This impact continues throughout history.

In several more stanzas Dryden continues to dramatize the effect of various instruments and their particular music on human beings. The trumpet's "clangor," along with the drum's beat, provokes us to battle, the sweetly sad flute evokes the "woes of hopeless lovers," and the "sharp violins" express the pain, jealousy, and anger of frustrated, passionate love. Only the organ, the poet suggests, seems able to restore humans to a sense of God's higher love:

> But O! what art can teach,
> What human voice can reach,
> The sacred organ's praise?
> Notes inspiring holy love,
> Notes that wing their heavenly ways
> To mend the choirs above.   (42–47)

In a short and simple stanza Dryden pays the highest tribute to this special instrument that can lead us back to our true home. With his initial rhetorical question Dryden implies that nothing can match the organ's ability to do this, or even to express the proper praise for it; it is beyond our natural power to articulate such celestial thoughts or feelings in words or song. The organ, Dryden indicates, can not only transcend the limits of earthly music, but also provide some correction to the choirs of angels in heaven, a bit of hyperbole meant to emphasize how powerful it is.

In the seventh stanza Dryden suggests that the organ is even more powerful than Orpheus's lyre, which in classical myth prompted animals, as well as rocks and trees, to follow the musician around. Cecilia's music, he avers, brought an angel down from heaven, thinking it was divine sounds it heard from here. In the final stanza, the "Grand Chorus," Dryden describes the crucial role music will play at the end of the world:

> As from the power of sacred <u>lays</u>   *songs*
>   The spheres began to move,
> And sung the great Creator's praise
>   To all the blest above;
> So, when the last and dreadful hour
> This crumbling <u>pageant</u> shall devour,   *life on earth*
> The trumpet shall be heard on high,
> The dead shall live, the living die,
> And Music shall untune the sky.   (55–63)

As music was the medium for the creation, so shall it be for the Last Judgment and the dissolution of the cosmos. It was God's instrument for expressing His will in the beginning and will be again at the end, when the trumpet blows its warning that the apocalypse has come. Life in all its showiness and degeneration, its superficial spectacle, will be completely destroyed, while, paradoxically, the "dead shall live," and "the living die." The final paradox is that music itself "shall untune the sky," as everything returns to its original chaos and cacophony. Dryden retains a fairly simple structure for this final stanza, starting with a quatrain composed of alternating lines of iambic tetrameter and trimeter (four and three stressed syllables) and alternating rhyme. With the last three lines rhyming in a triplet, Dryden provides a resounding conclusion to the whole history of the universe. Handel renders it, in his music for this poem, with matchless beauty and majesty.

Ten years later Dryden wrote another ode for the St. Cecilia's Day celebration called "Alexander's Feast," about the power of music to affect even the most powerful and ruthless warrior from the ancient world (see Chapter 1, p. 11, for a brief comment). It, too, is worth analyzing "Had we but world enough and time" (as Marvell put it), but we must now go on to other poets. It is appropriate, however, to quote one final short poem, Dryden's "Epigram on Milton," which reveals once again how deeply poets can appreciate, and pay warm tribute to, their immediate predecessors:

> Three poets, in three distant ages born,
> Greece, Italy, and England did adorn.
> The first in loftiness of thought surpassed,
> The next in majesty, in both the last:
> The force of Nature could no farther go;
> To make a third, she joined the former two.   (1–6)

These lines were written in 1688 for an edition of *Paradise Lost* only twenty years after it had been first published, already indicating the high esteem in which Dryden, a royalist poet, held Milton, a dedicated republican and Puritan. Despite these strong political differences, Dryden still ranks his fellow poet higher even than Homer and Virgil, the two great epic poets of classical antiquity. It is a tribute to Dryden's generosity of spirit and deep appreciation for literary achievement of the highest order that he can praise this controversial poet in such terms.

Dryden himself must be reckoned second only to Milton as a poet at this time for his own achievement in several different genres, from satire to lyric and narrative verse. He was perhaps most original in satire, but his significant achievement in many other kinds of verse makes him one of the most versatile of all poets, though, unfortunately, one of the least read and admired. Yet, it should be clear from this discussion that Dryden can be exceptionally evocative in his use of images, lucid and imaginative in the discussion of ideas, and highly skilled in the rhetorical employment of his verse form. With a little understanding of his historical context and the topical references found in his poetry, his work can afford us a remarkably deep and abiding pleasure. What more can we hope or want from a poet?

CHAPTER 9

Jonathan Swift (1667–1745):
Satirist, Preacher, and Lover

Jonathan Swift's presence in this book may surprise some readers since he is usually thought of as a writer of prose, especially of *Gulliver's Travels*, one of the great satires in English literature. Swift, however, also wrote a large number of poems in his career, many of them light and casual, but some of a high order, distinguished by humor, wit, and wordplay, along with serious themes. Though much of his work is satiric, some of it is social and political commentary, religious reflection, and, some, even about love. Indeed, Swift wrote poetry we can still enjoy today, though we may need help with some of his allusions and complex irony. His poetry, like his prose, is, at its best, the product of a lively imagination joined with a fundamentally moral purpose.

Swift was born in Ireland of English parents who had emigrated there not long before. His father died before he came into the world, but an uncle enabled him to receive a good education, first at Kilkenny School and then at Trinity College in Dublin. He became secretary to Sir William Temple, a retired diplomat and writer who lived in England. Swift lived and worked at Temple's estate for several years, eventually deciding to take holy orders and become a priest in the Church of England in 1695. After Temple's death in 1699 when he served as Temple's literary executor, Swift returned to Ireland to serve as a clergyman until he was sent back to England to work as a kind of lobbyist for the Irish church. As he visited various government leaders in pursuit of his appointed tasks, he naturally became more and more involved in politics, since laws that affected the Church were under intense debate at the time. As a result of his new acquaintances and of his own publications, both polemical (in support of the Church) and poetical, Swift was hired in

1710 by Robert Harley, the new Tory leader, to write periodical essays and other pieces for the ministry as it endeavored to negotiate a peace to the War of the Spanish Succession. Despite the Whigs' fierce opposition, this effort was successful and ended the war against France with the Treaty of Utrecht in1713. In the same year Swift was appointed dean of St. Patrick's Cathedral in Dublin, much to his disappointment, for he dearly wanted to become a bishop or at least be appointed to a prominent clerical post in England. When Queen Anne died in 1714, the Whigs returned to power under George I of Hanover and persecuted those who were associated with the making of the peace, finding some reasons to suspect them of treason and subversion. Swift retired to Ireland to serve as dean in Dublin, where he lived for the rest of his life.

After several years of keeping a low profile and adjusting to his new position, however, he emerged from retirement to become an Irish patriot, defending the country with his pen against economic oppression by the English. His success in this caused him to become an Irish national hero and much acclaimed by the people, despite his scorn for much that was Irish. The English government, led by Robert Walpole, viewed him as a serious enemy and put a price of £300 on the head of the anonymous author of some popular tracts that vigorously opposed English policies toward Ireland (most notably, the *Drapier's Letters*). Although everyone knew Swift had written them, no one ever betrayed him, and the government did not dare arrest him, for that would have provoked a riot. In 1726, on a visit to England, Swift carried the manuscript of *Gulliver's Travels* with him and had it published anonymously in October after he had returned to Ireland. It generated much commentary and controversy then and has since become a classic of English satire. The next year Swift returned to England for his final visit and published two volumes of *Miscellanies in Prose and Verse* with Alexander Pope, his good friend and fellow poet. He continued to write occasional poetry and prose in the later years of his life, including the well-known satiric essay "A Modest Proposal . . ." (1729), concerning the terrible plight of the poor Irish people after several years of bad harvests. After suffering for some years with serious health problems, Swift died in 1745, leaving his small fortune to establish an asylum for the insane in Dublin (it opened in 1757 and still operates today).

One of the earliest poems Swift published is called "A Description of the Morning," published in *The Tatler*, a society journal edited by Richard Steele, in 1709. It is a kind of "dawn" poem, in which the poet greets the beginning of a new day with hope and anticipation of pleasure to come, often with the expectation of seeing his beloved again. Here Swift focuses rather on the awakening of a great city as it stirs into life, describing some typical activities associated with a normal day. Since it is short and has no convenient break points, here is the complete poem:

Now hardly here and there a <u>hackney coach</u>	*a carriage for hire*
Appearing, showed the ruddy morn's approach.	
Now Betty from her master's bed has flown,	
And softly stole to discompose her own.	
The slipshod prentice from his master's door	
Had pared the dirt, and sprinkled round the floor.	
Now Moll had whirled her mop with dexterous airs,	
Prepared to scrub the entry and the stairs.	
The youth with broomy stumps began to trace	
The <u>kennel-edge</u>, where wheels had worn the place.	*gutter*
The <u>smallcoal man</u> was heard with cadence deep;	*coal street vendor*
Till drowned in shriller notes of chimney-sweep.	
<u>Duns</u> at his Lordship's gate began to meet;	*debt collectors*
And <u>Brickdust</u> Moll had screamed through half a street.	*scouring powder*
The <u>turnkey</u> now his flock returning sees,	*jailer*
Duly let out a-nights to steal for fees.	
The watchful bailiffs take their silent stands;	
And schoolboys lag with satchels in their hands.	(1–18)

It is clearly a realistic picture of the metropolis awakening, with a good many details that are amusing and picturesque. Swift begins with the sun about to appear like the "rosy-fingered dawn" of Homer. It is heralded by a hired coach that is probably returning someone home from a night's debauch in the city; only the well-off could afford such a luxury. The other characters that appear are from the low side of life, the servants and poor whose existence is usually not noticed, especially in poetry. This unusual focus and the ironic view of urban life, blended with some elements of a pastoral poem, is highly original.

Swift presents the activity both inside the house and in the street outside without any clear logical progression. It is a snapshot of life in the great city as it begins the day, the good and the not so good, the moral and the immoral. Betty the maid hurries from "her master's bed" to her own in order to pretend that she has been where she should have been all night. The sloppy apprentice has cleaned (more or less) his master's shop for the day, and Moll the chambermaid has begun her mopping of the interior, seemingly pleased with her ability to handle her cleaning implement. A more pathetic note is struck, implicitly, with the young boy sweeping the gutter for old nails or other treasures he might find there. Other street sellers appear, from the coal man to the chimney sweep (usually a small boy), whose voices clash and contrast as they bid for customers. The duns are gathering at the nobleman's door to suggest the common view of the arrogant lord as either unable or unwilling to pay his bills. "Brickdust Moll" adds to the noise in the street by shouting out her wares, as the jailer welcomes his prisoners back having let them out at night to earn (or steal) money for the special goods and services they could buy from him. The bailiffs are legal officers attempting to serve writs or other court orders, again revealing the more disorderly side of life in the city, while, in a delightful picture, schoolboys reluctantly trudge to school with their book bags in hand. All in all, Swift paints a wonderfully true-to-life picture of the city as it begins a new day, with both satiric and sympathetic elements. He does not moralize over or bemoan the corruption evident in this portrait, but depicts for the readers of Steele's journal the life around them from an unusual slant. As his verse form, Swift uses the heroic couplet, end-stopped and regular, which would normally be employed for much more important subjects. Here as the daylight breaks into the city, Swift looks around him and sees much that is interesting and striking, especially in the low life that is not usually put into formal verse. Later in his career he probably would not have been as gentle with what he observed as he is here. His vision darkened considerably as he grew older.

Swift published a second "description" poem in *The Tatler* the following year, which also focuses on the city, this time called "A Description of a City Shower." Again he provides some snapshots of urban life that are both positive and negative. The realism is most prominent, but there are also moments of comedy and suggestions of larger implications. The first twelve lines set the scene with some amusing details:

> Careful observers may foretell the hour
> (By sure prognostics) when to dread a shower:
> While rain depends, the pensive cat gives o'er   *is imminent*
> Her frolics, and pursues her tail no more.
> Returning home at night, you find the sink
> Strike your offended sense with double stink.
> If you be wise, then go not far to dine;
> You'll spend in coach-hire more than save in wine.
> A coming shower your shooting corns presage,
> Old achés throb, your hollow tooth will rage.
> Sauntering in coffeehouse is Dulman seen;
> He damns the climate and complains of spleen.   *melancholy, boredom*
> (1–12)

Here Swift offers some supposedly practical advice on how to tell if it is going to rain, by suggesting how it will affect your cat, your sewer, and yourself. One's physical vulnerabilities, as found in the feet and the teeth, are perhaps the most telling in the situation, images that hardly exalt human pride. The coffeehouse was a popular social gathering place at the time, where men-about-town such as Dulman came to converse with others or read the newspapers. His comments about the weather and his dull feelings suggest a mind full of trite phrases with nothing original to offer. They reflect a common stereotype of the time, that the rainy English climate was the reason for the pervasive sense of melancholy in the island. Swift thus creates an urban scene that potentially holds the seeds of a social drama, as in some of the comedies of manners in the theater.

The actual coming of the rain evokes even more ugly images in the poet's mind. Such images recall the Flood that swamped the earth at the time of Noah, as Milton described it in *Paradise Lost* (11: 238–240). As he usually does, Swift adapts them to his purpose and setting by making them ridiculous, and composes lines that reinforce and enhance this effect. Some of the characters here remind us of ones in the previous poem:

> Meanwhile the South, rising with dabbled wings,
> A sable cloud athwart the <u>welkin</u> flings,   *sky*
> That swilled more liquor than it could contain,
> And, like a drunkard, gives it up again.
> Brisk Susan whips her linen from the rope,
> While the first drizzling shower is borne aslope:
> Such is that sprinkling which some careless <u>quean</u>   *wench*
> Flirts on you from her mop, but not so clean:
> You fly, invoke the gods; then turning, stop
> To rail; she singing, still whirls on her mop.   (13–22)

Swift personifies (or animates) the south wind, making it a winged creature that seems to act with a specific intention. His language at first is rather formal and archaic, with such words as "athwart" and "welkin." His syntax is too, as he puts the object of the verb "flings" at the beginning of the line instead of keeping the normal subject-verb-object order. The contrast with the colloquial, even ugly next two lines thus shocks us with double force when he likens the rain to a drunkard's regurgitation of his drink. Incongruity is often the method of the comic and satiric writer, as it is here. While Susan, a typical maid, is saving her laundry from the rain, the speaker cannot escape getting wet and compares it to the shower caused by some busy (and perhaps mischievous) maid shaking her mop outside as you walk by her house. This is clearly one of the common dangers of going about in the great city, a comically annoying incident but not truly serious. In the last two lines of this passage Swift artfully uses several caesuras to imitate the movement and speech of the speaker and the maid, as he swears and moves quickly away from her mop's splatter, then stops and turns to glare at her as she continues to go about her work without, apparently, noticing him.

The scene becomes even more interesting as the rain turns into a downpour and the people in the streets need to seek shelter quickly. Here the satiric note increases as Swift focuses on their different reactions to the situation, thus exposing human nature as rather less than ideal:

> Now in contiguous drops the flood comes down,
> Threatening with deluge this devoted town.
> To shops in crowds the <u>daggled</u> females fly,   *splattered*
> Pretend to <u>cheapen</u> goods, but nothing buy.   *bargain*
> The <u>Templar</u> spruce, while every spout's <u>abroach</u>,   *law student / awash*
> Stays till 'tis fair, yet seems to call a coach.
> The tucked-up sempstress walks with hasty strides,
> While streams run down her oiled umbrella's sides.
> Here various kinds, by various fortunes led,
> Commence acquaintance underneath a shed.
> Triumphant Tories and desponding Whigs
> Forget their feuds, and join to save their wigs.   (31–42)

Here the rain becomes a flood of nearly biblical proportions, though it does not affect the people very significantly in ways that one might expect, that is, with repentance and prayer, but rather with further pretense and annoyance. The irony of "devoted" is clear, as the shoppers and others merely act as if they are interested in the store's goods while the rain lasts. The specific details of the seamstress's appearance, with her long dress neatly "tucked-up" and her "oiled" umbrella provide a wonderfully concrete portrait of a woman who, in contrast to the others, is prepared for the rain and does not find it necessary to seek shelter under false pretense. The democratic mingling of the people caused by the rain is ironically heightened by the bringing together of political adversaries who have just experienced a change of ministry: the Whigs (Swift's former allies) were out and the Tories (Swift's new party) were in. They share the laughter, however, that is directed at them as they all attempt to save their appearances from the power of the storm.

The next passage develops the social satire on the people caught in the downpour, as Swift looks critically at a typical young man-about-town in his covered chair (carried by two men with poles). This "beau" is not only annoyed by the storm but frightened by its seeming violence and potential danger:

> Boxed in a chair the beau impatient sits,
> While spouts run clattering o'er the roof by fits,
> And ever and anon with frightful din
> The <u>leather</u> sounds; he trembles from within.   *on the roof*
> So when Troy chairmen bore the wooden steed,
> Pregnant with Greeks impatient to be freed
> (Those bully Greeks, who, as the moderns do,
> Instead of paying chairmen, run them through),
> <u>Laocoon</u> struck the outside with his spear,   *Trojan priest*
> And each imprisoned hero quaked for fear.   (43–52)

Of course it is absurd that the beau should be so cowardly given the nature of the situation, but Swift suggests that such is the character of modern "heroes." To underscore his point, he then compares the modern young man to the Greek heroes of old, who hid inside the wooden horse from which they emerged to overthrow Troy once they were inside the walls. This is an effective example of a mock epic simile, with the subject ridiculed by such a comparison. The contemporary hero looks pathetic when seen in contrast to the ancient ones, though Swift also indicates that he can be just as brutal and unscrupulous as they were in not rewarding the chairmen with their fares but rather with death (an amusing exaggeration, of course). Swift alludes specifically to an incident in the *Aeneid*, when Laocoon tried but failed to warn the populace of Troy against the Greek trick by striking the horse with his spear. Here the epic allusion produces only mockery and scorn, though it raises the tone of the poem to a more sophisticated level. Swift may have learned this technique from Dryden.

The final lines of the poem revert to the nastiness produced by the downpour. The gutters of the streets are overwhelmed by all the trash and sewage collected by the streaming rain. It is not a pretty sight:

> Now from all parts the swelling <u>kennels</u> flow,   *gutters*
> And bear their trophies with them as they go:
> Filth of all hues and odours seem to tell
> What street they sailed from, by their sight and smell.

They, as each torrent drives with rapid force,
From Smithfield or <u>St. Pulchre's</u> shape their course,   *church in Holborn*
And in huge confluence joined at Snow Hill ridge,
Fall from the conduit prone to Holborn Bridge.
Sweepings from butchers' stalls, dung, guts, and blood,
Drowned puppies, stinking <u>sprats</u>, all drenched in mud,   *small fish*
Dead cats, and turnip tops, come tumbling down the flood.   (53–63)

The sewers were in the streets at that time, and Swift's description of the drainage is apparently quite accurate. The rain, we see, brings out much more than the foibles of human nature. This is the ultimate degradation of the great metropolis, drowned in its own filth. The cattle markets were located in Smithfield, while the citation of the church is probably ironic in the context.

The graphic recital of the various items caught in the deluge underscores Swift's powerful realistic vision and shows how poetry can be strikingly ugly; it is not always about beauty and goodness. The final triplet (three rhyming lines in succession) with an alexandrine (twelve syllables, six stressed) in the last line enhances the force of the flood with its heavy, re-peated sounds (both rhymes and alliteration) and movement. The whole poem wittily dramatizes the collection of all the sordid aspects of urban life that are usually not seen but brought into prominence by the downpour. It is a satiric look at the great city in its worst light, not as the center of civilization but as the greatest concentration of pretense and affectation as well as filth and garbage found anywhere. One of Swift's most important goals in his writing is to ridicule human pride, which he does here with a relatively light touch.

Swift's tone and themes acquired a sharper edge when he took up his pen once again after spending several relatively quiet years in Dublin as dean. In 1719 he wrote several "progress" poems, including ones on beauty and po-etry as well as the one we are about to consider, "Phyllis, or, The Progress of Love." Although "progress" could indicate improvement as it does today, it could also be used ironically to indicate a step-by-step decay and degrada-tion, as it was in other poems besides Swift's. Here he recounts the story of an elopement and its consequences for the couple, and shows what can happen to an impulsive and inconsiderate love. His narrative moves rapidly and is filled with suspense, surprise, comedy, and tragedy.

Swift begins by describing Phyllis's character. His remarks give some clues to what happens to her, and why. It is the portrait of a young woman who

feels she is reaching the limit of her marriageable age and is behaving in ways
that, unconsciously or not, reflect a growing desperation:

Desponding Phyllis was <u>endued</u>	*endowed*
With every talent of a prude:	
She trembled when a man drew near;	
<u>Salute</u> her, and she turned her ear:	*kiss*
If o'er against her you were placed	
She <u>durst</u> not look above your waist:	*dared*
She'd rather take you to her bed,	
Than let you see her dress her head;	
In church you heard her, through the crowd	
Repeat the absolution loud;	
In church, secure behind her fan	
She durst behold that monster, man:	
There practised how to place her head,	
And bit her lips to make them red;	
Or on the mat devoutly kneeling	
Would lift her eyes up to the ceiling,	
And heave her bosom, unaware,	
For neighbouring beaux to see it bare.	(1–18)

Phyllis obviously pretends to be modest, pious, and good, when she is anything but that. Her misplaced priorities are especially clear in her willingness
to sleep with a man, but not let him see her arrange her hair. Her behavior in
church is also indicative of her character and would be particularly outrageous to a clergyman. Her loud repetition of the absolution in the church
service is an amusing detail to suggest her desire to appear holy, but the act
only fixes her hypocrisy in the reader's mind. Swift takes the stereotype of
such a woman and fills it with life, using concrete details and an abundance
of exaggeration. It is diverting but also serious.

The poet quickly relates what happens to the young woman. Phyllis ac-
quires a suitable fiancé through the good offices of her father, who wants to
ensure she marries the right kind of husband. She makes all the preparations
for her wedding, seemingly happy and ready, yet she does not show up for
it. Where has she gone? Everyone is stunned and bewildered by her disappearance, until they discover that the butler, John, has also disappeared along
with the family's horse and an extra cushion. They soon discover a letter Phyllis
has left in her room explaining her departure. It is a masterpiece of special
pleading filled with clichés and self-deception. She begins by telling how

a fortune teller predicted she would run off with a servant and goes on to
defend and justify her action:

> 'It was her fate, must be forgiven,
> For marriages were made in heaven:
> His pardon begged, but to be plain,
> She'd do't if 'twere to do again.
> Thank God, 'twas neither shame nor sin;
> For John was come of honest kin.
> Love never thinks of rich and poor,
> She'd beg with John from door to door:
> Forgive her, if it be a crime,
> She'll never do't another time.

⁓&⁓

> One argument she summed up all in,
> The thing was done and past recalling:
> And therefore hoped she should recover
> His favour, when his passion's over.
> She valued not what others thought her,
> And was—his most obedient daughter.'   (55–64; 67–72)

Phyllis resorts to the trite phrases of romantic love to explain herself, she
shows no concern for the shock she has given to her parents and her fiancé,
and she assumes she will be forgiven when all is said and done. To sign
herself as her father's "most obedient daughter" is, of course, completely absurd. Swift has composed a wickedly revealing letter in her voice that fore-
shadows the serious consequences of her actions.

    The couple begins to have problems immediately after their departure and
soon both regret their hasty decision. Their poverty and their isolation ac-
centuate their differences until they are forced into immoral behavior in
order to survive. It is a picture that becomes less amusing and more de-
grading than before, but does not reach the end we might expect:

>   But what adventures more befell 'em,
> The muse hath now no time to tell 'em.
> How Johnny wheedled, threatened, fawned,
> Till Phyllis all her trinkets pawned:
> How oft she broke her marriage vows
> In kindness to maintain her spouse,
> Till <u>swains</u> unwholesome spoiled the trade;   *lovers*

For now the surgeon must be paid,
To whom those perquisites are gone,
In Christian justice due to John.

   When food and <u>raiment</u> now grew scarce,   *clothing*
Fate put a period to the farce,
And with exact poetic justice;
For John is landlord, Phyllis hostess:
They keep, at Staines, the Old Blue Boar,
Are cat and dog, and rogue and whore.   (85–100)

Phyllis, we see, has become a prostitute, and John expects the profits. When these must be used to pay the doctor for the resulting disease, he is obviously upset and ironically invokes "Christian justice" on his side. Instead of dying, though, Phyllis and John continue to ply their trade at an inn on the main road west out of London. This is perhaps the "poetic justice" that the poet discovers here, not the moral kind that would have led to a painful and ignominious death. As Swift's images suggest, they have essentially abandoned their humanity to become animals in mutual antagonism and immoral lives. Swift's generally end-stopped octosyllabic couplets convey the action with economy and speed, and his rhymes return with amusing quickness, often oddly paired as in the two "ells" and "ems" at the start of this passage. Here he also uses an extra unstressed syllable at the end of the line for variation and humor, as he does with "justice" and "hostess" later in the passage. It is clearly a didactic tale, but Swift does not hammer his theme home with easy moralizing. Rather, he allows the story and the characters themselves to point up the meaning.

   Not all of Swift's writing was satiric, though much of it was. His poems for Stella, that is, Esther Johnson (the daughter of Temple's steward who moved with a friend to Dublin in 1701 to live near Swift) reveal another side of this complex man. They were written mainly for her birthdays beginning in 1719 and celebrate her with appropriate compliments but also with great feeling, which is usually masked by wit and irony. Swift called her Stella (Latin for star), probably following Sir Philip Sidney's use of the name for the heroine of his sonnet sequence in the late sixteenth century. His *Journal to Stella* was a series of letters to her about his daily activities when he lived in London in 1710–1711 writing for the Tory cause. It is a fascinating look at life in the time, but especially at the relationship between Swift and this young woman whom he had befriended and mentored since their time together at Temple's. She was the woman Swift was most attached to in his life (some have even tried to make a case for their being married), and his poems for her display a tenderness and affection that are not commonly associated with him.

The last birthday poem Swift wrote for Stella came in 1727, less than a year before her death, and is more serious and more openly loving than the other ones he wrote for her. Her health had never been very good, and through the year it became increasingly precarious. Swift seems to anticipate her imminent passing with a somber look at their past together and present situation. He begins by confronting directly time's harsh effects on their bodies, but, as usual, with some humor and irony:

> This day, whate'er the fates decree,
> Shall still be kept with joy by me:
> This day then, let us not be told,
> That you are sick, and I grown old,
> Nor think on our approaching ills,
> And talk of spectacles and pills.
> Tomorrow will be time enough
> To hear such mortifying stuff. (1–8)

It is a realistic opening, but Swift says they should not think about the present and their physical ailments, but rather rejoice in the past. He clearly includes himself along with Stella in the physical decay, having suffered from Ménière's disease for many years. They are increasingly infirm, he admits, but they can still rise above their pain and decay to celebrate what they have been, without denying the reality of their present condition. His play on the sense of "mortifying," which means both "humiliating" and "dying," captures some of this irony.

Swift's basic argument to Stella is that her virtuous behavior in the past should provide some solid comfort to her in the midst of her suffering. He delineates for her all her goodness, describing her charity, compassion, justice, hatred of evil, and patience in severe pain. No doubt these refer to some actual episodes in her life that they both would recognize, but which have since been lost to history. Swift develops his argument using some analogies to reinforce his sense of the lasting effects of her good works:

> Shall these, like empty shadows pass,
> Or forms reflected from a glass?
> Or mere chimeras in the mind,
> That fly and leave no marks behind?
> Does not the body thrive and grow

By food of twenty years ago?
And, had it not been still supplied,
It must a thousand times have died.
Then, who with reason can maintain,
That no effects of food remain?
And, is not virtue in mankind
The nutriment that feeds the mind?   (51–62)

Her good deeds, Swift maintains, are more substantial than such shadows
and chimeras, which leave no presence on the mind or in the memory as they
pass by. They are more like the nourishing food from the past that still feeds
the body. Whatever its philosophical validity, Swift's images couched in this
series of rhetorical questions surely must have given some comfort to Stella,
knowing that her eminent friend thought so highly of her past actions.

In the final verse paragraph Swift becomes most personal and touching.
He urges Stella to believe in her friends' compassion and love for her, which
may allude to a difference they had had, though we do not know for sure
what it was. (Swift was going to England for several months that spring,
which may have had something to do with it.) He concludes with a remarkable acknowledgment:

   O then, whatever heaven intends,
Take pity on your pitying friends;
Nor let your ills affect your mind,
To fancy they can be unkind.
Me, surely me, you ought to spare,
Who gladly would your sufferings share;
Or give my scrap of life to you,
And think it far beneath your due;
You, to whose care so oft I owe,
That I'm alive to tell you so.   (79–88)

Swift says that he owes his life to her care for him and that he would gladly
give up his own life for her, a highly unusual testimony for the time, but one
he published only a couple of months after her death (January 1728) in the
volume of *Miscellanies* that he and Pope did together, as well as later in the
collected edition of his works in 1735. Despite his deep feelings, Swift can
still play with words and generate images such as his "scrap of life." But he
has dropped his mask of banter with very direct statements to make sure
Stella understands his profound love and gratitude for her. All in all, it
reveals a strikingly different Swift than we see in his other works.

Swift's autobiographical poem, "Verses on the Death of Dr. Swift" (a short passage of which is quoted in Chapter 1, p. 12) starts with a maxim written by La Rochefoucauld, a French moralist of the previous century, who wrote, "In the misfortune of our best friends we always find something that does not displease us." This may seem a highly cynical remark to us, but Swift believed, as a good Protestant Christian did then, that humans were far more sinful than saintly. Poetry, for him, became one of his principal modes of exploring this belief and of attempting to open his readers' eyes to these pervasive failings. In this poem Swift depicts all his good friends and others who, if they do not rejoice in his passing, at least find some comfort in the fact that it involves him and not them. We do not like to admit we have such feelings, he says, but realistically it is true, and includes himself in this indictment. Since he foresees his own death in the poem, he imagines how his friends and acquaintances will react to it. In the following passage some of his friends converse together as they wait about his deathbed:

"See how the Dean begins to break!
Poor gentleman! he droops apace!
You plainly find it in his face.
That old vertigo in his head
Will never leave him till he's dead.
Besides, his memory decays;
He recollects not what he says;
He cannot call his friends to mind;
Forgets the place where last he dined;
Plies you with stories o'er and o'er,
He told them fifty times before." (80–90)

It is a typical picture of an old man whose mind and body are clearly weakening, with his friends speaking in a tone of rather complacent and self-satisfied pity. There is of course some truth in what they say, as they cite his disease of the inner ear and his love of telling the same stories over and over. They even suggest his literary talent is not what it once was:

"For poetry, he's past his prime;
He takes an hour to find a rhyme;
His fire is out, his wit decayed,
His fancy sunk, his Muse a jade.
I'd have him throw away his pen—
But there's no talking to some men." (99–104)

It is an amusing look at Swift as poet from his "friends'" point of view, with their superior knowledge of what is best for him and their condescending attitude toward his physical and mental decay. Their comments in the middle two lines on his fading poetic capabilities are particularly trenchant and witty, as Swift employs the two halves of each line to parallel the several ways in which they think his talent has declined. According to them, his personal Pegasus, the winged horse of the imagination in classical mythology, has turned into a broken down old nag. It is ironic, of course, since Swift himself is writing these lines and thereby disproving them.

Perhaps the most remarkable of these pictures of false sorrow comes with some of his "female friends" who hear of his death while they are playing cards, a fashionable pastime. Again Swift displays an acute sense of their colloquial language and tone as they might have used in such a situation. The social scene is wickedly described:

> "The Dean is dead (and what is trumps?)
> Then, Lord have mercy on his soul!
> (Ladies, I'll venture for the <u>vole</u>.)   *a kind of grand slam*
> Six deans, they say, must bear the <u>pall</u>.   *the coffin and its cover*
> (I wish I knew what king to call.)
> Madam, your husband will attend
> The funeral of so good a friend?"
> "No, madam, 'tis a shocking sight;
> And he's engaged tomorrow night.
> My Lady Club would take it ill,
> If he should fail her at <u>quadrille</u>.   *a fashionable card game*
> He loved the Dean—(I lead a heart)
> But dearest friends, they say, must part.
> His time was come; he ran his race;
> We hope he's in a better place."   (228–242)

The news of Swift's death barely interrupts the course of the card game, as the ladies continue to bid and comment on the play, thus displaying only the most superficial concern with the report. They express pious sentiments toward the deceased without the least real feeling. To say that one's husband could not possibly attend the funeral since it would terribly upset the lady to whose house he is committed for cards, despite the fact that Swift was "so good a friend," is to reveal a total lack of sympathy for him. The contrast between the ostensible "love" of her husband for Swift and her bidding a "heart" is surely not accidental. The clichés of the last few lines along with the "hope" the lady expresses in Swift's salvation indicate her true opinion of him, that he scarcely deserved to go to heaven. Here Swift dramatically exposes the great hypocrisy of the social world through its own words, not by preaching against it. The reader laughs at the pretense of the women without being put off by a sense of self-righteousness on the part of the poet.

Swift then imagines one year having passed after his death when a customer, "a country squire," enters the bookshop of Bernard Lintot, a well-known publisher of the day, trying to find some of Swift's works. Lintot vaguely recalls his name but cannot find any of his works in the shop, finally recalling that he has recently sent all his unsold stock to a bakery in a nearby street, where they were to be ripped up and used as liners for baking pans and dishes and for wrapping packages. Lintot's speech is another amusing glance at society's values and attitudes:

> "Sir, you may find them in Duck Lane:
> I sent them, with a load of books,
> Last Monday to the pastry-cook's.
> To fancy they could live a year!
> I find you're but a stranger here.
> The Dean was famous in his time,
> And had a kind of knack at rhyme.
> His way of writing now is past:
> The town has got a better taste.
> I keep no antiquated stuff;
> But <u>spick and span</u> I have enough."   *new, fresh*
> (258–268)

The bookseller is only concerned with being up-to-date, since that is what sells. He obviously has no qualms about unloading the old (anything more than a year old) to keep up with the new. His irony at finding someone naive enough to believe that a "book could live a year" is delicious, since Swift's real target here is the rapid change in the taste of the town and those who cater to it. The true test of the value of a book for someone like Swift is how long it lasts, not how much noise it makes in the world for however brief a time. Lintot's dismissive use of "antiquated stuff" for Swift's works perfectly captures this misguided attitude. We can see here the beginning of the importance of best-sellers for the modern world that determines what is read, and the gradual, or sometimes rapid, disappearance of the classics.

The last part of Swift's "Verses" is generally regarded as less successful, since it makes a more direct defense of his own life (though spoken by a supposedly "impartial" character at the Rose tavern). In one passage, however, this voice characterizes Swift's poetic practice vigorously and concisely.

His satires, the character claims, were all intended for the betterment of his readers:

"As with a moral view designed
To cure the vices of mankind.
  "His vein, ironically grave,
Exposed the fool and lashed the knave;
To steal a hint was never known,
But what he writ was all his own."   (313–318)

This is, I believe, an accurate view of Swift's purpose and method, although it obviously idealizes his motives and intentions. Swift presents himself, through the words of this outsider, as a noble, purely altruistic commentator on a corrupt society, no doubt exaggerating his virtue and disinterestedness. Yet he was sincerely concerned with both his countries, and he made many recommendations, usually in the form of essays and pamphlets, to improve the lot of the people and defend the Church. Swift was also highly original in his poetry (as in his prose), though he did take hints and sometimes more from other writers. What he took, he always adapted to his purpose, transformed it in the process, and gave it a new slant or twist.

Because of its negativity and implied superiority, satiric poetry may not appeal to everyone, but, clearly, from these samples Swift was more than a simple cynic in his poems. He no doubt ridicules his targets with a mordant wit, but his purpose is to open his readers' eyes to their (and others') pervasive pride, foolishness, and affectation. It is a moral and educational end that he sets himself, and one, I believe, he often achieves. Moreover, effective satire, like other forms of art, requires a serious purpose, careful selection and organization of details, and original language. Swift's poetry meets all these tests and reveals a special flair for the impersonation of different voices and an often complex and dark irony. As a result, with a little help from editors and scholars, we can still appreciate his work today. Swift was a fascinating man who was very much concerned about his society, and wrote about it in his poetry and in his prose. His concise, witty verses can and should be enjoyed by many.

CHAPTER 10

Alexander Pope (1688–1744): Satirist and Moralist

Alexander Pope, a small, frail, infirm hunchback from a despised minority, became the greatest English poet of his generation. Because of his Catholicism, Pope could not go to university, vote in elections, or hold public office. After being trampled by a cow at the age of 12, he suffered from a disease of the spine, which caused him to be increasingly bent as he aged. He probably grew no taller than 4 feet, 6 inches. Yet he became a great writer and friends with some of the other great writers of his time, including Jonathan Swift, John Gay, and, earlier in his life, Joseph Addison.

Pope's father had been a successful London merchant, who moved his family to a small property at Binfield in Windsor Forest in 1700. There, as a youth, Pope read widely in the classics, learned several languages, ancient and modern, with a tutor and on his own, and began to write poetry with the encouragement of his father. He started publishing in 1709 with some pastoral poems and soon established himself as a major poetic voice with his *Essay on Criticism* (1711). He confirmed his status with the first version of *The Rape of the Lock* in 1712 (in two cantos), *Windsor Forest* (1713), a pastoral political poem, and his translation of the first four books of the *Iliad* in 1715. It was Pope's complete translation of Homer's epic in a subscription edition that enabled him to buy the small villa and five acres on the Thames called Twickenham (pronounced Twit'nam) in 1718. Here he lived for the rest of his life, adding a translation of the *Odyssey* in 1726 that supplemented his small fortune. After this, his poetry became increasingly satiric, though occasionally mixed with more philosophical or ethical poems, like his *Essay on Man* and his moral epistles. In the first version of the *Dunciad* (1728) in three books, Pope attacked all the dunces he found in English society who were contributing to its corruption in the arts. In the second version published not long before his death, he added a fourth book and widened the attack to include the whole of English society, beginning at the top. Meanwhile, in the 1730s Pope used the classical satirists, Horace and Juvenal, to guide him in developing his critical look at contemporary English society. Pope also studied and practiced painting throughout his life and developed an interest in landscape gardening that led to his becoming a leader in the "natural" school with his small estate as the model for his theories and experiments. For the first time in England, Pope demonstrated that one could make a living at writing without compromising one's standards or depending on a wealthy patron. His favorite vehicle for conveying his often controversial ideas and judgments was the heroic couplet, of which he became a master.

In the *Essay on Criticism* (1711) the young Pope articulates his general aesthetic standards, sometimes with a sharp tongue. In its three parts he defines the true critic, describes the pitfalls of criticism, and reviews the history of criticism. He establishes the importance of criticism as a literary activity and connects it to the development of a sophisticated taste. He does all of this in a style that is relatively informal and colloquial, with some passages of pointed satiric attack that enliven his remarks. Unexpectedly, the poem proved to be a great success for the young poet, prompting high praise from several leading writers, including Joseph Addison in the *Spectator* papers (No. 253), who called it a "Master-piece in its kind." As we will see, criticism for Pope represents an activity that every reader engages in, including interpretation and evaluation.

In Part 1 Pope covers some of the basic principles in the art of criticism. Many of these contain broad terms that give only a vague indication of the values Pope asserts. An example is "Nature," one of the most complex and elusive concepts in his discussion. Here is how Pope describes it early on in his recommendations for a literary critic:

> First follow Nature, and your judgment frame
> By her just standard, which is <u>still</u> the same;   *always, ever*
> Unerring Nature, still divinely bright,
> One clear, unchanged, and universal light,
> Life, force, and beauty must to all impart,
> At once the source, and end, and test of art.

❧

> Those rules of old discovered, not devised,
> Are Nature still, but Nature methodized;

Nature, like liberty, is but restrained
By the same laws which first herself ordained.   (1: 68–73; 88–91)

Critics are to judge works by the universal standard of "Nature," which provides a permanent and comprehensive principle. This is ultimately divine, the source of all life and order in the universe as we know it. Nature's laws were first revealed by the ancient writers of the Greek and Roman classics, who put them into coherent form in their works. Homer embodied them in his epics, and Virgil followed him in composing his own epic about the Roman Empire. These and other similar works that have passed the test of time, Pope urges, should be the chief study of critics who wish to know the standards by which to judge literature.

But there is another principle Pope identifies that supplements and qualifies "Unerring Nature." It is one that accepts a subjective and variable role in art, the idea of inspiration or genius that cannot be explained by a law or a precept. One cannot simply apply a formula to a work of art to determine its value:

Some beauties yet no precepts can declare,
For there's a happiness as well as care.
Music resembles poetry, in each
Are nameless graces which no methods teach,
And which a master hand alone can reach.

∾

Great wits sometimes may gloriously offend,
And rise to faults true critics dare not mend;
From vulgar bounds with brave disorder part,
And snatch a grace beyond the reach of art,
Which, without passing through the judgment, gains
The heart, and all its end at once attains.   (1: 141–145; 152–157)

There still is a mysterious element in art that one cannot fully explain, a "grace beyond the reach of art." This is the "je ne sais quoi" (literally, "I don't know what") part that eludes rational description, a gift that transcends our limited ability to define or characterize art. Clearly, great artists are not subject to simple rules of writing and creation; their "faults" may even be offensive to some, a "brave disorder" that appeals to the heart, not the mind. Through such violations of good judgment, though, the artist may reach a higher level of creativity and significance than can be explained in traditional terms. Critics, Pope suggests, must be able to recognize and appreciate such moments when they find them, rather than sticking rigidly to their preconceived notions.

In Part 2 Pope surveys the reasons for critics' failure to recognize great writing when they meet it. Here Pope becomes the moralist with a sense of general human limitations that derive from his religious values. He begins by citing the chief of the Seven Deadly Sins as a central culprit in causing critics to misjudge a work. Pride, "the never failing vice of fools" (2: 204), leads many to mistake the writer's intention and feel superior to his execution. This operates through all areas of human activity, but especially the academic:

> A little learning is a dang'rous thing;
> Drink deep, or taste not the Pierian spring.   *sacred to the Muses on*
>   *Mt. Olympus (Greece)*
>
> There shallow draughts intoxicate the brain,
> And drinking largely sobers us again.   (2: 215–218)

Only by immersing ourselves in learning can we fully realize how complex and difficult a true judgment can be. The more we know, the more we realize how little we actually understand. Pope effectively develops the metaphor for learning as drinking, with the paradox that it can become intoxicating in small quantities, whereas more drinking will make us more reasonable. To put this idea in different terms, Pope introduces an epic simile:

> So pleased at first the tow'ring Alps we try,
> Mount o'er the vales, and seem to tread the sky,
> Th'eternal snows appear already past,
> And the first clouds and mountains seem the last;
> But, those attained, we tremble to survey
> The growing labors of the lengthened way,
> Th'increasing prospect tires our wandering eyes,
> Hills peep o'er hills, and Alps on Alps arise!   (2: 225–232)

The natural image of the beautiful mountains with the near ones hiding the higher, more difficult ones farther on is an excellent way to depict concretely this sense of early exultation that leads to more and more weariness and disappointment as one finds the path toward the summit of true knowledge steeper and more challenging than anticipated. Pope displays a fine sensitivity to the experience of learning in this passage, emphasizing one's need for humility, in contrast to the arrogance that often results from gaining some academic knowledge.

Illustrating his knowledge of poetic technique, Pope comments in detail on some of the practices that he deplores. Again he turns to satire to develop his ideas, brilliantly parodying some of the faults of those pretenders to poetry who may write smoothly and correctly, but not with genius. He ridicules those who fill their lines with "expletives" to make up the right number of feet, and create absurd lines like this simplistic one: "And ten low words oft creep in one dull line" (2: 347). Others write in clichés and "expected rhymes," so that

> Where'er you find "the cooling western breeze,"
> In the next line, it "whispers through the trees...."   (2: 350–351)

Pope further mocks the use of the hexameter or alexandrine, a line of six iambic feet, used to conclude a work or a passage:

> A needless Alexandrine ends the song
> That, like a wounded snake, drags its slow length along.   (2: 356–357)

His simile of the snake perfectly captures his sense of this kind of line, slowing down the thought so that it loses its bite and coiled compression. Pope proves a master at imitating such inartistic poetic practices that he scorned.

In the next passage Pope moves to the positive side of the account, describing his ideal poetic practice. He shows how the poet must adapt his sound and rhythm to his subject. In some well-known lines, he advises readers to listen carefully to the sound of the verse as well as to its meaning:

> True ease in writing comes from art, not chance,
> As those move easiest who have learned to dance.
> 'Tis not enough no harshness gives offense,
> The sound must seem an echo to the sense.
> Soft is the strain when Zephyr gently blows,   *the west wind*
> And the smooth stream in smoother numbers flows;
> But when loud surges lash the sounding shore,
> The hoarse, rough verse should like the torrent roar.
> When Ajax strives some rock's vast weight to throw,   *powerful Greek warrior*
> The line too labors, and the words move slow;
> Not so when swift Camilla scours the plain,
> Flies o'er th'unbending corn, and skims along the main.   *grain*
>   (2: 362–373)

Pope clearly believes in a poetic art that is carefully adjusted to reinforce every nuance in the sense of the words. He was, no doubt, the most polished poet of his generation, but also one of the most skilled at his craft. The smooth lines run fluently, the rough seas sound loudly with hard consonants, and Ajax's slow, heavy lifting moves haltingly. Alliteration, assonance, and internal rhyme all contribute to the lines' effective imitation of the sounds the words describe. The alexandrine in the last line quoted above gives him the length he needs to suggest the speed of the "swift Camilla." By his early twenties Pope was already a master of poetic technique.

In Part 3 Pope advises critics on their personal morality. He asserts the importance in criticism of truth, honesty, and sincerity, but he also recommends that the critic should practice prudence and discretion. People may be seriously upset if you criticize them in print, so be careful, but still be faithful to your judgment. Pope seems not to have strictly followed his own advice here, for in the next passage he ridicules a prominent critic, even as he is advising caution. Critics, he suggests, should be able to "bear reproof" if they are wise:

> 'Twere well might critics still this freedom take;
> But Appius reddens at each word you <u>speak</u>,   *rhymes with "take"*
> And stares, tremendous! with a threatening eye,
> Like some fierce tyrant in old tapestry.   (3: 584–587)

These lines made John Dennis, the critic mocked, an enemy for life. Pope seems to have given his satiric tongue a little too much latitude here, though it must be said that his brief character portrait of Dennis is highly effective. One can see the pride welling up in the critic as his judgment is questioned and his blood pressure rises. Reference to the old wall hanging helps us to visualize the scene, with the suggestion of an old-fashioned, almost medieval point of view.

Pope balances this portrait with a description of the ideal critic. He emphasizes the importance of humility and generosity in one who wants to judge a work of art fairly and justly. It is, clearly, no mean feat:

> But where's the man, who counsel can bestow,
> Still pleased to teach, and yet not proud to know?
> Unbiased, or by favor, or by spite:
> Not dully prepossessed, nor blindly right;
> Though learned, well-bred; and though well-bred, sincere;
> Modestly bold, and humanly severe:

Who to a friend his faults can freely show,
And gladly praise the merit of a foe?
Blessed with a taste exact, yet unconfined;
A knowledge both of books and humankind;
Gen'rous converse; a soul exempt from pride;   *well-bred conversation*
And love to praise, with reason on his side?   (3: 631–642)

It takes a good man to be a good critic, Pope suggests, and, as we know, such a man is hard to find. Not only must he be well-read and humble, but he must also be able to criticize a friend and praise a foe, when it is justified by their works. Such disinterestedness and balance are not easily achieved. Notice how Pope builds his portrait from different qualities that are often opposed (like modesty and boldness) and how the whole passage is a series of questions, indicating the difficulty in finding such a person. Thus Pope demonstrates in his *Essay* how the fair and just interpretation of literature is a profoundly difficult task, yet an extremely important one. He also shows how ideas can be shaped into effective, interesting poetry, never an easy task. All of this constitutes excellent advice for every reader as well as for the critic.

In his next important poem, *The Rape of the Lock* (1712), Pope achieved contemporary recognition almost immediately, though he did not please the people for whom it was written. He was asked by a friend, John Caryll, to compose a poem that might heal the rift between two Catholic families, who had been alienated by Lord Petre's act of snipping off a lock of the beautiful young Arabella Fermor's hair. The first version of the poem was in two cantos, but Pope expanded this into five in 1714 with all the activity of the sylphs, the game of ombre, and other elements, and finally added the lines spoken by Clarissa in the last part in 1717. Although the poem was not successful in bringing together the two families, it soon became a popular success and a recognized classic of the mock-epic genre. Readers have loved it ever since, for its wit, fancy, and incisive verse.

As a kind of epic, *The Rape* tells a story with several major characters, including a heroine and a hero as well as some supernatural figures, and some surprising events, with strange twists and turns. Pope even makes card playing and drinking coffee into pivotal episodes. Belinda is the beautiful if somewhat vain young society woman who undergoes a traumatic experience. The Baron, love-struck and impulsive, is the villain with the scissors, while many of the sylphs are the souls of deceased coquettes, who turn out to be rather weak guardian angels of human virtue. The poem opens with a mock-epic statement of theme and an invocation of the muse:

What dire offense from am'rous causes springs,
What mighty contests rise from trivial things,
I sing—This verse to Caryll, Muse! is due:
This, ev'n Belinda may vouchsafe to view:
Slight is the subject, but not so the praise,
If she inspire, and he approve my <u>lays</u>.   *songs, poems*
    Say what strange motive, Goddess! could compel
A well-bred lord t'assault a gentle belle?
Oh, say what stranger cause, yet unexplored,
Could make a gentle belle reject a lord?
In tasks so bold can little men engage,
And in soft bosoms dwells such mighty rage?   (1: 1–12)

We recognize that Pope is imitating the epic's introduction, putting the object of the sentence before the subject like Milton, but with his "I sing" coming only in the third line, not in the sixth as in *Paradise Lost*. Pope makes sure we understand the nature of his poem by explicitly naming the origin of his action as "trivial things" and designating the subject as "slight." Yet it has led to a "dire offense," a surprising assault, and a violent reaction. All this seems mysterious at first and requires elaborate discussion and narration, conveyed with delicate wit and some sparks of satire. The self-deprecation of Pope's "little men" who take on the large task of describing all this is appropriately light and modest, especially in view of all these upper-class characters. The heroic couplet is here reduced to narrating a kind of comedy of manners rather than a complex tale of epic proportions.

The scene opens with a sylph named Ariel hovering around Belinda's head as she awakes at noon, causing her to dream about fashionable young courtiers and instructing her in the role of the sylphs. Ariel's real purpose is to warn her about the impending dangers that surround her as she goes about the pleasurable social business of visiting and parties. After describing the sylphs' nature and function as well as the gnomes (former prudes), Ariel warns Belinda about the ominous signs that exist for this day:

"Of these am I, who thy protection claim,
A watchful sprite, and Ariel is my name.
Late, as I ranged the crystal wilds of air,
In the clear mirror of thy ruling star
I saw, alas! some dread event impend,
Ere to the main this morning sun descend,
But Heav'n reveals not what, or how, or where:
Warned by the Sylph, O pious maid, beware!

This to disclose is all thy guardian can:
Beware of all, but most beware of Man!"   (1: 105–114)

Ariel makes clear to Belinda that something dire could happen to her involving a man, but he cannot say exactly what. His sympathy and care for her
is evident, as are his limited powers of protection. Unfortunately, after Shock,
her lapdog, licks her face to wake her up and she sees that a love letter awaits
her, she forgets all about the warning she has had. It disappears from her
consciousness like a dream as we see what really occupies her attention—
love.

Pope now pictures Belinda in front of her dressing table, preparing to face
the beau monde in all her splendor. He describes all the products from
around the world that she uses to make herself beautiful, drawing on London's central role in global trade. This passage is a bit long to quote in its
entirety, but a couple of shorter parts will show why it has become a classic
of satiric description. The first part characterizes the nature of this activity:

> And now, unveiled, the <u>toilet</u> stands displayed,   *dressing table*
> Each silver vase in mystic order laid.
> First, robed in white, the nymph intent adores,
> With head uncovered, the cosmetic pow'rs.
> A heav'nly image in the glass appears;
> To that she bends, to that her eyes she rears.
> Th'inferior priestess, at her altar's side,
> Trembling, begins the sacred rites of Pride.   (1: 121–128)

Clearly, for Belinda, this is a religious rite, with her adoration directed at the
"cosmetic pow'rs" and her rich treasures solely designed to enhance her
beauty. This is what she lives for, and, it must be admitted, what she is quite
successful in creating: her divinely beautiful image is reflected in her mirror
as her maid, the "inferior priestess," starts to conduct the holy service. It is a
triumph of narcissism and of well-honed satire, yet also a compliment to her
real loveliness.

Further description of this rite suggests other values in our heroine. We
see that she is a skilled and successful participant in the amorous games of
her society. In these she has many resources on which to call:

> This <u>casket</u> India's glowing gems unlocks,   *box*
> And all Arabia breathes from yonder box.
> The tortoise here and elephant unite,

> Transformed to combs, the speckled and the white.
> Here files of pins extend their shining rows,
> Puffs, powders, patches, Bibles, billet-doux.
> Now <u>awful</u> Beauty puts on all its arms;   *awe-inspiring*
> The fair each moment rises in her charms,
> Repairs her smiles, awakens ev'ry grace,
> And calls forth all the wonder of her face....   (1: 133–142)

She has the finest products the world can offer—jewelry, combs, pins—with which to create her lovely appearance. The mixture, however, of all these beauty aids, love letters, and sacred scriptures reveals something of her own confusion of values. The Bible seems especially out of place on her dressing table, showing by contrast how far Belinda is from true grace. It clearly has nothing to do with her life or her real interests, but only serves to give them a pseudo-sacred veneer. One can begin to see why the real Belinda might not have appreciated Pope's poem.

In Canto 2, as Belinda sails down the Thames toward Hampton Court Palace and her social life, the Baron is preparing to make his attack on her, especially on the two carefully arranged locks of her hair with which he has become especially taken. Ariel, meanwhile, warns all his troops of spirits that they must guard Belinda carefully because of the ominous signs that surround her fate. His speech to them evokes both the trivial and the dire possibilities:

> "This day black omens threat the brightest fair,
> That e'er deserved a watchful spirit's care;
> Some dire disaster, or by force or slight,
> But what, or where, the Fates have wrapped in night:
> Whether the nymph shall break <u>Diana</u>'s law,   *goddess of chastity*
> Or some frail china jar receive a flaw,
> Or stain her honor, or her new brocade,
> Forget her pray'rs, or miss a masquerade,
> Or lose her heart, or necklace, at a ball;
> Or whether Heav'n has doomed that <u>Shock</u> must fall.   *her lapdog*
> Haste, then, ye spirits! to your charge repair...."   (2: 101–111)

Ariel says that they must be ready for anything that might happen, assigning specific areas of concern to each one and putting fifty sylphs in charge of her petticoat. Even he seems to equate such opposed things as Belinda's honor and her new dress, her heart and her necklace, as Pope ironically joins them in the rhetorical structure of his couplet, which pairs and contrasts them by making them objects of the same verb (the technical name for this is zeugma). The suggestion is that Belinda does not see much difference between compromising her honor or ruining her new dress, thus contributing to the portrait of her moral blindness. The scene is set for the dramatic confrontation between Belinda and the Baron.

Canto 3 depicts the battle between them over ombre, a popular card game of the time. Pope describes this as an epic contest between hero and heroine with the face cards (King, Queen, Jack) as the major combatants and the other cards as the foot soldiers in the battle. In the game Belinda triumphs over the Baron just as he thinks he is about to win, prompting her to exult prematurely in her glorious feat. The poet comments on her thoughtlessness and hubris (excessive pride), which blinds her to an even worse fate. Before the final attack occurs, they brew and drink coffee (recently introduced to England), which causes "vapors" to rise up "to the Baron's brain" that prompt him to decide to take one of her beautiful locks of hair by force. Ariel realizes that this is the crucial moment:

> Just in that instant, anxious Ariel sought
> The close recesses of the virgin's thought;
> As on the nosegay in her breast reclined,
> He watched th'ideas rising in her mind,
> Sudden he viewed, in spite of all her art,
> An earthly lover lurking at her heart.
> Amazed, confused, he found his pow'r expired,
> Resigned to fate, and with a sigh retired.   (3: 139–146)

Ariel finds he is powerless to defend her because Belinda is in love, and he cannot do anything about it. Her internal acceptance of this man is enough to negate all his supernatural force. She shares the blame for what happens, since she secretly loves him. However, when the Baron suddenly snips a lock from her head and exults in his triumph, she is outraged and cries out in horror:

> Not louder shrieks to pitying heav'n are cast,
> When husbands, or when lapdogs breathe their last;
> Or when rich china vessels fall'n from high,
> In glitt'ring dust and painted fragments lie!   (3: 157–160)

Again Pope mocks the scene by equating the deaths of lapdogs and husbands in the eyes of this society. But he also suggests that Belinda's "rape" is a serious fall from grace, in the broken Chinese vase lying in pieces in the dust.

It is an image that hints at the tragic loss of innocence and beauty in this scene, the human sin that brought about the original fall. Pope manages to evoke this idea with great delicacy, at the same time that he satirizes the couple and their social values. His art is nicely to balance mockery with sympathy, to take the violation of Belinda's hair seriously without making it into a fully tragic event.

The consequences of this act continue to reverberate through the action in Canto 4. Umbriel, a melancholy gnome, hurries down to the underworld where the Queen of Hades, Spleen, resides. She represents all the ill humor, anger, and resentment that Belinda feels after her violation. Spleen was a fashionable ailment that could mean serious depression, or, more commonly, a temporary melancholy or peevishness. This episode reflects the visit to Hades that the epic hero usually takes as part of his role in the poem. Here Umbriel, as he proceeds to Spleen's palace, has to pass through a most unusual group of figures:

> Unnumbered throngs on ev'ry side are seen
> Of bodies changed to various forms by Spleen.
> Here living teapots stand, one arm held out,
> One bent; the handle this, and that the spout:
> A <u>pipkin</u> there, like Homer's tripod, walks;   *earthen pot*
> Here sighs a jar, and there a goose pie talks;
> Men prove with child, as pow'rful fancy works,
> And maids, turned bottles, call aloud for corks.   (4: 47–54)

Madness is clearly a possible consequence of the spleen, but Pope again draws some humor out of this by making the various psychoses of these human figures into ridiculous manifestations. In the last two lines of this passage the sexual fantasies of these figures reflect the bizarre effect spleen can have on love. These may be seen as warnings against indulging such feelings for too long. It is a wonderful example of Pope's fertile imagination, fancifully building on an epic convention.

Umbriel requests that Spleen allow Belinda to be infected, which she does, and sends him back with a bag full of emotions, sighs, and tears. Belinda is then encouraged by her friend Thalestris (the name of an Amazon queen) to denounce the Baron and indulge her resentment at the "loss" of her honor. Thalestris hurries to ask her suitor, Sir Plume, to become Belinda's champion and go to the Baron to retrieve the lock. The conversation between the two men is one of the funniest parts of the poem, as Sir Plume, "of amber snuffbox justly vain," challenges the Baron to give up his prize:

With earnest eyes, and round unthinking face,
He first the snuffbox opened, then the case,
And thus broke out—"My Lord, why, what the devil!
Z----ds! [Zounds] damn the lock! 'fore Gad, you must be civil!   *God's wounds*
Plague on't! 'tis past a jest—nay prithee, pox!
Give her the hair"—he spoke, and rapped his box.
    "It grieves me much," replied the Peer again,
"Who speaks so well should ever speak in vain."   (4: 125–132)

Sir Plume's sputtering, broken speech filled with exclamations is nicely contrasted to the smooth irony of the Baron, who clearly feels no fear from the lady's champion. Pope's ability to incorporate such dialogue within his heroic couplet is a tribute to his skill in managing the verse to characterize these men through their speech. The flexibility of this seemingly rigid poetic form proves to be remarkable in the hands of a master.

In Canto 5 Belinda continues to be subject to spleen. Clarissa, another lady of the court, tries to restore peace by offering words of advice to her friend, counsel that seems to represent Pope's own point of view. Her speech is filled with maxims that set the action into its proper perspective:

"How vain are all these glories, all our pains,
Unless good sense preserve what beauty gains;
That men may say when we <u>the front box</u> grace,   *at the theater*
'Behold the first in virtue as in face!'
Oh! if to dance all night, and dress all day,
Charmed the smallpox, or chased old age away,
Who would not scorn what housewife's cares produce,
Or who would learn one earthly thing of use?
<u>To patch</u>, nay ogle, might become a saint,   *to wear beauty marks*
Nor could it sure be such a sin to <u>paint</u>.   *use cosmetics*
But since, alas! frail beauty must decay,
Curled or uncurled, since locks will turn to gray;
Since painted, or not painted, all shall fade,
And she who scorns a man must die a maid;
What then remains but well our pow'r to use,
And keep good humor still whate'er we lose?"   (5: 15–30)

In the perspective of time, human beauty is transient and relatively unimportant, certainly not something one should seriously quarrel about. Good humor is more than constant cheerfulness: it is to accept the conditions of human life with grace and civility. The only lasting values are goodness, generosity of spirit, and control of one's passions. Pope's poetry condenses these wise words into memorable couplets that summarize his point, using just enough conversational idioms in such words as "Oh!," "nay," and "alas!" with their breaking up of the rhythm, to keep the speech from being too formal.

Unfortunately, Belinda does not heed this advice and shrieks out for the Baron to "Restore the lock!" He is not about to do that, but the lock is taken from him by the gods and sent into the skies, where it becomes a constellation to be contemplated by the "beau monde" as a reminder of the sorrows of love and of Belinda's beauty. Unfortunately, too, the families were not reconciled by the poem, with the main figures in the story eventually marrying other people later on. Pope's poem, however, has remained as a classic of the mock-heroic kind, a brilliant, polished gem of wit, wisdom, and delight.

Pope's *Epistle to Dr. Arbuthnot* (1735), an imaginary personal letter to a real friend of his who was suffering from his final illness, is a defense of the poet's life and career against the many slanders and attacks on him over the years. It is loosely based on various classical poems (especially by Horace), but adapted to Pope's situation and concerns. Dr. Arbuthnot had been a distinguished physician, man of letters, and friend of Pope for many years. The poem was published early in 1735, just twenty-five days before Arbuthnot died. Pope has Arbuthnot speak some lines of dialogue in the poem, which probably represent, at least roughly, his actual position on the issue of satire that Pope discusses in the poem. Pope's main point is that for satire to be effective, it must be specific and name names. Arbuthnot, the prudent man of the world, cautions him to be more careful and more general. As this is quite a lengthy poem (over 400 lines), we will be able to look at only a few passages from it.

Pope begins in exasperation by ordering his gardener, John Searle, to close up his house and estate, so that no more people will be able to hound him for free advice about their own poetry. He has been deluged with requests that have left him no time for his own life and work. It is an amusingly vehement and colloquial opening:

P[ope]. Shut, shut the door, good John! (fatigued, I said),
Tie up the knocker, say I'm sick, I'm dead.
The <u>Dog Star</u> rages! nay 'tis past a doubt   *Sirius (associated with August)*
All <u>Bedlam</u>, or Parnassus is let out: *Bethlehem hospital*
Fire in each eye, and papers in each hand,
They rave, recite, and madden round the land.

What walls can guard me, or what shades can hide?
They pierce my thickets, through my grot they glide,
By land, by water, they renew the charge,
They stop the chariot, and they board the barge.
No place is sacred, not the church is free;
Ev'n Sunday shines no Sabbath day to me....   (1–12)

Pope vividly expresses his frustration with all these would-be poets, whom
he characterizes as madmen driven wild by the heat of the season. It seems to
him that Bethlehem Hospital for the insane, that is, Bedlam (from whence
our word), has opened wide its doors and unleashed its patients on the city.
They infiltrate his land, besiege his house, and plague his outings. They even
invade his dear grotto, a subterranean passage Pope had built under the main
London road in order to connect his house with the land on the other side,
and a favorite escape that he had richly decorated with shells and rock crys-
tals. This epistle projects an imaginative vision of the total lack of privacy
that some celebrities today would no doubt find all too accurate. The short
phrases, colloquial language, and broken lines in this passage suggest the
multitude of people who beset him as well as his own fevered emotional
state.

   Pope then asks Arbuthnot if he can offer any cure for this noxious crowd
of pests. Arbuthnot has little to say in reply until Pope starts to impugn
royalty in a brief allusion to the parable of King Midas, who, for favoring
Pan's flute playing over Apollo's music, was given ass's ears by the gods. At
this point, Arbuthnot interrupts Pope's diatribe to caution him to tone down
his criticism, which could land him in serious trouble:

A[rbuthnot]. Good friend, forbear! you deal in dang'rous things.
I'd never name queens, ministers, or kings;
Keep close to ears, and let those asses prick;
'Tis nothing—P[ope]. Nothing? if they bite and kick?
Out with it Dunciad! let the secret pass,   *Pope's satiric epic*
That secret to each fool, that he's an ass:
The truth once told (and wherefore should we lie?)
The queen of Midas slept, and so may I.
   You think this cruel? take it for a rule,
No creature smarts so little as a fool.   (75–84)

Pope thus assumes the mantle of truth teller, one whose integrity will never
allow him to be cowed even by the most powerful people in his society. His
colloquial language and his fiery interjection, cutting off Arbuthnot's mild

advice, underscore his passionate commitment to make bold statements of intellectual and moral honesty. After all, he argues, the people he attacks even by name will not feel his lash since they are much too dense. Pope absolutely refuses to abandon his independence as a writer and a moral being to become a flatterer or a toady.

The poet then reflects on why he became a writer in the first place. Why should he suffer all this abuse for a career that began in innocence and goodwill? His statement of his beginnings as a poet is a classic of rhetorical idealizing:

> Why did I write? What sin to me unknown
> Dipped me in ink, my parents', or my own?
> As yet a child, nor yet a fool to fame,
> I lisped in <u>numbers</u>, for the numbers came.   *verses, poetic meter*
> I left no calling for this idle trade,
> No duty broke, no father disobeyed.
> The Muse but served to ease some friend, not wife,
> To help me through this long disease, my life,
> To second, Arbuthnot! thy art and care,
> And teach the being you preserved, to bear.   (125–134)

Pope's account of his beginnings as a writer emphasizes how naturally poetry came to him. It was, he claims, not something he had to acquire, but inherent in his makeup from the start. Nor did he rebel against his parents or quit a trade or profession to become a poet. He found that poetry was helpful to console others and to enable him to endure, as he puts it, "this long disease, my life." It is an ideal vision, of course, but largely true, in the sense that he had found his calling in the innocence of his youth.

Moreover, Pope says that he was encouraged by knowledgeable critics of the early eighteenth century and that his earliest poems were completely innocuous in subject and tone. How could anyone react viciously to these first efforts, he wonders:

> Soft were my <u>numbers</u>; who could take offense   *verses*
> While pure description held the place of sense?
> Like gentle Fanny's was my flow'ry theme,
> A painted mistress, or a purling stream.
> Yet then did <u>Gildon</u> draw his venal quill;   *a minor writer*
> I wished the man a dinner, and sat still.
> Yet then did <u>Dennis</u> rave in furious fret;   *John Dennis, a critic*
> I never answered, I was not in debt.

If want provoked, or madness made them print,
I waged no war with Bedlam or the Mint.   *safe area for debtors in London*
                                                                       (147–156)

His first poetry was pastoral, concerned with natural beauty or artificial love. But he began to be attacked with venom by some people for political or personal reasons. These were either madmen or mercenary writers, Pope suggests, but from then on, others took up their pens to revile his character, person, and writings. Yet he continued to restrain himself until he finally published his *Dunciad* (1728), enshrining all his attackers in a mock epic of fools and knaves.

The satire becomes more pointed in the character portraits Pope paints of his enemies. Some of them were actually fine writers, blessed with great talent, but they turned against him because of politics, a sense of rivalry, or an arrogance that could not accept the independence of others. Joseph Addison (1672–1719), a poet, dramatist, and essayist (in the *Spectator* and the *Tatler*), was one of these. He had "True Genius" Pope admits, but he also tried to rule the literary world like a tyrant. Addison could, Pope declares,

Bear, like the Turk, no brother near the throne;
View him with scornful, yet with jealous eyes,
And hate for arts that caused himself to rise;
Damn with faint praise, assent with civil leer,
And without sneering, teach the rest to sneer;
Willing to wound, and yet afraid to strike,
Just hint a fault, and hesitate dislike. . . .   (198–204)

Addison could, in other words, undermine his rivals indirectly and without appearing that that was what he was doing. He would manipulate others for his own personal gain, especially if they threatened his power. His is the most insidious kind of opposition, difficult to prove and impossible to counteract. This was a shame, as Pope concludes, for its waste of great talent in schemes of subtle personal denigration:

Who but must laugh, if such a man there be?
Who would not weep, if Atticus were he?   *Addison*
                                                                               (213–214)

Atticus was the name of a good friend of Cicero, a generous and wise man of letters in Roman times, both like and unlike Addison. Pope's portrait of

Addison is not wholly satiric, but a mixed one with both good and bad elements, though with the emphasis on the serious flaw in his character.

Other portraits are not so mixed, including one of the proud, tasteless patron, Bufo, a type who loved to be flattered by fawning authors, yet was stingy with his gifts. Pope had been successful enough not to have to depend on such a patron, but he knew well that others had to rely on such a benefactor. His portrait of John, Lord Hervey, courtier and friend of Queen Caroline, is one of the most devastating in all of literature. In a recent poem Hervey had viciously attacked Pope, so Pope here replies with a vengeance. Because of Hervey's apparent bisexuality, Pope calls him "Sporus" (the boy whom the emperor Nero married in public), and treats him with great contempt. At the beginning of the diatribe, as soon as Pope mentions his name, Arbuthnot himself breaks in to call Hervey some scathing names, showing how much even the moderate doctor hates this man (and forgets his own advice to Pope not to name names). Pope continues with comments on Hervey that are even more highly charged:

> Yet let me flap this bug with gilded wings,
> This painted child of dirt, that stinks and stings;
> Whose buzz the witty and the fair annoys,
> Yet wit ne'er tastes, and beauty ne'er enjoys;
> So well-bred spaniels civilly delight
> In mumbling of the game they dare not bite.
> Eternal smiles his emptiness betray,
> As shallow streams run dimpling all the way.
> Whether in florid impotence he speaks,
> And, as the prompter breathes, the puppet squeaks;
> Or at the ear of Eve, familiar toad,
> Half froth, half venom, spits himself abroad,
> In puns, or politics, or tales, or lies,
> Or spite, or smut, or rhymes, or blasphemies.
> His wit all seesaw between *that* and *this*,
> Now high, now low, now master up, now miss,
> And he himself one vile antithesis.
> Amphibious thing! that acting either part,
> The trifling head or the corrupted heart,
> Fop at the toilet, flatt'rer at the <u>board</u>,   *dinner table*
> Now trips a lady, and now struts a lord.   (309–329)

Sporus has a fine, genteel appearance, always smiling it seems, but underneath the surface lies a nastiness that can only be suggested through animal and other lowly imagery. Sporus's special talent seems to be in slander and lies spread in secret. Pope even alludes to *Paradise Lost*, when he compares Sporus to a toad, which was one form Satan took when he first tried to seduce Eve (who, in this case, would be Hervey's good friend, Queen Caroline). Sporus, thus, is not just vile, but evil personified. His split personality is neatly divided into the two halves of the couplet in the last two lines of this passage, as Pope employs its structure, using alliteration and repetition to mark the division points. As powerful personal satire, this portrait can scarcely be matched anywhere.

Pope ends his letter on a strongly positive note, contrasting his parents with the corruption and decadence he has just described. He greatly admired his father, whom he portrays as embodying the very ideals he has been promoting throughout the poem:

> Born to no pride, inheriting no strife,
> Nor marrying discord in a noble wife,
> Stranger to civil and religious rage,
> The good man walked innoxious through his age.
> No courts he saw, no suits would ever try,
> Nor dared an oath, nor hazarded a lie.
> Unlearn'd, he knew no <u>schoolman</u>'s subtle art,   *medieval philosopher*
> No language but the language of the heart.
> By nature honest, by experience wise,
> Healthy by temp'rance, and by exercise;
> His life, though long, to sickness passed unknown,
> His death was instant, and without a groan.
> Oh, grant me thus to live, and thus to die!
> Who sprung from kings shall know less joy than I.   (392–405)

Goodness, honesty, sincerity, and independence all are Pope's inheritance from his father. He lived a long and healthy life, was true to his faith (he refused to take oaths of allegiance and against the pope, thus making him subject to the anti-Catholic laws), and died easily and quickly (a sign of God's favor). The poem thus ends in hope and peace, with goodness rewarded and evil punished. Pope's exasperation at the outset has been resolved, and he prays for Arbuthnot's quick recovery. He goes far beyond his broad model, Horace, in both his praise of virtue and the harshness of his satire. It is a poem of deep feeling, with much anger and bitterness, but also great joy and pleasure, as he reviews and defends his life and career.

For the final poem by Pope, we will look briefly at Book 4 of the *Dunciad*, a mock epic he originally published in three books in 1728, adding the last book in 1742. In 1729, he brought out a "Variorum" edition, with mock notes, commentary, and appendices, to parody the learned editions recently being published. In his extensive poem Pope attacks those who have ridiculed and slandered him as he surveys the many follies, vices, and crimes that have crippled English society over the past generation. Although published anonymously, the poem was soon attributed to Pope, generating even more attacks on him afterwards. He depicts Queen "Dulness" presiding over the action such as it is, with Colley Cibber, the Poet Laureate of England and prominent actor, as hero in the final edition. By dullness Pope really means knavery as well as folly, and by the end of Book 4 it reigns supreme over England. This is Pope's most pessimistic review of the state of English life and letters.

In the first three books of the *Dunciad* Pope focused on the abysmal condition of literature, caused by the many hack writers who produced trash for a newly burgeoning popular market. In Book 4 Pope takes aim at larger issues, including the degradation he found in education, politics, and morality. In the first lines he invokes the great powers of "dread Chaos" and "eternal Night," who now control the destiny of his land. He urges them to allow him a little time to speak his mind before he passes into oblivion:

> Yet, yet a moment, one dim ray of light
> Indulge, dread Chaos, and eternal Night!
> Of darkness visible so much be lent,
> As half to show, half veil the deep intent.
>   Ye Pow'rs! Whose mysteries restored I sing,   *Chaos and Night*
> To whom Time bears me on his rapid wing,
> Suspend a while your force inertly strong,
> Then take at once the poet and the song.   (4: 1–8)

Instead of invoking a benevolent Muse or the gods, Pope pleads with the forces of darkness and destruction for a few moments of respite before he, along with everyone else, is engulfed by the waters of annihilation. The world, he believes, is returning to its original disorder. He evokes the "darkness visible" of Hell in *Paradise Lost*, when Satan first views his new home (1: 63), to suggest his own world's condition. Pope thus creates a new mythology to describe this current state, which is anything but comforting or hopeful. Clearly, nothing of value can survive in the face of such an inert, but overwhelmingly destructive power.

In the central part of the poem, various historical and typical figures representing contemporary decadence come to Queen Dulness to receive her blessing and request her favor. A good example is Dr. Busby (1605–1695), former headmaster of Westminster School and infamous for his severity and iron discipline, who describes his harsh educational methods and asks her approval. Words alone are the main emphasis in his school, and the "narrower" way in learning is the better, Busby claims, so that the imaginations of his boys will not be allowed to roam freely:

> We ply the memory, we load the brain,
> Bind rebel wit, and double chain on chain,
> Confine the thought, to exercise the <u>breath</u>;   *in rote recitations*
> And keep them in the <u>pale</u> of words till death.   *enclosure*
> Whate'er the talents, or howe'er designed,
> We hang one jingling padlock on the mind....   (4: 157–162)

Any creative endeavor or independent thinking is strictly suppressed. Perhaps surprisingly, Pope becomes the advocate for freedom of thought and the cultivation of the imagination in education. The imagery of imprisonment and the "jingling padlock" clearly carries his disapproval of the opposite approach, with its cruel attempt to maintain absolute control over the young boy's mind.

After other foolish and trivial petitioners (like the carnation grower who complains of the butterfly collector) have had their say, the final triumph of Chaos occurs. Queen Dulness blesses all her subjects and urges them to go back to their lives and "MAKE ONE MIGHTY DUNCIAD OF THE LAND" (line 604). The poet relates, as his final, apocalyptic vision, the ultimate death of all art, truth, and philosophy as "Night primeval" covers the land:

> Religion blushing veils her sacred fires,
> And unawares Morality expires.
> Nor public flame, nor private, dares to shine;
> Nor human spark is left, nor glimpse divine!
> Lo! thy dread Empire, CHAOS! is restored;
> Light dies before thy uncreating word:
> Thy hand, great Anarch! lets the curtain fall;
> And Universal Darkness buries All.   (4: 649–656)

The last act of the human drama has been performed, and utter mindlessness has conquered all. Civilization has disintegrated with nothing left to redeem society from the forces of destruction. Like Swift's, Pope's outlook darkened seriously at the end of his life, though I believe there is something pleasurable in the imaginative vision Pope offers us. His use of personification for the abstract values that suffer under the tyranny of Dulness, like "skulking Truth" who is forced to return to her cave (line 641), his inventive actions involving these figures, and his use of the structure of the heroic couplet to emphasize important words through alliteration and rhyme all testify to the brilliance of Pope's own creative imagination still hard at work even as his body is decaying.

In sum, Pope treats themes and issues still important today, and he does so in his verse with great suggestiveness, trenchancy, and verve. He is a fine craftsman as well as a clear thinker and moralist in his poetry, setting forth his ideas with power and passion in a variety of genres. Readers today may need help with some of his allusions and references (especially in the satire), but this is surely a small price to pay for the insight and pleasure that results. Few poets in English have ever put so many significant ideas so memorably as Alexander Pope. In his hands, satire became an art form worthy of the highest respect.

CHAPTER 11

Samuel Johnson (1709–1784): Moralist and Satirist

Samuel Johnson overcame some significant obstacles in his life, from disease to poverty and a melancholy temperament, to become the foremost man of letters in England in the late eighteenth century. He was born in Lichfield, the son of a provincial bookseller whose financial situation gradually deteriorated over time. As a baby Johnson contracted scrofula, a form of tuberculosis that seriously affected his eyesight, hearing, and appearance. Nevertheless, he proved to be an excellent student and, after completing the standard classical curriculum at the local grammar school, he eventually went off to Oxford University at the age of 19 (somewhat late for the time). He was able to stay at Oxford for just a year before he had to return home for lack of money. He continued to live at home for a time, working in his father's shop until his father's death in 1731. Moving to Birmingham, then, to try his luck, he attempted different kinds of work, including teaching, but nothing seemed satisfactory. In 1735, despite the objection of her family, Johnson married Elizabeth Porter, a widow twenty years older than he was, acquiring two stepsons and a stepdaughter at the same time. Two years later, after failing to succeed in a private school venture, he decided to move to London permanently, along with his student David Garrick, who, like his mentor, later became famous. At first Johnson worked as a hack writer, but he soon became a regular contributor to and later editor of the *Gentleman's Magazine*, the most prominent review of news, history, and literature in England. He gradually published works on his own, including poetry, essays, translations, and a biography of his friend, Richard Savage. To Johnson's great distress, his wife died in March 1752, adding sorrow to his struggles with indebtedness and his work on his own (and others') writing projects (he was always helping others with their poems and prose).

In spite of these difficulties, Johnson emerged in the 1750s as the most important writer of his time, starting with a poem called *The Vanity of Human Wishes* in 1749, the essays in *The Rambler* (1750–1752), and the monumental *Dictionary of the English Language* (1755). He extended his influence and achievement into other areas of literature with his philosophical tale, *Rasselas* (1759); an excellent edition of Shakespeare's plays with a brilliant introduction and notes (1765); a notable travel book, *A Journey to the Western Islands of Scotland* (1775); and, finally, an extensive edition of English poetry with his biographical and critical comments on each poet, *Lives of the Poets* (10 vols., 1779–1781), a remarkable accomplishment for an aging author. Moreover, from 1766 to 1768, Johnson, though he had no formal training in the subject, helped write a series of lectures on various aspects of the law for Robert Chambers, the Vinerian Professor of Law at Oxford. Johnson also composed several trenchant and sometimes controversial essays on political issues during the 1770s, including one on the American revolution called *Taxation no Tyranny* (1775), arguing against the colonists' right to rebel. Despite all these significant writings, Johnson suffered several periods of depression and morbid melancholy in his career, sometimes doubting the value of his life and even the possibility of his salvation. Yet he managed to surmount these afflictions to compose several extraordinary literary works which ensure that his name will survive as long as English is known and its literature read.

After Johnson's death in 1784, James Boswell, a young Scotsman who had been Johnson's friend for twenty years, published the *Life of Johnson*, a work that is still regarded as one of the great biographies in the English language. For many years Johnson was at the center of a circle of friends who were some of the most prominent men in their fields, including his former student David Garrick, a great actor and theater manager; Edmund Burke, an eloquent statesman and philosopher; Sir Joshua Reynolds, a distinguished painter and first president of the Royal Academy; and Oliver Goldsmith, poet, essayist, and playwright. These and other distinguished men met regularly at a tavern for dinner to discuss literature, art, politics, and other topics of general interest. Boswell's account of several of these dinners, which he describes with extraordinary vividness, is one of the delights of his *Life of Johnson*. Johnson's exceptional learning, knowledge of language and literature, capacious memory, and witty conversation made him the natural leader of their informal club, so the second half of the eighteenth century is now often called the Age of Johnson in his honor. Such a title may exaggerate his influence, but it does indicate how important Johnson had become as a literary figure, despite formidable hurdles, by the end of his life.

Although not primarily a poet, Johnson wrote poetry of one sort or another all his life. He took up the torch of satire early on from Pope and Dryden, beginning with his imitation of Juvenal's third satire, an attack on Rome of the first century C.E., with his poem called simply *London* (1739). An imitation is not a translation but a free paraphrase of the original, transferring the scene to the contemporary world with recent historical events and more modern characters replacing the older ones. Juvenal's poem is about the corruption and vices of Rome under Nero, with one character leaving the city to go live in the country to escape the moral contagion. Most of this Latin poem is a diatribe against the sharpers and parasites who appear to succeed in the Roman metropolis at the expense of the virtuous, who are usually their victims. In the same manner Johnson describes Thales who, having lost most of his fortune to con artists in London, is about to depart for Wales, where he can live in peace and security far from the pervasive urban corruption. To make sure the reader sees the parallels, Johnson put the relevant lines from Juvenal at the bottom of each page.

In the first passage we will consider from Johnson's poem, the narrator, a friend of Thales, describes the conditions in London that have made Thales decide to leave. He regrets losing his friend but understands why Thales must quit the metropolis, given the appalling life (and death) found there. These thoughts, along with the place where they are waiting for a boat, give rise to memories of the glories of Queen Elizabeth's reign, when England experienced peace and greatness in abundance:

For who would leave, unbribed, Hibernia's land,	*Ireland*
Or change the rocks of Scotland for the Strand?	*a major street in London*
There none are swept by sudden fate away,	
But all whom hunger spares, with age decay:	
Here malice, rapine, accident, conspire,	
And now a rabble rages, now a fire;	
Their ambush here relentless ruffians lay,	
And here the fell attorney prowls for prey;	
Here falling houses thunder on your head,	
And here a female atheist talks you dead.	
While Thales waits the wherry that contains	*a small boat*
Of dissipated wealth the small remains,	
On Thames's banks, in silent thought we stood,	
Where Greenwich smiles upon the silver flood:	
Struck with the seat that gave Eliza birth,	

We kneel, and kiss the consecrated earth;
In pleasing dreams the blissful age renew,
And call Britannia's glories back to view;
Behold her cross triumphant on the main,
The guard of commerce, and the dread of Spain,
Ere masquerades debauched, excise oppressed,
Or English honor grew a standing jest.   (9–30)

Johnson's suggestion at the beginning of this passage that no one would leave Ireland or the "rocks of Scotland" without a bribe to come live in London is deeply ironic, given the assumption of many that those were primitive places without the cultural advantages of the big city. London may have once been the seat of civilization, but it is no longer a desirable place to live or perhaps even livable. If the muggers or con men do not get you, the narrator suggests, then accidents will. In lines 13–14, Johnson compresses some of the dangers into a single couplet, using a list, repetition, alliteration, and parallelism to emphasize the many possibilities that can threaten a resident. Buildings, too, do not just collapse, but "thunder" down on your head, echoing the frightening noise of the crash. In a note of sardonic humor, Johnson suggests that the worst danger in the city may be the "female atheist," who threatens to kill you with an endless diatribe on her favorite subject.

Meanwhile, the two friends share a moment of nostalgic peace in recalling past glories in English history. Here Johnson becomes more political than his original, suggesting that one of the main reasons for the decadence of London is the corruption of the country's leaders. With a dramatic gesture Thales and the narrator kneel and kiss the sacred ground to demonstrate their love for their country and their hope for its future, recalling its former triumphs over Spain under Queen Elizabeth I. They know their memories are "pleasing dreams," for they can never hope to recover such idyllic times, given the nature of reality now. The two friends are, clearly, not discontented rebels who despise their own land or wish to overthrow the government and restore the Stuarts, like the Jacobites. But they do deplore the oppressive taxes, especially the infamous excise that had recently been the focus of much of the opposition's attack on Robert Walpole, the de facto prime minister. And they mourn the loss of "English honour" in the world, as well as the corruption in the social life of the time. Johnson thus develops the contrast between past and present far more than Juvenal. And he creates a formal verse pattern with the inversions of normal syntactical order in lines 20–21 (and elsewhere), where phrases that normally follow the verb or the object are placed first. This can occasionally make his lines difficult to understand, but it also gives them a less conversational tone as well as dignity and weight.

Thales then begins his extended tirade on life in contemporary London. One of the most decadent aspects, he declares, is the importation of French manners and morals. His portrait of the French focuses on their hypocrisy and greed, continuing a long tradition of such attacks by English writers:

> Studious to please, and ready to submit,
> The supple <u>Gaul</u> was born a parasite: *Frenchman*
> Still to his interest true, where'er he goes,
> Wit, bravery, worth, his lavish tongue bestows;
> In every face a thousand graces shine,
> From every tongue flows harmony divine.
> These arts in vain our rugged natives try,
> Strain out with faltering diffidence a lie,
> And get a kick for awkward flattery.
> Besides, with justice, this discerning age
> Admires their wondrous talents for the stage:
> Well may they venture on the mimic's art,
> Who play from morn to night a borrowed part;
> Practised their master's notions to embrace,
> Repeat his maxims, and reflect his face;
> With every wild absurdity comply,
> And view each object with another's eye;
> To shake with laughter ere the jest they hear,
> To pour at will the counterfeited tear,
> And as their patron hints the cold or heat,
> To shake in dog-days, in December sweat.   (123–143)

Johnson suggests in this portrait how false the Frenchman is, and how skillful he is at flattering the great and pleasing the wealthy. The poor Englishman is no match for the cynical French parasite, for when he tries to do the same, he is only rejected and humiliated for his bumbling efforts. The contrast between the two is amusing, but, as Johnson suggests, it is really to his credit that the Englishman cannot lie and flatter in the same manner, for it shows his honesty and sincerity. The Frenchman, Johnson ironically adds, must be admired for his acting ability, for the way he can ingratiate himself into his master's favors by seeming to adopt his ideas and opinions with perfect empathy. He appears to have no independent existence other than to agree with whatever nonsense his master spouts or does. Of course, everything the Frenchman says or does is for his own gain. In the last line of this passage

Johnson neatly contrasts the absurd extremes to which the Frenchman will go by paralleling his shaking with cold in the heat of August to his sweating with heat in the chill of December. Note that Johnson divides the line into two parts separated by a caesura, with the second half reversing the order of the first with the prepositional phrase placed before the infinitive (with the "to" before "sweat" understood). This contrasting syntactical structure gives special emphasis to the absurd behavior of the Frenchman.

Finally, Thales wonders if there is no escape from this situation anywhere in the world, no deserted island where greed and servility do not reign. The poor and the virtuous in particular have no chance in the world as it currently exists, especially given the power of "oppression" and its "insolence." Exploitation and degradation seem to be their only possible fates, but there may be even worse in store for them in the crowded city:

> Has heaven reserved, in pity to the poor,
> No pathless waste, or undiscovered shore;
> No secret island in the boundless main?
> No peaceful desert yet unclaimed by Spain?
> Quick let us rise, the happy seats explore,
> And bear oppression's insolence no more.
> This mournful truth is everywhere confessed,
> SLOW RISES WORTH, BY POVERTY DEPRESSED:
> But here more slow, where all are slaves to gold,
> Where looks are merchandise, and smiles are sold;
> Where won by bribes, by flatteries implored,
> The groom retails the favours of his lord.
> But hark! th'affrighted crowd's tumultuous cries
> Roll through the streets, and thunder to the skies;
> Raised from some pleasing dream of wealth and power,
> Some pompous palace, or some blissful bower,
> Aghast you start, and scarce with aching sight
> Sustain th'approaching fire's tremendous light;
> Swift from pursuing horrors take your way,
> And leave your little ALL to flames a prey;
> Then through the world a wretched vagrant roam,
> For where can starving merit find a home?
> In vain your mournful narrative disclose,
> While all neglect, and most insult your woes.   (170–193)

When even "smiles are sold" in their society, as Johnson puts it, there seems no hope for an honest person to succeed, and little chance to find a place that is not infected with greed. It is a truth universally acknowledged, the poet suggests, that merit has little or no hope of success in the world, but especially in London. The law of life that Johnson puts in capital letters in line 177 is a central theme in the poem and seems to have special meaning for his own destiny, as he struggled in London with no name or fortune, but a strong sense of his own worth. The sudden drama of the fire that spreads quickly, destroying houses and possessions, is brought home to all readers by his use of the second person, "you," pointedly indicating that everyone who lives in London may be at risk of such a calamity. The poor would be utterly ruined by such an event, with no relief agencies, charities, or insurance to aid them. Moreover, the homeless and the destitute would have few friends afterward, even if they had some before the fire. It was a harsh, cruel world, according to Johnson, which his little vignette effectively dramatizes.

Johnson concludes the poem by describing some of the ways violent death can strike in the city, as well as the many criminals executed for their cold-blooded activities. Thales boards his boat to leave forever, offering to help the poet write his satire on life in London once he decides to leave as well. Johnson's harsh truths about life in the city, no doubt inspired in part by personal experience, gain general application through his imaginative rendering of them and passionate expression. The contrast between the dangerous, decadent city and the innocent country was traditional, but one that Johnson evokes with considerable power. The political elements of the poem, including some implied criticism of the king (George II), created quite a stir at the time, causing it to go through numerous editions in Johnson's own lifetime. For the time being, then, Johnson turned to prose and less inflammatory subjects.

In 1749 Johnson published the first work to appear under his own name, a poem called *The Vanity of Human Wishes*. It was, like *London*, an imitation of one of Juvenal's satires (No. 10), redone in contemporary dress. Although it follows the general lines of Juvenal's work, Johnson introduces much material that is original and makes changes in the theme and in many of the examples he uses. His subject is much broader than his previous imitation as he surveys human nature and history in somber and occasionally harsh reflections that sometimes reach tragic levels. This poem was never as popular as *London* in his own time, but it is now generally considered Johnson's finest poem, with a density and power that can still impress.

His main theme is how misplaced and even foolish our great expectations for life are, how we continue to build castles in the air and dream impossible dreams despite their constant failure. The "vanity" in the title combines the excessive sense of pride we all feel in our hopes and desires with the futility that inevitably envelops most of them. Nothing in life works out quite as we imagined or planned. Yet we continue to indulge our schemes for the future as if we had learned nothing from the past. In the first lines Johnson takes a global point of view from which to survey human experience. From this universal perspective he details the many different ways we go wrong, including the false idols we worship and the inflated expectations we indulge. Two of the most powerful and therefore most dangerous of these are the pursuits of money and power:

> But scarce observed, the knowing and the bold
> Fall in the general massacre of gold;
> Wide-wasting pest! that rages unconfined,
> And crowds with crimes the records of mankind;
> For gold his sword the hireling ruffian draws,
> For gold the hireling judge distorts the laws;
> Wealth heaped on wealth, nor truth nor safety buys,
> The dangers gather as the treasures rise.
> 　Let History tell where rival kings command,
> And dubious title shakes the madded land,
> When statutes glean the refuse of the sword,
> How much more safe the vassal than the lord;
> Low skulks the <u>hind</u> beneath the rage of power,　　　　　　*peasant*
> And leaves the wealthy traitor in the Tower,
> Untouched his cottage, and his slumbers sound,
> Though Confiscation's vultures hover round.　　　　　　　　(21–36)

The irony in these lines is that even the supposedly educated and energetic people who should be immune to the temptations of wealth succumb to the false hopes it raises. No one can escape its delusions, it seems. Johnson's powerful image for it is as a plague that runs rampant through society, causing all sorts of crimes and miserable deaths. Inverting normal syntax in the lines about gold (lines 25–26) puts the emphasis on that glittering precious metal as the reason for the murder of innocents and the subversion of the laws. From the top of society to the bottom, gold rules, to the detriment of all. The more it accumulates, the more danger it poses. Neither "truth" nor security may be bought with it.

　Nor is power any more secure than gold. Those at the top of society, in fact, may be even more subject to danger than those at the bottom because of their position. Civil war may erupt when the throne is in dispute, and ravage the entire country. The people then become polarized, enmity rages, and the law is exploited to take possession of the little that is left. The lowly peasant may seem able to escape the general disaster, but he too may suffer from the carnage all around. Madness and anger permeate society, and the "vultures" of confiscation soar nearby waiting patiently for their prey. Images of violence, fear, and injustice convey the general insecurity with powerful concreteness.

Yet most people do not appear to have learned from the past. They still desperately seek to gain the rewards society offers, from material wealth to high positions. They may succeed for a time, Johnson suggests, but this will not last. It will all end quickly and definitively:

> Unnumbered suppliants crowd Preferment's gate,
> Athirst for wealth, and burning to be great;
> Delusive Fortune hears th'incessant call,
> They mount, they shine, evaporate, and fall.
> On every stage the foes of peace attend,
> Hate dogs their flight, and Insult mocks their end.
> Love ends with hope, the sinking statesman's door
> Pours in the morning worshiper no more....   (73–80)

The drive to seek higher status and fortune is a compulsive one, as Johnson suggests, akin to a driving thirst and an internal combustion. The goddess Fortune fools such obsessed people with her lures, so they seem to rise only to disappear immediately into thin air. Once these temporarily successful people begin their downward spiral, their friends abandon them and their enemies redouble their attacks. Johnson combines his personifications with active verbs, like "dogs" and "mocks," to infuse the abstractions with a powerful force. The declining officeholder can no longer delude himself with hope to continue his climb, as his room, which was filled with well-wishers and parasites, is now empty. His fall is dramatic and final. The pattern of rise and fall, in fact, is a continuing motif in this poem.

So far, the poet's comments have been only general and hypothetical. Johnson turns to English history to provide some specific examples. In one of the most famous he describes how Cardinal Wolsey, though the son of a butcher, reached the heights of fame and fortune under Henry VIII as Lord Chancellor of England and Archbishop of York:

> In full-blown dignity, see Wolsey stand,
> Law in his voice, and fortune in his hand: (99–100)

Such extraordinary good fortune, however, could not last. In a few years Wolsey had lost everything—position, power, and wealth. Johnson's description of this process is graphic:

At length his sovereign frowns—the train of state
Mark the keen glance, and watch the sign to hate.
Where'er he turns, he meets a stranger's eye,
His suppliants scorn him, and his followers fly;
At once is lost the pride of <u>awful</u> state,   *awe-inspiring*
The golden canopy, the glittering plate,
The regal palace, the luxurious board,
The liveried army, and the menial lord.
With age, with cares, with maladies oppressed,
He seeks the refuge of monastic rest.
Grief aids disease, remembered folly stings,
And his last sighs reproach the faith of kings.   (109–120)

As soon as Henry turns away from him, Wolsey, stripped of all his magnificent luxuries, ill and isolated, dies a pathetic death in bitterness and regret. It is a sad ending for a brilliant figure, but the world is cold and cruel, not just. Johnson is a master at summing up the fate of such tragic figures in a few trenchant lines, using the strong beat of the heroic couplet to emphasize his point. Note how he underscores the words "age" and "cares" (line 117), not only with the iambic stress but also with a caesura after each, preventing the reader from hurrying on.

Another temptation in life may be found in the seemingly quiet life of the scholar, happily working away in his library searching for esoteric knowledge, far from the turmoil and troubles of the world. This is a myth too, however, for there is still much to disturb and distract him from his purpose, from sloth to beauty and melancholy. Johnson suggests that anyone who aspires to such a life and thinks this is not true should look again more closely:

Deign on the passing world to turn thine eyes,
And pause awhile from <u>letters</u>, to be wise;   *learning, study*
There mark what ills the scholar's life assail,
Toil, envy, want, the patron, and the jail.
See nations slowly wise, and meanly just,
To buried merit raise the tardy bust.
If dreams yet flatter, once again attend,
Hear Lydiat's life, and Galileo's end.   (157–164)

Johnson substituted the word "patron" in this passage (line 160) for the original "garret," because of his unhappy experience with his own patron, Lord Chesterfield, who had at first encouraged him to undertake his dictionary, only to ignore him and his work until it was about to be published. His letter to Chesterfield rejecting the nobleman's late offer of help is a model of restrained scorn and irony. Here Johnson also notes that even famous scientists, like Galileo and Lydiat (an Oxford mathematician) who had made significant contributions to their fields, could suffer unjustly in their lives. With the "tardy bust" (line 162) Johnson appears to allude to the placement (in 1737) of Milton's sculpture in Westminster Abbey, to honor him, finally, sixty years after his death. Again, the world is not just, even toward its most famous scholars and poets.

Johnson also uses the example of great warriors to show how unstable success can be for them as well. He cites Alexander the Great from the ancient past and Charles XII of Sweden in his own century as leaders who were at first exceptionally triumphant, only to fall at last into degradation and death. Charles seemed from the outset of his career to have all the qualities needed for continued success:

> A frame of adamant, a soul of fire,
> No dangers fright him, and no labors tire;
> O'er love, o'er fear, extends his wide domain,
> Unconquered lord of pleasure and of pain;
> No joys to him pacific scepters yield,
> War sounds the trump, he rushes to the field;
> Behold surrounding kings their power combine,
> And one capitulate, and one resign;
> Peace courts his hand, but spreads her charms in vain;
> "Think nothing gained," he cries, "till naught remain,
> On Moscow's walls till Gothic standards fly,
> And all be mine beneath the polar sky."   (193–204)

Charles's physical and mental powers were remarkable, and he lived only for war and conquest. In the first two lines of this passage Johnson parallels the two aspects (mental and physical) of Charles's strength, dividing the lines into two parts to assert how unusually powerful he was in both, reversing the order of the aspects in the second for emphasis. Charles's control over his passions was equally strong. When "Peace" courted him with all her charms, he rejected her out of hand. But his growing hubris led him to attack Russia, and, like Napoleon later, he failed miserably. He ended his life in exile, dying in a minor battle. Johnson notes the irony of his life and career, and draws the obvious lesson:

> His fall was destined to a barren <u>strand</u>,   *shore*
> A petty fortress, and a dubious hand;

He left the name, at which the world grew pale,
To point a moral, or adorn a tale.   (219–222)

Charles's greatness turned into monumental folly for the ages to contemplate. No one has dramatized this failure more forcibly than Samuel Johnson.

After the historical examples, Johnson turns to more general temptations, such as the normal human desire to live a long life. Of course we tend to forget all the ills that flesh is heir to, and that the longer we live, the more we can suffer both mentally and physically. Johnson's description of the aging process is memorably concrete:

    Unnumbered maladies his joints invade,
Lay siege to life and press the dire blockade;
But unextinguished avarice still remains,
And dreaded losses aggravate his pains;
He turns, with anxious heart and crippled hands,
His bonds of debt, and mortgages of lands;
Or views his coffers with suspicious eyes,
Unlocks his gold, and counts it till he dies.   (283–290)

The physical side of life, he suggests, is a kind of warfare, with time besieging the body, blocking up the senses, and crippling the joints. But even more pathetic is the mental side, with its insecurity and greed: fear leads to an obsession with one's wealth and the constant need to hold it in one's hands to make sure it is still all there. In the process one loses one's life, and perhaps one's soul. The extreme example of mental deterioration is, for Johnson, sheer mindlessness, which he briefly evokes with reference to two recent figures, the Duke of Marlborough, the great general, from whose "eyes the streams of dotage flow" and Jonathan Swift, who had died a few years before this poem was published, "a driv'ler and a show" (lines 317–318). No one, however brilliant or successful, can escape the ravages of time.

Johnson has a few words for youth as well. He depicts parents wishing dearly for beauty for their children, and young people who think only about their appearances and their pleasures. Beauty, however, is a much greater danger than any of them imagine. He addresses the young ladies of fashion especially:

Ye nymphs of rosy lips and radiant eyes,
Whom Pleasure keeps too busy to be wise,
Whom Joys with soft varieties invite,

By day the frolic, and the dance by night;
Who frown with vanity, who smile with art,
And ask the latest fashion of the heart;
What care, what rules your heedless charms shall save,
Each nymph your rival, and each youth your slave?
Against your fame with Fondness Hate combines,
The rival batters, and the lover mines.
With distant voice neglected Virtue calls,
Less heard and less, the faint remonstrance falls;
Tired with contempt, she quits the slippery reign,
And Pride and Prudence take her seat in vain.   (323–336)

Like Swift's "Progress of Love," Johnson develops a moral tale proceeding from thoughtless youth to the psychological gamesmanship of love. The beautiful young woman at first exerts her power in this contest with skill and joy, but then she succumbs to the rivalry with others, and gradually virtue loses its influence on her behavior. Personified abstractions play the characters that vie for her soul, but in the end she is lost. The final couplet of this passage deftly summarizes her fate:

Now Beauty falls betrayed, despised, distressed,
And hissing Infamy proclaims the rest.   (341–342)

The s sounds effectively convey the power of shame to convict the young woman of her outcast state. It is a sad tale of the conflict of good and evil over the soul of a young woman. Such a tale may no longer have the relevance it had in the eighteenth century, but Johnson still makes his point with economy and force.

After such a dismal catalogue of failure and tragedy, where do we arrive? Is there any hope at all for us? As may be expected, Johnson finds a glimmer in a traditional vision:

Where then shall Hope and Fear their objects find?
Must dull Suspense corrupt the stagnant mind?
Must helpless man, in ignorance sedate,
Roll darkling down the torrent of his fate?
Must no dislike alarm, no wishes rise,
No cries invoke the mercies of the skies?
Inquirer, cease, petitions yet remain,
Which Heaven may hear, nor deem religion vain.
Still raise for good the supplicating voice,

But leave to Heaven the measure and the choice.
Safe in his power, whose eyes discern afar
The secret ambush of a specious prayer.
Implore his aid, in his decisions rest,
Secure, whate'er he gives, he gives the best.   (343–356)

This is not the Stoicism of Juvenal but rather a broadly Christian vision, which urges us to find our contentment in God's sovereignty, goodness, and love. We can and should pray for wisdom, patience, and faith, but we must not expect an easy road in life or a safe and comfortable journey. Only by accepting God's will can we find a measure of happiness. It is a modest hope, to be sure, but one that postulates a religious outlook that acknowledges our limited powers. Johnson has dramatized fully and concretely in the poem how difficult it is for humans to be wise, good, or even moderately happy. Here he suggests how even our prayers may be false and insincere, but God will not be fooled. Whatever happens, we must trust in Him, for we do not have ultimate control over our lives. In the end such a humble hope is, for Johnson, all we can reasonably expect in life.

The last poem we will consider by Johnson is more personal than the previous ones. It is an elegiac tribute to Robert Levet, who was one of several indigent dependents that lived in Johnson's house for many years. Without a university degree Levet practiced a rudimentary form of medicine among London's poor, doing what he could to relieve their suffering. He died in 1782 at the age of 76. Johnson's poem, "On the Death of Dr. Robert Levet," was published the next year in the *Gentleman's Magazine* when he was nearly 74 years old. It represents heartfelt praise for someone whose benevolence Johnson knew intimately and deeply admired.

Abandoning the heroic couplet for his elegy, Johnson composed it in quatrains with alternating rhyme, employing iambic tetrameter for his basic rhythmic pattern (eight syllables in each line, four of them stressed). In this poem the prevailing tone is one of sincere praise for this good man within an overall melancholy outlook. In contrast to Milton's "Lycidas," Johnson employs no pastoral elements or classical references (which he thought were much too artificial) to commemorate his friend, but he does use some of his usual poetic techniques such as personification and other figures of speech to dramatize the theme. He begins in a general way by commenting on life's cycle of loss and decline, then turns more specifically to Levet and his death:

Condemned to Hope's delusive mine,
    As on we toil from day to day,

By sudden blasts, or slow decline,
   Our social comforts drop away.

Well tried through many a varying year,
   See Levet to the grave descend;
<u>Officious</u>, innocent, sincere,   *helpful, kind*
   Of ev'ry friendless name the friend.

Yet still he fills Affection's eye,
   Obscurely wise, and coarsely kind;
Nor, lettered Arrogance, deny
   Thy praise to merit unrefined.   (1–12)

Everyone is subject to the false encouragement of hope, Johnson suggests, even as "we" labor each day in the tedious, seemingly meaningless tasks of life, like prisoners condemned to slavery in mines. The somber mood of such a view is appropriate to mourning a good friend who has passed away. Meanwhile, our lives are deprived of their "social comforts" by accidents and the aging process. Even the experienced Levet, however good he was, is subject to this iron law of life—no one can escape. Nevertheless, Levet will be remembered with affection and admiration, though he was not perfect. He lacked social grace, was unsophisticated and not learned, but he was also deeply kind and caring. Note how Johnson contrasts the figures of Affection and Arrogance in their attitudes toward Levet. Johnson directly addresses the latter figure to challenge him (or her) not to condescend to this man who has been of such good service in his life. Virtue, for Johnson, was more important than education, manners, or social status.

    In the next three stanzas Johnson expands his commentary on Levet's life and charitable actions. Levet, he says, was not afraid of visiting even the most difficult places in the slums:

When fainting Nature called for aid,
   And hov'ring Death prepared the blow,
His vigorous remedy displayed
   The power of art without the show.

In Misery's darkest caverns known,
   His useful care was ever nigh,
Where hopeless Anguish poured his groan,
   And lonely Want retired to die.

No summons mocked by chill delay,
   No petty gain disdained by pride,

> The modest wants of every day
>> The toil of every day supplied. (13–24)

Again Johnson employs personification, to which he gives active qualities, to embody Levet's caring work into concrete characters representing many different cases over the years. The idea of Anguish "pouring" out his grief and pain suggests the depth and passion in this misery. Yet even in the most desperate situations Levet was able to render useful service to the suffering poor. His efforts were energetic and effective, but without the ostentation that some doctors no doubt used. Clearly, no one else had dared to enter these lowly, even sordid places to offer any help. Nor did Levet ever refuse to go on such a visit or delay it to show how important or powerful he was. He did not scorn to accept small fees for this work because he was not trying to enrich himself. His personal humility was matched by his own humble desires.

In the last three stanzas Johnson becomes somewhat more positive on Levet's life as he completes his portrait. He even offers some consolation in contemplating its ultimate meaning:

> His virtues walked their narrow round,
>> Nor made a pause, nor left a void;
> And sure th'Eternal Master found
>> The <u>single talent</u> well employed.   *allusion to Matthew 25:14–30*

> The busy day, the peaceful night,
>> Unfelt, uncounted, glided by;
> His frame was firm, his powers were bright,
>> Though now his eightieth year was nigh.

> Then with no throbbing fiery pain,
>> No cold gradations of decay,
> Death broke at once the vital chain,
>> And freed his soul the nearest way. (25–36)

Levet's goodness may have been limited in scope, as Johnson acknowledges, but it was active, constant, and comprehensive within its sphere. His talent may have been single, in the terms of Jesus's parable, but it was fully employed, and so must have pleased God. Levet's salvation seems implied by this comment, and the manner of his death reinforces this impression. It occurred quickly and easily, after Levet had lived beyond the usual life span of an eighteenth-century man as well as the biblical span of three score and ten. He was vigorous until the end and did not suffer long then. Death was kind to him and liberated his soul from the burden of the body, so that, it would seem, his soul could return to his Father. The reward for a good life is clear, though not explicitly stated. Johnson does not idealize his friend or make him into a saint. He acknowledges Levet's limitations, but shows how he still fulfilled his life in a way that was unusual but most meaningful: in compassionate service to others, especially the very poor. For Johnson, this was one of the most important duties in life, one that he himself fulfilled in various ways, including keeping several needy individuals like Levet in his own home for many years.

The elegy for Levet is representative of Johnson's poetry in general in its solid moral seriousness and its desire to make goodness appealing. His poems, like his works in prose, always contain a core of realism based on concrete human experience as well as a deeply felt concern for both individuals and society at large that keep them from being too abstract or narrowly didactic. Moreover, Johnson's command of English and his imaginative powers invigorate his poetic themes with fresh images and original thoughts and phrases to make his poetry a continuing pleasure. Johnson is perhaps the most incisive poet in English in urging his readers to adopt a realistic vision of life along with a passionately moral, and ultimately religious, sense of its significance.

CHAPTER 12

Four Eighteenth-Century Poets:
Finch, Gray, Goldsmith, and Cowper

This chapter differs from the previous ones in covering four different poets, but only one poem by each. All of these poems were popular in their own time, have retained their popularity since they were first published, and are likely to do so into the future. Each of these poets wrote a good many other poems, but the ones considered here stand out in their works and merit special attention. These particular poems span the eighteenth century from the beginning to the end and introduce us to some ideas and feelings that we have not encountered so far. We will find new themes emerging and old ones being refashioned, sometimes in radical ways. It should be noted, however, that one poem will not give us a full idea of the poetic achievement of these writers. A single poem, even one that has resonated with many readers over several generations, is not necessarily representative of the poet's outlook in general. That can come only by reading a substantial number of poems by each. Interested readers will find suggestions for other poems by these authors in the "Further Reading" section.

ANNE FINCH, COUNTESS OF WINCHILSEA (1661–1720):
POET OF NATURE

Only recently have women come to be recognized as important poetic voices in the eighteenth century. Before that time only a few ever published their poetry, and never to much acclaim. It is true, of course, that most women until then had access only to basic literacy, though a few fortunate wealthy ones did receive an education nearly equal to a young man's of comparable status.

One of those fortunate ones was Anne Kingsmill, who came from an ancient Hampshire family. She lost both of her parents by the time she was 3, and was raised first by a grandmother in London and later by an uncle. After her uncle died in 1682, she became maid of honor to Mary of Modena, Duchess of York, later queen of England when James, Duke of York, succeeded to the throne. In 1684 Anne married Col. Heneage Finch, a courtier and soldier, who became Earl of Winchilsea in 1712. During the short reign of James II (1685–1688), the young couple flourished at court, but with the Glorious Revolution they were forced to retire to the country because of their close ties to the king. Anne's husband was arrested in 1690 for Jacobite activities, but he was apparently released later that year. Over the years, Anne composed various kinds of poems, from pastorals to epistles and dialogues, and collected them into two large manuscripts. In 1713 she published some of them in one volume called *Miscellany Poems*, adding her name to the volume only several months after it first appeared. After returning to London around 1708, she became acquainted with some of the best writers of the time, including Jonathan Swift, who wrote a poem for her ("Apollo Outwitted"), and Alexander Pope, who included several of her poems in a miscellany he published in 1718. Although widely respected as a poet in her time, Finch's real influence probably only began after Wordsworth praised her poetry for its concern with nature and for its style that is, as he said, "often admirable, chaste, tender, and vigorous" (quoted in the *Norton Anthology*, p. 2291). Through much of her adult life, she suffered from "spleen," periods of melancholy and depression, and wrote a poem about it called "The Spleen" that became one of her most celebrated works. The poem we will discuss, however, is "A Nocturnal Reverie," because it appears to be more widely read and appreciated today.

One of the typical themes in Finch's poetry is the pleasure to be found in solitude and quiet, which she often discovered in nature. Here she escaped from the turmoil of a busy social life and an often troubled political situation, to find the peace and security she deeply needed. In "A Nocturnal Reverie" Finch explores the night and its ability to refresh and renew her sense of life's meaning that seemed to be lost in the daylight world. It is unusual in that time, especially for a woman, to celebrate the rural nighttime for its potential to restore and revive. She opens the poem by focusing on various sensory experiences in the darkness:

> In such a night, when every louder wind
> Is to its distant cavern safe confined;
> And only gentle <u>Zephyr</u> fans his wings,   *the west wind*
> And lonely <u>Philomel</u>, still waking, sings;   *the nightingale*

Or from some tree, famed for the owl's delight,
She, hollowing clear, directs the wanderer right:
In such a night, when passing clouds give place,
Or thinly veil the heavens' mysterious face;
When in some river, overhung with green,
The waving moon and trembling leaves are seen;
When freshened grass now bears itself upright,
And makes cool banks to pleasing rest invite,
Whence springs the woodbind, and the bramble-rose,
And where the sleepy cowslip sheltered grows;
Whilst now a paler hue the foxglove takes,
Yet checkers still with red the dusky <u>brakes</u>.... *thickets*
(1–16)

At the outset, Finch evokes an idyllic atmosphere for this night, beginning with an echo of Shakespeare's *The Merchant of Venice*, with the repeated phrase "in such a night." In the play Lorenzo and Jessica use this phrase several times in their conversation near the end, partly mocking and ironic, about several tragic lovers of mythology. This is the scene in which Lorenzo, a few moments later, lyrically describes the beauty of their love and its fulfillment with these familiar words: "How sweet the moonlight sleeps upon this bank," allowing the music of the night and of the spheres to create the "touches of sweet harmony" within them (5.1.62–65). Even if one does not recognize the allusion, the words still have the effect of marking a special moment for the poet, though here it doesn't involve love. By using the classical names for the west wind and the nightingale, the poet evokes a personified being with some pictorial elements such as wings and the sad, lonely woman at the mythical origin of the bird's song. But there is also definite reassurance here in the suggestion that the wandering traveler may find direction from the song. The heavens remain "mysterious," but the riverbank is inviting with its grass refreshed by the dew and its cool shade. Nature seems well disposed to human rest and reflection at this time, with the wild flowers adding their muted colors to the beauty of the scene. It is not a formal garden with strictly organized beds, defined paths, and symmetry, but a natural one with a pleasant disorder to it. Here human beings may find a soothing harmony between themselves and nature.

Finch continues in the same vein in the next part of the poem, but adds some human elements to the mix. She cannot resist a compliment to her friend Lady Salisbury, for her perfect beauty and virtue that are obvious in any light, thus introducing a moral dimension to the scene. Other human dimensions follow:

When scattered glow-worms, but in twilight fine,
Show trivial beauties watch their hour to shine;
Whilst <u>Salisbury</u> stands the test of every light,   *Anne Tufton*
In perfect charms, and perfect virtue bright:
When odors, which declined repelling day,
Through temperate air uninterrupted stray;
When darkened groves their softest shadows wear,
And falling waters we distinctly hear;
When through the gloom more venerable shows
Some ancient <u>fabric</u>, awful in repose,   *edifice, building*
While sunburnt hills their swarthy looks conceal,
And swelling haycocks thicken up the vale:
When the loosened horse now, as his pasture leads,
Comes slowly grazing through the adjoining meads,
Whose stealing pace, and lengthened shade we fear,
Till torn-up forage in his teeth we hear:
When nibbling sheep at large pursue their food,
And unmolested kine rechew the cud;
When curlews cry beneath the village walls,
And to her straggling brood the partridge calls;
Their shortlived jubilee the creatures keep,
Which but endures, whilst tyrant man does sleep. . . .   (17–38)

It is an interesting picture of the English field at night, with an ancient building silhouetted in solemn dignity in the distance, while various domesticated animals enjoy the peacefulness to continue their feeding. They add a realistic element to the scene, so that we do not think this is pure fantasy or an idealized vision. These animals, of course, work hard for humans during the day, as well as provide basic food for their needs. The images of the "torn-up forage" being crunched by the horses' teeth and the cattle chewing their cud make concrete the animals' real presence and add another sensory dimension. They also indicate, indirectly, that the poet is not too far from civilization or too isolated in some rugged part of nature. The animals are free to roam about as they wish (within limits, of course), untied and "unmolested," enjoying their freedom quietly, not wildly or rambunctiously. Even though the shadow of the horse may raise some fear in the observer at first, it soon dissipates when the sounds make it clear that nothing threatening is going on. Everything contributes to the peace and repose of the scene, as the animals quietly enjoy their temporary liberty from toil.

In the last few lines of the poem Finch turns more directly to the meaning of this quiet scene for her. She is clearly interested in the power of the night to affect her psyche, not just to make an impression on her senses:

When a sedate content the spirit feels,
And no fierce light disturbs, whilst it reveals;
But silent musings urge the mind to seek
Something, too high for syllables to speak;
Till the free soul to a composedness charmed,
Finding the elements of rage disarmed,
O'er all below a solemn quiet grown,
Joys in the inferior world, and thinks it like her own:
In such a night let me abroad remain,
Till morning breaks, and all's confused again;
Our cares, our toils, our clamors are renewed,
Or pleasures, seldom reached, again pursued.   (39–50)

For a brief time, the poet can forget the cares of the world and allow her mind and soul to roam freely like the animals. In so doing, she discovers the world of the spirit where she can find a profound serenity based on a sense of the harmony of all things, a higher reality than the physical world but one that does not reject it. Although what she discovers may seem vague and general, it is still "Something" that speaks to her soul. Only here can she attain the kind of deep tranquility she needs, for she realizes the return of the day will inevitably bring confusion and frustration again. It is an epiphanic moment that brings her refreshment and renewal, if only for a few hours.

As was common for poets in the time, Finch employs the heroic couplet, usually end-stopped and regular, in which to embody her vision. In line 41 she uses a run-on to suggest the quest that takes one beyond the bounds of regularity. Interestingly, she uses almost no figures of speech, so that her poem at first seems rather plain and straightforward. But her words often evoke an overtone of feeling or meaning beyond the literal, such as the "sleepy cowslip" (line 14) on the sheltered bank, and the "stealing pace" (line 31) of the horse as it calmly searches for grass to eat, but also suggesting possible criminal activity that may be dangerous. All these elements enhance the effectiveness and pleasure of the poem.

Anne Finch's "Nocturnal Reverie" thus portrays an introspective, musing atmosphere that was rarely found in the poetry of her time, the early part of the eighteenth century in England. It is a psychological portrait that seems to be autobiographical, though how far it is not clear. The poet is driven to escape the busy, noisy daylight world to find solitary refuge outside in the quiet of the night. In its deep appreciation of nature, the night, and solitude, it anticipates the Romantic poets at the end of the century, who discovered in the natural world a spiritual quality that could refresh and bring solace to the suffering soul. It is no wonder, then, that Wordsworth praised her poetry and that many readers since have responded to it with enthusiasm and delight.

THOMAS GRAY (1716–1771): POET OF COMMON HUMANITY

Thomas Gray became the author, most improbably, of one of the most popular poems ever written in English, the "Elegy Written in a Country Churchyard" (1751). His success was unlikely because he was a shy, reticent man who led a retired, scholarly life in Cambridge with a small circle of friends. Most of his life was spent in esoteric studies, such as pre-Elizabethan poetry and Old Norse literature. He was the son of a London exchange broker and went to Eton, one of the oldest English "public" (i.e., private) schools, then to Cambridge University where he left before taking a degree (he completed it a few years later). Like many educated young men of the time, he went on a "Grand Tour" of France and Italy from 1739 to 1741, studying the languages, history, and culture of these countries. When his father died in 1741, Gray became financially independent but by no means exceptionally rich. He moved to Cambridge and lived there, quietly and studiously, for the rest of his life, never marrying. He occasionally studied in the newly opened British Museum and traveled to places like Scotland and the Lake District in northwestern England, drawing inspiration for his poetry from their landscapes and cultures. In 1757 Gray was nominated Poet Laureate, but he declined it. In 1768 he published his collected poems and was appointed to the honorary post of Professor of Modern History at Cambridge, though he was not required to give a lecture or tutor any students. Three years later he died as he had lived, quietly and without fanfare. Though widely admired as a poet, Gray was buried in the graveyard at Stoke Poges, his home, next to his mother, far from Westminster Abbey where many poets rested.

Gray lived and wrote at a time when England was expanding its empire in North America and India, fighting France over Canada, and establishing trading outposts in the Far East, but he has little to say about these global conflicts and movements. He was clearly more interested in the past than the present. It was also a time of vigorous intellectual debate in the country when the Enlightenment was raising burning questions involving social justice, truth, and scientific progress. The "philosophes" in France, including such writers as Voltaire, Rousseau, and Diderot, were publishing controversial works of social commentary, philosophy, and fiction that stirred the very foundations of French society. These concerns are largely missing from Gray's poetry, though he does display some interest in related issues, showing a deep sympathy for the common people, a delight in nature, and a desire to learn about different ethnic cultures. In his poetry Gray combines an excellent classical education with a love of history and a fine sensitivity. At this time in England, sentiment was in the process of becoming more important than ideas in artistic endeavors. This change marks an important shift in English cultural life.

Gray published the "Elegy Written in a Country Churchyard" in 1751, since it was about to appear in an unauthorized edition from a copy that had circulated in manuscript. The poem was an immediate success, going through several editions in its first year, and was later translated into other languages, including Latin. From the outset, it was quoted, imitated, and parodied. Gray clearly had struck a chord with the English public, in part because of the vogue for "graveyard" poetry at the time with its brooding, gloomy melancholy, but also because of his skill at blending these feelings with some social and philosophical concerns. It is an elegy not written for a specific person, but for all people who have failed to fulfill their potential in life. For his form Gray uses a quatrain with alternating rhyme and generally end-stopped lines of regular iambic pentameter, which provides a relatively simple thematic unit within which to develop his pastoral elegy. Each stanza is generally a single sentence and adds one further dimension in the description of the scene or the thought generated by it. The first four stanzas set the scene and establish an aura of somber melancholy:

> The curfew tolls the knell of parting day,
> The lowing herd wind slowly o'er the lea,   *meadow*
> The plowman homeward plods his weary way,
> And leaves the world to darkness and to me.
>
> Now fades the glimmering landscape on the sight,
> And all the air a solemn stillness holds,
> Save where the beetle wheels his droning flight,
> And drowsy tinklings lull the distant folds;   *pens, enclosed ground*
>
> Save that from yonder ivy-mantled tower
> The moping owl does to the moon complain
> Of such, as wandering near her secret bower,
> Molest her ancient solitary reign.
>
> Beneath those rugged elms, that yew tree's shade,
> Where heaves the turf in many a moldering heap,
> Each in his narrow cell forever laid,
> The rude forefathers of the hamlet sleep.   *uneducated*
>   (1–16)

It is evening in the English countryside, with the sun declining in the west and the farm worker returning home after a day of plowing. Darkness is gradually spreading across the land as the village church bell sounds the time for rest, and the only creatures left outside are the cattle and the solitary poet. He observes the twilight slowly fading into night with the light lingering on as long as possible and the sounds of darkness gradually emerging. The hooting of the owl disturbs the night as it protests against the intrusion into its territory by a foreign element, but the air is still and the atmosphere solemn. In many ways it recalls Finch's "A Nocturnal Reverie." The climax of this description, however, is the focus on the graveyard where the ancestors of the villagers are buried and death reigns in all its finality. They were mostly poor and uneducated, and have now found their final resting place in the land that surrounds the village church. It is a scene of quiet reflection on the meaning of their lives.

Gray stresses the fact that their enjoyment of life on earth is over: no more will they wake to the pleasant sounds of the morning or return to the cozy family hearth in the evening. Their life was largely hard manual labor, but they took joy in working the fields and cutting the timber. Despite the hard work, they found fulfillment in this life, so, as the poet notes, we need not feel superior to them for their narrow, simple existence:

> Let not Ambition mock their useful toil,
>   Their homely joys, and destiny obscure;
> Nor Grandeur hear with a disdainful smile
>   The short and simple annals of the poor.
>
> The boast of <u>heraldry</u>, the pomp of power,   *noble birth*
>   And all that beauty, all that wealth e'er gave,
> Awaits alike the inevitable hour.
>   The paths of glory lead but to the grave.   (29–36)

Gray uses personification here to animate the abstract attitudes some people might take toward such limited lives. Their work has, after all, been useful, their pleasure in life real, and their renown sufficient. Gray thus puts the haughtiness of the more fortunate into perspective, by showing how they all end in death in any event. An ancient family with its own heraldic device cannot change that, nor can power, beauty, or money. The alliteration in the key words of the last line in this passage linking glory with the grave discreetly underscores the irony of Gray's point. The theme of human mortality is of course a common theme among poets going back to the classics, but Gray lends it force and quiet drama with his figures of speech and the aphorism at the end.

The poet says further that we should not scorn these people because they have no elaborate memorials or tombs in great churches, as may be found elsewhere. Such impressive tributes in stone or brick cannot bring the dead back to life, nor can their souls in death be pleased by such remembrances. Nevertheless, the people buried here might have proved in other circumstances to be heroes or great leaders, had they not been so confined by their personal fates. Gray then sympathetically describes some of the ways their lives were seriously hampered:

> But Knowledge to their eyes her ample page
>   Rich with the spoils of time did ne'er unroll;
> Chill Penury repressed their noble <u>rage</u>,   *rapture, inspiration*
>   And froze the <u>genial</u> current of the soul.   *warm, creative*
>
> Full many a gem of purest ray serene,
>   The dark unfathomed caves of ocean bear:
> Full many a flower is born to blush unseen,
>   And waste its sweetness on the desert air.   (49–56)

It is not surprising that Gray the scholar puts a lack of education at the top of this list. Again he personifies this concept, here as a female book that discovers all the richness of life in the past through its pages that are like ancient scrolls of parchment. The oppressive power of poverty is dramatized in the personified figure of Penury, who freezes the creative powers of the individuals caught in its unforgiving sway. Gray then evokes two analogues for such unfulfilled souls, the beautiful precious stone lost in the ocean (like a pearl) and the blooming flower in the desert that no one ever sees. The jewel is given a specially bright sparkle and the flower a human blush, both suggesting purity and beauty far beyond the normal. Such images evoke the regret for lost potential that the poet laments.

In the passage from this poem quoted in Chapter 1 (p. 9), Gray cites several historical figures from the time of the English Civil War, including Hampden, Milton, and Cromwell, as national heroes whom the villagers may, fortunately, not equal in the blood they shed or the disruption in the country they caused. The good side of this is, then, that by remaining simple villagers, their lives have retained their innocence and purity. They have not had to "wade through slaughter to a throne" (line 67) or "heap the shrine of Luxury and Pride" (line 71) in order to prove themselves, as have the others:

Far from the madding crowd's ignoble strife,
　　Their sober wishes never learned to stray;
Along the cool sequestered vale of life
　　They kept the noiseless <u>tenor</u> of their way.   *course, drift*

Yet even these bones from insult to protect
　　Some frail memorial still erected nigh,
With uncouth rhymes and shapeless sculpture decked,
　　Implores the passing tribute of a sigh.   (73–80)

In these familiar lines Gray notes with scorn the urban mob's frantic search for
the selfish fulfillment of their desires. "Madding" suggests both madness and
irrational group action and is contrasted with the sober, restrained, and quiet
life of the poor villagers. They kept to the straight and narrow, and were rewarded with small, rustic tombstones, unsophisticated epitaphs, and roughly
carved figures. Both the feelings and the artistic endeavors these represent
command Gray's respect, but not his admiration or artistic approval. He knows
they derive from a common human need, a deep desire to be remembered after
death, but does not find their efforts in that way to be very satisfying. In fact, he
is writing their elegy in this poem, a more artistic effort, he implies, than their
stones. Gray stands above this scene of graveyard memorials to describe it and
note its emotional source, but not to endorse it completely.

In the final lines Gray shifts the focus of the poem to the poet himself as the
memorialist of these unrecognized villagers. (Some critics, it should be noted,
believe he addresses a third figure, the village poet, as "thee.") He imagines
this poet's life in the countryside, as seen by one of the older members of the
community, as well as his disappearance and death. The picture is pathetic
and sad, but also rather amusing:

For thee, who mindful of the unhonored dead
　　Dost in these lines their artless tale relate;
If chance, by lonely contemplation led,
　　Some kindred spirit shall inquire thy fate,

Haply some <u>hoary-headed</u> swain may say,   *white-haired*
　　"Oft have we seen him at the peep of dawn
Brushing with hasty steps the dews away
　　To meet the sun upon the upland lawn.

"There at the foot of yonder nodding beech
　　That wreathes its old fantastic roots so high,

His listless length at noontide would he stretch,
   And pore upon the brook that babbles by.

"Hard by yon wood, now smiling as in scorn,
   Muttering his wayward fancies he would rove,
Now drooping, woeful wan, like one forlorn,
   Or crazed with care, or crossed in hopeless love."   (93–108)

In line 93 Gray appears to address himself as poet in the second person (though this has been much debated), and imagines how he will be viewed in the future. If some "kindred spirit" should seek out information about the poet in the future, the villagers will not necessarily be sympathetic or understanding. As expressed by the older man, their point of view toward the odd poet is that he seemed to have nothing better to do but wander around the countryside muttering to himself and lying under a tree. They suppose, as Gray imagines them thinking, that he must have been suffering from some terrible grief or that he was an unhappy lover, both far from the truth. The irony is that he was celebrating their lives in his poem, while they completely misunderstood his sympathy for them. Society, it seems, will never comprehend the poet's role in their midst; he will forever remain an outsider.

The "Elegy" concludes with a three-stanza epitaph for the poet that has been inscribed on his tombstone. In contrast to the villager's portrait, it celebrates his life for its learning ("Science") and its empathy for the poor. The poet's "Melancholy," with which he is identified, had come to represent at this time not simply a gloomy temperament, but a heightened sensitivity toward those less fortunate and a desire to better their condition. The poet's charitable impulses are celebrated in the epitaph, as well as his reward in heaven. It cautions the passerby not to inquire more deeply into the poet's life, either for its "merits" or its "frailties," implying that God has judged him favorably, and that is all we need to know. Like the villagers, the poet has died unknown and unappreciated, but at least he has demonstrated a profound sympathy with the poor people among whom he lived and wrote, however different they were.

This time period, the second half of the eighteenth century, has come to be often called the "Age of Sensibility" in English literature, to suggest how important a role emotion had come to play in its scale of values, as evidenced by the popularity of novels like *The Man of Feeling* (1771) by Henry Mackenzie and *A Sentimental Journey through France and Italy* (1768) by Laurence Sterne. Gray anticipates this emotional emphasis in his elegy, with its focus on the unfortunate fate of the poor. His poem embodies some of the growing spirit of democracy that was spreading throughout Western Europe, with common human sentiments concerning death expressed in memorable English phrases and set in a landscape to which everyone could relate. It is a poem that still speaks to us today with its deep sympathy, quiet power, and resonant language.

OLIVER GOLDSMITH (c.1730–1774): POET OF EXILE

The third poet in this group is another oddity, an Irishman who was undistinguished in appearance, background, and conversation, but who distinguished himself in several different literary genres and became the friend of many of the greatest writers of the time. He was the son of a provincial Irish clergyman, grew up in rural Ireland, and, although a mediocre student, went to Trinity College, Dublin, where he graduated in 1749. He studied medicine for a time, wandered around the continent on his own not-so-Grand Tour, and returned to England in 1756. He tried different lines of work, including medicine and teaching, succeeded at none, and eventually became a hack writer for a kind publisher. His essay titled *An Inquiry into the Present State of Polite Learning in Europe* (1759) brought him some recognition, as did other prose writings, most notably his series of "Chinese Letters," containing satiric comments on English life by a supposed visitor from the Far East, whose letters reflect a point of view that ironically contrasts with that of the average Englishman. These letters were collected together and published separately as *The Citizen of the World* (1762), earning him steady employment as a writer for John Newbery, the publisher who is remembered especially for his work in children's literature. Goldsmith soon became acquainted with Samuel Johnson and his circle of distinguished friends, and, though socially awkward and often inept, he became a charter member of The Club for their biweekly dinners at a London tavern. In 1764 he published his poem, "The Traveller, Or a Prospect of Society," which heralds several of the themes found in "The Deserted Village" several years later. In 1766 his novel *The Vicar of Wakefield* was published and became, especially after Goldsmith's death, one of the most popular novels through the nineteenth century, though not much read any more. Goldsmith became a dramatist next, with the production of *The Good Natured Man* in 1768, but his best play, and one of the most delightful of all English comedies, *She Stoops to Conquer*, was produced with great success in 1773. During these years Goldsmith kept publishing biographies, anthologies, histories, and other works with incredible rapidity. He earned quite a bit from his writings but never enough to cover his expenses and his charity. At the time of his death Goldsmith owed the extraordinary sum of £2,000, a small fortune in its time, mostly to publishers who had advanced him money for other projects never completed. Though his life was cut short by disease at the age of 44, Goldsmith had already established himself as one of the foremost writers of the Age of Johnson.

The Deserted Village (1770), Goldsmith's best-known poem, exemplifies some traditional themes as well as several contemporary concerns. It immediately captured the interest of the public, going through six editions in the first year. Though a few readers objected to Goldsmith's basic thesis, that the villages of England were being depopulated by the growth of trade and increasing greed, many responded favorably to his emotional presentation of this idea. From the beginning Goldsmith makes his case personal and speaks with feeling:

> Sweet Auburn! loveliest village of the plain,
> Where health and plenty cheered the laboring swain,
> Where smiling spring its earliest visit paid,
> And parting summer's lingering blooms delayed:
> Dear lovely bowers of innocence and ease,
> Seats of my youth, when every sport could please,
> How often have I loitered o'er thy green,
> Where humble happiness endeared each scene;
> How often have I paused on every charm,
> The sheltered <u>cot</u>, the cultivated farm,   *cottage, shelter*
> The never-failing brook, the busy mill,
> The decent church that topped the neighboring hill,
> The hawthorn bush, with seats beneath the shade,
> For talking age and whispering lovers made. . . .   (1–14)

It is a highly idealized vision of his hometown, with the poet's memory recalling only the "innocence and ease," the beauty and the happiness he experienced there growing up. Spring came early and summer lingered on, he remembers, not in its intense heat or its storms or drought, but in the nostalgic perfection of his selective recall. Both youth and age found their bliss in the shade of the hawthorn. The images he uses focus on the golden moments of life in the village, when conflict, suffering, and malice are absent. Humans live and work there in harmony with nature and with each other.

The poet continues by illustrating the social harmony in the small community, with the people playing various games and sports on the village green to find relief from the everyday toil, but now, he declares, "all these charms are fled" (line 34). None of these games or sports, none of this happiness and innocent pleasure, is present any more. What has happened to spoil this charming scene? A tyrant, in the form of a wealthy merchant, has come to rule their little world for his own pleasure and profit. So the people, disappointed and unemployed, have begun to leave the area for faraway lands. Their homes and shops are closed and falling into ruin, and the wilderness is reasserting its presence. Goldsmith generalizes this theme with powerful claims:

> Ill fares the land, to hastening ills a prey,
> Where wealth accumulates, and men decay;
> Princes and lords may flourish, or may fade;
> A breath can make them, as a breath has made;
> But a bold peasantry, their country's pride,
> When once destroyed, can never be supplied.
> A time there was, ere England's griefs began,
> When every <u>rood</u> of ground maintained its man; *a quarter acre*
> For him light labor spread her wholesome store,
> Just gave what life required, but gave no more;
> His best companions, innocence and health;
> And his best riches, ignorance of wealth.
> But times are altered; Trade's unfeeling <u>train</u> *followers*
> Usurp the land and dispossess the swain;
> Along the lawn, where scattered hamlets rose,
> Unwieldy wealth, and cumbrous pomp repose;
> And every want to opulence allied,
> And every pang that folly pays to pride. (51–68)

Here is the heart of the problem. The wealth of the country has increased but to the detriment of the people. Goldsmith gives eloquent voice to the sad fate of the yeoman farmers who are being displaced by the newly rich merchants that are buying up the land and converting it to their own personal playground. In the process they are destroying the backbone of the country, even its innocence and health. The profit motive has little concern for the people who have lived on the land for many generations and now are being forced to move into the city or to emigrate to another land. Only greed and ostentation prosper. Goldsmith uses several medial caesuras (as in lines 52–53) to emphasize the opposition between wealth and human welfare, or the doubling of the effects of such trends. Repeating the first two words in the last two lines of this passage also stresses the contrast between the luxury for a few and the pain for many.

The poet feels this pain personally because he had hoped to retire to the little village where he had grown up, only to find that it scarcely exists now.

Only a "wretched" widow still lives there, eking out a subsistence by picking watercress from the nearby stream. Musing about his past, the poet recalls some of the people of the village who used to live there, like the preacher who was one of its central figures:

> There, where a few torn shrubs the place disclose,
> The village preacher's modest mansion rose.
> A man he was, to all the country dear,
> And passing rich with forty pounds a year;
> Remote from towns he ran his godly race,
> Nor e'er had changed, nor wished to change his place;
> Unpracticed he to fawn, or seek for power,
> By doctrines fashioned to the varying hour;
> Far other aims his heart had learned to prize,
> More skilled to raise the wretched than to rise.
> His house was known to all the vagrant train,
> He chid their wanderings, but relieved their pain....   (139–150)

The wilderness is taking over the village where civilization used to be, with the village preacher one of the most civilized of the former population. He was one who truly fulfilled his role as spiritual leader of the community and comforter for the suffering. He himself was not ambitious for gain or material wealth, but only for the spiritual health of his parish. He was sympathetic, charitable, and sociable, the ideal minister for any village. In every way he was the opposite of the wealthy man who was assuming control of the area now.

The village schoolmaster was another one of the prominent figures in the town. He, too, was in many respects an ideal teacher, learned and wise, but he also had some faults that Goldsmith does not hide. This portrait has a humorous dimension to lend it credibility:

> Yet he was kind, or if severe in aught,
> The love he bore to learning was in fault;
> The village all declared how much he knew;
> 'Twas certain he could write, and cipher too;
> Lands he could measure, terms and <u>tides</u> presage,   *changing annual feast days*
> And even the story ran that he could <u>gauge</u>.   *measure the capacity of a cask*
> In arguing too, the parson owned his skill,
> For even though vanquished, he could argue still;
> While words of learned length, and thundering sound,
> Amazed the gazing rustics ranged around;

And still they gazed, and still the wonder grew,
That one small head could carry all he knew.   (205–216)

The schoolmaster is knowledgeable, but he also is opinionated and likes to impress the uneducated with his large vocabulary. The implication is that he pretends to more learning than he really has in order to win arguments and dazzle any less-educated listeners as well as opponents. Still, the irony in Goldsmith's portrait of the teacher is not harsh, but warm and forgiving, portraying a man with a good heart and a solid mind, but with a few human failings. The time for the harsh moral irony of Swift and Pope has now passed, replaced by a generous acceptance of common foibles. Goldsmith also manages to give his verses a modest musical effect with the occasional use of discreet alliteration and repetition, as in lines 213–215. Nor does he invert the normal syntax very much or employ a learned diction, keeping for the most part to common English.

Goldsmith even salutes the old, but neat tavern of the village, now in ruins, where "graybeard Mirth" and "smiling Toil" (line 222) used to meet for a cup of ale and conversation. Where can the poor go now to escape the encroachment of the wealthy landowner and find a new life? If they try the city, corruption and crime await them. If they emigrate to the New World, wild animals (including "crouching tigers" [line 355]), "savage men" (line 356), and harsh weather, like the "mad tornado" (line 357), will greet them. But leave they must, for they cannot remain in the country where they have lived since time immemorial. Their departure is wrenching, but the power of luxury is inexorable. The poet imagines the unhappy scene of separation:

Even now, methinks, as pondering here I stand,
I see the rural Virtues leave the land.
Down where yon anchoring vessel spreads the sail,
That idly waiting flaps with every gale,
Downward they move, a melancholy band,
Pass from the shore, and darken all the strand.
Contented Toil, and hospitable Care,
And kind connubial Tenderness are there;
And Piety, with wishes placed above,
And steady Loyalty, and faithful Love....   (397–406)

Clearly, the poet is witnessing a tragic episode, both for the people involved and for the country at large, for this movement represents the fundamental decay of the moral fabric of English society. Such virtues will not be found anywhere else, and so will be lost forever. The image of the darkened shore suggests both the multitude of people leaving with their values, as well as the gloom of despair of those leaving and those remaining. The personification generalizes the impact and indicates something of the moral scope of the destruction. The pathos of the scene may be exaggerated for effect, but it is, no doubt, a troubling vision.

One additional virtue is leaving, too: "sweet Poetry," the "loveliest maid" who feels terribly uncomfortable "where sensual joys invade" (lines 407–408). The poet believes that poetry is being neglected like the other virtues, and will also have to leave, to his great regret. She has been, after all, as he says, the

>   source of all my bliss, and all my woe,
> That found'st me poor at first, and keep'st me so;
> Thou guide by which the nobler arts excel,
> Thou nurse of every virtue, fare thee well.   (413–416)

The poet says he has not been enriched by his dedication to her, but that is not important to him. What is important is the key role she plays in developing and guiding the arts and the morality in the land. Wherever she goes, the poet hopes she will continue to provide that kind of nurturing:

> Still let thy voice, prevailing over time,
> Redress the rigors of the inclement clime;
> Aid slighted truth, with thy persuasive strain
> Teach erring man to spurn the rage of gain;
> Teach him that states of native strength possessed,
> Though very poor, may still be very blest. . . .   (421–426)

Poetry, it seems, is the only answer to the country's woes, the antidote to the poison of materialism and greed, but it is doubtful that even poetry can counteract this spreading disease. The poet does not offer an optimistic vision, but one that at least has the possibility of restoring some order and reason to society. If poets would celebrate the virtuous poor and traditional values, perhaps they could do something to redress the balance in a failing land. Goldsmith's elegy for a traditional way of life is not completely bleak, though it could hardly be called hopeful.

As readers will have noticed, Goldsmith employs the heroic couplet as his primary verse form, and his verse is traditionally moral and didactic, but we also see that the themes and values of poetry are changing, at least in emphasis. Goldsmith is more overtly sociological in his concern for the poor and for the life of rural England, using pathos and melodrama to dramatize their plight. But he also uses humor, especially in his depiction of human beings, and a gentle irony that often bathes them in a warm glow of sentiment. Sentiment is perhaps even more important than ideas in his verse, with sympathy and generosity being the most prominent feelings displayed. In "The Deserted Village," then, Goldsmith combines traditional poetic forms and devices with contemporary concerns, creating a verse that is fluent, moving, and humane. It is, thus, still a pleasure for us to read and savor today.

WILLIAM COWPER (1731–1800): POET OF DESPAIR

Another poet who exemplifies some of the changes occurring in English society and intellectual life is William Cowper (pronounced Cooper), a more openly religious and socially conscious writer than most other poets we have discussed. Cowper's poetry is often highly personal and subjective, even deeply emotional, reflecting a life of troubled adaptation to contemporary society. It is often pious as well, especially in his hymns, which have a strong Protestant outlook. Perhaps not surprisingly, given this combination of qualities, Cowper was probably the most popular poet of the last quarter of the eighteenth century.

He was born the son of a rector in Hertfordshire. His mother died when he was age 6, after giving birth to his brother, so Cowper was sent away to private schools, including Westminster School, and then to the Inner Temple in London to study law. Although Cowper was called to the bar, he never practiced, suffering a nervous breakdown when preparing to take an exam for a position as Clerk to the House of Lords. Although he recovered from this serious depression, Cowper's mental condition for the rest of his life was fragile and unstable. He suffered several periods of depression and melancholia, and spent some time in an asylum. Because he had attempted suicide, he felt he was a vile sinner who was alienated from God and was certainly headed for eternal damnation. For the rest of his life, he owed much to the care of two individuals: Mary Unwin, widow of an Evangelical preacher to whom he became engaged, and John Newton, a prominent Evangelical minister and author of the well-known hymn, "Amazing Grace." For most of his life Cowper lived a retired existence in the company of a few friends, taking walks in the countryside, caring for his pets, writing letters, and composing various kinds of poems from satires to tales and lyrics. In 1779 he published the *Olney Hymns* with John Newton, including such classics as "God moves in a mysterious way" and "Oh, for a closer walk with God." His most substantial work was *The Task* (1785), a charming discursive poem in blank verse about country life that incorporates digressions on various topics, like the slave trade and colonial wars, to which he was strongly opposed. Over the years Cowper translated numerous classical poems into English, including a blank-verse rendition of Homer, which was not very successful. After Mary Unwin's death in 1796, Cowper's physical and mental state deteriorated until his own death four years later. He was, however, still able occasionally to write powerful poetry, as "The Castaway" (1799) illustrates.

Cowper found the story he used in "The Castaway" in Lord Anson's account of a voyage around the world, an incident that involved a sailor who was washed overboard during a storm. The setting is rather melodramatic, with its nocturnal storm at sea and heroic main character:

> Obscurest night involved the sky,
>   The Atlantic billows roared,
> When such a destined wretch as I,
>   Washed headlong from on board,
> Of friends, of hope, of all bereft,
> His floating home forever left.
>
> No braver chief could <u>Albion</u> boast   *ancient poetic name for England*
>   Than <u>he</u> with whom he went,   *the captain, Lord Anson*
> Nor ever ship left Albion's coast,
>   With warmer wishes sent.
> He loved them both, but both in vain,
> Nor him beheld, nor her again.   (1–12)

The absolute darkness has completely occupied and enveloped the sky, as though it were an active force itself. The wind is howling and the waves are crashing against the ship. The senses of sight, hearing, and touch are all besieged by the most extreme conditions imaginable. One sailor on board is suddenly swept into the sea, though he is not identified by name or position. The poet compares himself to this sailor, moreover, identifying both as "wretches" destined to be overwhelmed by the storms of life. Both are deprived of all hope and companionship, isolated and desperate. Yet the ship was captained by one of the great sailors in English history. If anyone could save him, it would be Lord Anson. The terrible storm, however, will not allow anyone caught in it to be rescued. Neither the good wishes of the people nor the sailor's love for the captain and the ship can defend him against the force of fate. The good feelings of all parties make no difference to the ruthless power of the storm. Cowper says little about the accident itself, but the situation is clearly irrecoverable and hopeless.

The focus turns to the sailor as he struggles in the water trying to gain control over his situation and arouse his shipmates. They become aware of his desperate condition, but are unable to provide any effective help. His distance from the ship rapidly increases:

> Nor long beneath the whelming brine,
>   Expert to swim, he lay;
> Nor soon he felt his strength decline,
>   Or courage die away;
> But waged with death a lasting strife,
> Supported by despair of life.
>
> He shouted; nor his friends had failed
>   To check the vessel's course,
> But so the furious blast prevailed,
>   That, pitiless perforce,
> They left their outcast mate behind,
> And scudded still before the wind.
>
> Some succor yet they could afford;
>   And, such as storms allow,
> The cask, the coop, the floated cord,
>   Delayed not to bestow.
> But he (they knew) nor ship, nor shore,
> Whate'er they gave, should visit more.   (13–30)

Amazingly, despite the raging sea, the sailor is able to recover his poise and swim vigorously in the powerful waves. For some time he displays surprising strength and courage in this unequal battle, shouting for help to his fellow shipmates. The wind, however, without pity, sweeps the ship away in spite of their efforts. They do throw several objects designed for rescue into the sea for him, but "cask," "coop," and "cord" have little chance of reaching him in such a situation. The men on board know it is without hope.

The poet then continues from his omniscient point of view to comment on the sailor's feelings as he watches the ship disappear. He praises the sailor's resilience in the situation and describes the gradual loss of the sailor's cries for help as the ship hurries away. The end of the action is inevitable:

> Nor, cruel as it seemed, could he
>   Their haste himself condemn,
> Aware that flight, in such a sea,
>   Alone could rescue them;
> Yet bitter felt it still to die
> Deserted, and his friends so nigh.
>
> He long survives, who lives an hour
>   In ocean, self-upheld;
> And so long he, with unspent power,
>   His destiny repelled;
> And ever, as the minutes flew,
> Entreated help, or cried, "Adieu!"
>
> At length, his transient respite past,
>   His comrades, who before
> Had heard his voice in every blast,
>   Could catch the sound no more.
> For then, by toil subdued, he drank
> The stifling wave, and then he sank.   (31–48)

In order to save themselves, the sailors on board are forced by the violent wind to allow the ship to run freely; otherwise, they would endanger everyone as well as the ship itself. Even the sailor in the water realizes that, although, according to Cowper, he still feels bitter about it. The ship and his shipmates were so close and now are speeding away. The poet notes that the sailor has fought the waves remarkably well given the circumstances, but that there was essentially no possibility of survival for him. Even so, he continues to cry out to his shipmates, and then, more pathetically, to bid them farewell. Gradually, the sound of his voice disappears as the ship sails away before the wind, and at last he is heard no more, his energy and strength gone. His disappearance beneath the waves is put with stark finality: "and then he sank." There is no weeping and gnashing of teeth, or moaning and complaining on the part of the poet or the other sailors. The drama and climax of the scene are perhaps more powerful because they are understated, being reported simply and objectively.

The poet then steps back to look at the aftermath of the story, the reporting of the incident in Anson's book and the response by other poets. He does not wish to prolong the sorrow or exploit it for his own purposes, but he does want to draw out the parallel suggested at the beginning. He identifies himself clearly with the sailor, though in quite different circumstances. The parallel between them contains the real meaning in the poem:

> No poet wept him; but the page
>   Of narrative sincere,
> That tells his name, his worth, his age,
>   Is wet with Anson's tear.
> And tears by bards or heroes shed
> Alike immortalize the dead.
>
> I therefore purpose not, or dream,
>   Descanting on his fate,
> To give the melancholy theme
>   A more enduring date:
> But misery still delights to trace
> Its semblance in another's case.
>
> No voice divine the storm allayed,
>   No light propitious shone,
> When, snatched from all effectual aid,
>   We perished, each alone;
> But I beneath a rougher sea,
> And whelmed in deeper gulfs than he.   (49–66)

The poet admits that writers may confer immortality on great actions, as Anson has done for this sailor. No poets have taken up his story, however, nor does the poet believe he can fulfill that role. He wants only to draw a parallel between the sailor and himself, in the overwhelming suffering and consciousness of impending death that he has experienced. He, too, has been deprived of all help and seems to have died, isolated and alone, from his terrible suffering. The past tense ("perished") suggests his sense that his life is over. He does not specify what caused his own death, but it is clearly psychological in nature, a suffering more in the mind than in the body. In either case there has been no divine intervention to rescue them, no saving grace to restore them to life. God has failed to protect them in their extremity. The implication is that one cannot count on help from above in times of great difficulties, even if they are not of one's own making. We are all isolated and alone in the tumultuous sea of life.

    The six-line stanza Cowper uses in this poem is well adapted to the blend of narration and reflection he offers us here. The first four lines act as a quatrain with alternating rhyme and alternating lines of iambic tetrameter and trimeter. The last two lines form a couplet that summarizes the action and often comments ironically on it. The lines are generally end-stopped and include some discreet alliteration, repetition, and variations in the rhythm. One example of the latter occurs in line 19, where the poet puts a strong pause after the sailor's shout, to suggest the silence in response to his desperate call for help. There are no metaphors to speak of in the poem, but the whole becomes, at the end, a kind of allegory of the poet's own mental condition. "The Castaway" is a remarkable achievement for anyone suffering mightily in mind and spirit as Cowper was. To compose such a carefully crafted work and make this tragic event somehow pleasurable in the reading is extraordinary, but that is what great art and artists do.

Cowper wrote many different kinds of poems, but none quite so emotionally charged as this one. Most of his poems are quietly reflective, gentle, and conversational. "The Castaway," however, is memorable for its powerful evocation of the poet's own sense of isolation and despair. Its passion is enhanced by the regular stanzas and generally objective tone he uses to tell the story, providing structure and restraint to the intense pathos of the tale. As a result, it continues to be read by many with sympathy and pleasure two centuries later.

CHAPTER 13

Robert Burns (1759–1796): Singer, Satirist, and Storyteller

In the eighteenth century, despite all the turbulence and deprivation it had suffered, Scotland became a hotbed of intellectual activity, centered in Edinburgh. A generation of writers and teachers created a period later known as the Scottish Enlightenment, with such eminent leaders as David Hume in philosophy, Adam Smith in economics and moral philosophy, and Hugh Blair in rhetoric, among others. Many of their works continue to attract readers today as they did in their own time. Furthermore, great interest developed in the native poetry and songs of the past, as well as in the dialect of English known as Scots, the spoken language of the people, which derives more directly from Anglo-Saxon than from English. (Gaelic was largely confined to the Highlands of Scotland.) Several collections of traditional songs were published in the eighteenth century, and poets composed in Scots (or a blend of Scots and English) to celebrate their native heritage.

Robert Burns, the last poet we will consider, was inspired by these various currents, coming as he did toward the end of the century. He wrote much of his verse in Scots English based on indigenous works and gathered, from local sources, a number of songs and their music for some of these collections of Scots poetry. Although his language can occasionally be difficult for the modern reader, that can be readily overcome with a few marginal glosses and notes. Often, it is sufficient to add or change only one letter to form a word that is quite familiar. Today's reader, thus, can enjoy Burns's poetry with relatively little effort. It is a poetry of great variety, filled with a pleasing vitality, a humor that can occasionally be sharp, and some sensitive evocations of the life around him. Though it is quite a different tradition from those we have encountered so far, it is one that has had a significant impact on later poets and readers.

Burns was born in Ayrshire on the west coast of the Scottish Lowlands, the son of a poor farmer, William Burnes (as he spelled it), who worked diligently but unsuccessfully in trying to scrape together a living from several small properties. Robert's education was sporadic, given that he had to help with the farm work at an early age, but as an adolescent he developed an interest in poetry, largely (as he said) from his own burgeoning interest in love. He read widely as a youth, and began writing poetry in earnest after his father's death in 1784, when he and his brother Gilbert moved to a farm near Mossgiel, rented to them by their friend, Gavin Hamilton. By 1786 Burns, hard-pressed for money, was thinking about leaving Scotland for Jamaica to start a new life, so he gathered his poems into book form and published them by subscription in July, in Kilmarnock. The volume was an instant hit, exciting attention even in Edinburgh, so Burns abandoned his plan to emigrate and went to Edinburgh, where he was encouraged to publish a second edition of his poems that included additional works. It was even more successful, and established Burns as "Caledonia's bard," as one writer put it. Another reviewer, Henry MacKenzie, famous author of *The Man of Feeling*, called him a "heaven-sent ploughman," thus beginning the tradition of treating Burns as a natural genius with little formal education or knowledge. Burns also became notorious for his love affairs, but in 1787 he married Jean Armour, who had already given birth to twins by him, and settled down first on another farm, and then in Dumfries, where he became an excise officer. For most of the rest of his short life, in addition to his regular work, Burns collected and wrote (or rewrote) Scottish folk songs to preserve and promote the Scots tradition. He died of heart disease in 1796 at the age of 37, cutting short a productive poetic career, but leaving behind a rich heritage of original and imaginative verse. He was a highly controversial figure in his own time, with his support for the American and French revolutions, his attacks on the Scottish Presbyterian Church, and his various adventures in love, but his work lives on today in the hearts and minds of many readers over the years who have responded to it with deep pleasure.

Burns recovered and rewrote many traditional Scottish folk songs, as he did with "Green Grow the Rashes," a hymn to love and life. The song was originally quite bawdy, but Burns eliminated the obscene parts to focus on the pleasure of love. Like most songs, this one is concerned with one central point reinforced through repetition and a refrain or "chorus." Burns employs a simple quatrain with a rudimentary rhyme scheme that he sometimes abandons. Here are the first two stanzas, along with the chorus, which sets forth the main theme of the song:

Green grow the <u>rashes</u>, O;	*rushes*
Green grow the rashes, O;	
The sweetest hours that e'er I spend,	
Are spent among the lasses, O.	
1	
There's nought but care on ev'ry <u>han</u>',	*hand*
In ev'ry hour that passes, O:	
What signifies the life o' man,	
An' 'twere na for the lasses, O.	
Green grow, etc.	
2	
The <u>warly</u> race may riches chase,	*worldly*
An' riches still may fly them, O;	
An' tho' at last they catch them fast,	
Their hearts can ne'er enjoy them, O.	(1–8)
Green grow, etc.	

The highest pleasure in life is love, he proclaims, finding in it the only thing that makes life worthwhile. It is a bold declaration, especially in view of the Scottish Church's emphasis on living an austere life for the glory of God. Burns stresses, though, the pervasive hardships of life, rather than the Church's doctrine, reminding his readers of their constant manual labor, little reward, and grinding poverty. The image of the green rushes, through their color, continual growth, and association with water, links them with love, nature, and the vital energy of life. Those people obsessed by the quest for wealth, he asserts, will never find happiness, for even if they are successful, they can never escape the care and anxiety of possessing it. This is a race that can never be won. Only the joy of love, Burns suggests, can compensate one for the troubles of life.

In the next two stanzas, Burns becomes more pointed and more colloquial in his development of this idea. In the first he contrasts his point of view with those who take the sober road in life (as advocated by the Church), and in the second he wittily and decisively rejects this road for his own. Here the Scots vernacular provides the dismissive voice and tone:

3

But gie me a <u>canny</u> hour at e'en,   *quiet*
    My arms about my Dearie, O;
An' <u>warly</u> cares, an' <u>warly</u> men,   *worldly*
    May <u>a</u>' gae <u>tapsalteerie</u>, O!   *all / topsy-turvy*
            Green grow, etc.

4

For you sae <u>douse</u>, ye sneer at this,   *sober*
    Ye're nought but senseless asses, O:
The <u>wisest Man</u> the warl' saw,   *Solomon*
    He dearly lov'd the lasses, O.   (9–16)
            Green grow, etc.

Instead of the endless pursuit of money, the poet prefers to enjoy a quiet time of love with his girl, when he can forget all the cares of the world. This, he believes, is time much better spent than in the quest for wealth. In the second of these stanzas (No. 4), the poet becomes much more outspoken in the terms he uses to and for his opponents, whom he addresses directly. This part may have been one of the reasons the poem was not included in the first edition of his poems. Moreover, he invokes one of the great patriarchs of the Old Testament to support his own penchant for the opposite sex, conveniently ignoring that they were generally blamed for Solomon's downfall.

In the final stanza Burns quotes Nature herself to provide the clinching evidence for his case. She represents the principle of life, energy, and vitality that created human beings in the first place:

5

Auld Nature swears, the lovely Dears
    Her noblest work she classes, O:
Her prentice han' she try'd on man,
    An' then she made the lasses, O.   (17–20)
            Green grow, etc.

This, too, would have been anathema to the Presbyterian Church of the time, since it reverses the traditional order and value of the human beings in the biblical account of creation. Women were hardly the "noblest" of beings because of their role in the Fall and in subsequent history. Burns is defying the Church and its strongly moralistic doctrines that had ruled Scotland with a firm hand for more than two centuries. Thus, the song is less innocent than it might seem on the surface, especially given that it was based on an old bawdy song that many would have known (or known about). One can see from this relatively simple example how Burns might generate passionate feelings, for or against him, in his contemporary readers.

In the next poem, "Holy Willie's Prayer," the poet's antagonism to the Scottish Church is far more overt. In it he imitates the inner voice of a Presbyterian elder who prays to God for help in combating his enemies. The poem is based on an actual dispute between Gavin Hamilton, Burns's friend and landlord, and his parish, which had been resolved in Hamilton's favor by the Presbytery, much to the chagrin of some of the elders like William Fisher. Burns imagines "Holy Willie" appealing to God for His help after suffering defeat in the Church hierarchy. In this interior dramatic monologue the satire on certain aspects of Scottish Calvinism (the "Old Light" wing) is sharp and unforgiving, so much so that Burns never published it in his lifetime, though it circulated in manuscript form among his friends. Burns portrays Willie as a self-righteous hypocrite whose belief in his own role as one of God's elect never wavers, despite his own failure to live up to the moral code of the Church. In strict Calvinistic thought, the elect are justified by their faith through God's mysterious grace, not by their actions on earth. Burns satirizes this idea with particular asperity.

The poem takes the form of a prayer, which has certain standard parts that Burns uses to mark its development in Willie's mind. First, the speaker invokes God and praises His power and grace, especially to himself as one of the elect. Willie's pride and complacency shine forth as he begins his petition to his maker:

> O thou that in the heavens does dwell!
> Wha, as it pleases best thysel,
> Sends ane to heaven and ten to h-ll,
>   A' for thy glory!
> And no for ony gude or ill
>   They've done before thee.
>
> I bless and praise thy matchless might,
> When thousands thou has left in night,
> That I am here before thy sight,
>   For gifts and grace,
> A burning and a shining light
>   To a' this place.   (1–12)

Willie glories in his own elect status since he believed most other people are damned to eternal punishment in Hell, not by their own misdeeds but by God's inscrutable wisdom. God, too, seems in Willie's eyes to glory in his apparently arbitrary choices, ignoring what people have actually done in His sight. Willie sees himself, in the image he uses, as a candle or torch that is lighting up the darkness of life for others to acknowledge and admire, even though they may not follow him. Willie's assumption of his own special role in life, with his "gifts and grace," enables Burns to have the speaker implicitly damn himself through his own words and complacency.

Readers may have noticed that Burns has chosen an unusual stanza for his poem. It is no longer the heroic couplet that dominated English poetry for much of the previous two centuries, but a compact, six-line stanza with four lines of iambic tetrameter and two lines of dimeter (four syllables with two of them stressed), and a rhyme scheme that uses only two rhyming sounds (*aaabab*). It is called the Standard Habbie, a traditional form that was used by other Scottish poets before Burns and which he adopted for many of his own poems. It is quite a feat to compose in such a complex, limited form and still retain the sounds and rhythms of a Scottish elder's voice. Most readers believe Burns has succeeded admirably.

In the next two stanzas Burns has Willie admit that he is a sinner from birth based on Adam's original fall, and wonders how God can be so gracious as to exalt him, rather than throw him into Hell along with everyone else to burn and "weep, and wail," as He could have done. Willie's vision of Hell is positively medieval in its picture of "damned devils [that] roar and yell" (line 23), revealing almost a comic-strip imagination at work. The two stanzas that follow (nos. 5 and 7) continue Willie's self-righteous sense of his own election, but add some particulars regarding his own sins. In the first Willie parades his own special role:

> Yet I am here, a chosen sample,
> To shew thy grace is great and ample:
> I'm here, a pillar o' thy temple
>   Strong as a rock,
> A guide, a ruler and example
>   To a' thy flock.

                          ❧

> But yet—O Lord—confess I must—
> At times I'm <u>fash'd</u> wi' fleshly lust;   *troubled*
> And sometimes too, in warldly trust
>   Vile Self gets in;
> But thou remembers we are dust,
>   Defil'd wi'sin.   (25–30; 37–42)

The images Willie employs here to describe his role, conventional though they are, convey his pride with simple economy. He is a "pillar" of the church, a "rock" like St. Peter, a "guide" and "ruler" to show the path of righteousness and lead (or command) the people. But then he also confesses (to God at least) that he is bothered by the force of his natural desires, including lust, selfishness, and the general sinfulness covered by the "dust" of human nature. For the reader, the juxtaposition of these aspects, with the sins coming after the virtues, seriously undermines his extremely positive self-image. Although Willie tries to discount his sins as he expects God to do, the reader sees that they effectively negate all his pride and purity.

In the stanza immediately following, Willie details one of his recent sinful episodes. Burns captures some of Willie's feelings in the rhythm of his voice as he talks about it:

> O Lord—yestreen—thou kens—wi' Meg— *last evening / know*
> Thy pardon I sincerely beg!
> O may't ne'er be a living plague,
>   To my dishonor!
> And I'll ne'er lift a lawless leg
>   Again upon her.   (43–48)

Such a specific instance of sin dramatizes Willie's own weakness. It occurred very recently and with a girl that Willie obviously knows well. It is probably not the first time and, by extension, probably will not be the last. The broken rhythm of the first line suggests Willie's sense of his own failure, as well perhaps as the memory of the pleasure he experienced in it. His guilt is obvious, and he asks for God's mercy as he should, but there is the strong sense that he is more worried about the possible human consequences of his sin, such as Meg's being made pregnant, that would compromise his honor, than he is about the sin itself. His promise not to do it again is seriously weakened by his not accepting full moral responsibility for his action, blaming his "lawless leg."

Willie goes on to talk about another sinful incident (or incidents) with a different girl but continues to hope that God will bless His chosen people and curse their enemies. Here his attack on God's earthly opponents becomes more direct and personal. He names some of them and their sins. The first is the vile Gavin Hamilton:

> Lord mind Gaun Hamilton's deserts!
> He drinks, and swears, and plays at cartes,   *cards*

Yet has sae mony taking arts
   Wi' Great and Sma',
<u>Frae</u> God's <u>ain</u> priest the people's hearts   *from / own*
   He steals awa.   (67–72)

Willie calls on the Lord to take note of Hamilton's sins. They are relatively minor ones, though, in contrast to Willie's own more serious failings with girls, and he admits that Hamilton is popular with practically everyone, both high and low, except the church. Hamilton has somehow stolen the people's hearts away from their spiritual leaders by his "taking arts," as if he were a magician or had supernatural powers. Willie cannot understand how God could allow this to happen, nor will he forgive Hamilton for doing it. He is particularly upset that Hamilton has made Willie and his friends look foolish for their attempt to reprimand him and correct his moral failings. He asks a special curse on Hamilton and his "Kail [broth] and potatoes" (line 78), echoing Deuteronomy (28:15) and bringing the curse down to specific Scottish food, to teach him a lesson. This is personal attack with a vengeance.

Moreover, Willie denounces the Presbytery, the body responsible for judicial matters concerning individual church members, that recently upheld Hamilton against the local parish authorities. He is stunned by their decision and outraged by what he considers a serious miscarriage of justice, especially since it is supposedly God's justice they are administering. As a result, he condemns them in no uncertain terms:

Lord hear my earnest cry and prayer
Against that Presbytry of Ayr!
Thy strong right hand, Lord, make it bare
   Upon their heads!
Lord visit them, and <u>dinna</u> spare,   *do not*
   For their misdeeds!   (79–84)

Willie does not simply criticize their judgment, but wants God to act against them, with His hand hurting their heads. If not quite literal acts Willie proposes, these are to be definite, actual responses to inflict suffering on them that they will notice. God must not be merciful to them, he urges, but act against them in anger and judgment. Willie, in his own bitterness, completely forgets Christ's admonition to forgive one's enemies. The sight of Willie condemning his own church for its support of Hamilton is highly ironic.

Willie also condemns Robert Aiken, the lawyer who defended Hamilton, for humiliating them in court, and he calls for a terrible "vengeance" from

God to "destroy them" all for the sake of His chosen people. He ends his prayer by asking God to reward those who have been faithful to Him, and reveals more of his own sinfulness in the process:

> But Lord, remember me and mine
> Wi' mercies temporal and divine!
> That I for grace and <u>gear</u> may shine,   *wealth*
>   Excell'd by nane!
> And a' the glory shall be thine!
>   Amen! Amen!   (97–102)

It is a fitting conclusion to this ironic self-portrait. Willie's main concerns are the benefits to himself and his own family. That these are to be more material than spiritual is evident in his hope not to be outdone by anyone else. Such a petty desire that he then ascribes to God's glory is, of course, ridiculous. To confuse his own interests with God's is the principal mistake Willie has made all along. His meanness and vindictiveness are fully exposed, along with his lust and selfishness, through his own words and deepest thoughts. Thus does Burns gain his own revenge on the Presbyterian elders who had condemned and humiliated him for his immoral behavior (he and Jean had been publicly admonished in church for their sin). It is obvious why this poem was not published in Burns's lifetime.

In a less contentious vein, Burns occasionally wrote poems about animals or other nonhuman subjects, though they still reflect on individuals or society in general. "To a Mouse" begins with an incident that may have actually happened to the poet. As he is plowing his field, he accidentally turns up a mouse's nest and reflects on what that means for the little creature, normally considered a pest on the farm. It is well to recall that plowing was done by hand behind a horse or ox, so the farmer was involved in hard physical labor close to the earth. There was little separation between him and the soil as there is today. Such an incident would have normally been considered trivial on a farm, but for Burns it becomes a kind of philosophical moment, as he ponders the extreme vulnerability of the field mouse that has just been deprived of her home with winter coming on. Through his colloquial language and humor, however, he keeps the poem from becoming too ponderous or pathetic.

Burns involves the reader in the scene from the outset, beginning with the plowman's discovery of what he has just done to the mouse. He sees it running away but protesting loudly as it goes, and directs his speech to the mouse, treating her with some irony. His language is idiomatic, and his attitude is amused but sympathetic:

Wee, <u>sleeket</u>, <u>cowran</u>, tim'rous beastie,   *sleek / cowering*
O, what a panic's in thy breastie!
Thou need na start awa sae hasty,
      Wi' <u>bickering brattle</u>!   *headlong scamper*
I wad be <u>laith</u> to rin an' chase thee   *loath*
      Wi' murd'ring <u>pattle</u>!   *plowstaff*

I'm truly sorry Man's dominion
Has broken Nature's social union,
An' justifies that ill opinion,
      Which makes thee startle,
At me, thy poor, earth-born companion,
      An' fellow mortal!   (1–12)

The plowman sees the mouse as a cute, but excessively frightened little creature because of her bias against humans. He tries to reassure her that he will not attempt to kill her, as the normal farmer would do, because he feels that humans too often misuse their God-given rule over the animal world. The first stanza is filled with colloquial language that expresses the plowman's amused immediate reaction to the mouse's flight, while the second is almost completely in standard English as he considers what this means, namely that the natural unity between man and mouse (i.e., the whole animal kingdom) has been inadvertently shattered. He ends the passage by asserting his wholehearted acceptance of equality and brotherhood with the mouse as part of the complex web of life that he does not want to disturb.

In the next two stanzas the plowman explains that he does not resent the mouse's presence in the field, even though she might steal from him. He is happy to share his crop with her and feels especially sorry that he has destroyed her house, which will be difficult to rebuild at this time of year. His language returns to the colloquial pattern of the first stanza:

I doubt na, <u>whyles</u>, but thou may thieve;   *sometimes*
What then? Poor beastie, thou <u>maun</u> live!   *must*
A <u>daimen-icker</u> in a <u>thrave</u>   *occasional ear / twenty-four sheaves*
      'S a sma' request:
I'll get a blessin wi' the <u>lave</u>,   *remainder*
      An' never miss 't!

Thy wee-bit housie, too, in ruin!
Its <u>silly wa's</u> the win's are strewin!   *feeble walls*
An' naething, now, to <u>big</u> a new ane,   *build*
      O' <u>foggage</u> green!   *coarse grass*

An' bleak December's winds ensuin,
      Baith <u>snell</u> and keen!
                                                    bitter
                                                (13–24)

The plowman's empathy for the mouse is remarkable, sensing as he does the animal's instinctive knowledge of the harsh winter at hand. Perhaps the farmer's own poverty and labor have sensitized him to the mouse's plight, since both are extremely vulnerable to any kind of serious accident. His use of the word "housie" suggests he has made the connection between them in his own mind. His generous offer to share his grain with the mouse also reveals an exceptional sympathy. Burns's use of the Scots dialect helps make it seem to be a real conversation in a field.

In the next two stanzas Burns reconstructs in detail the activities of the mouse before it was disturbed by the plow. Here he projects himself into the mouse's consciousness with a powerful sensitivity. The mouse seems to have a fully human imagination:

Thou saw the fields laid bare an' waste,
An' weary Winter comin fast,
An' cozie here, beneath the blast,
      Thou thought to dwell,
Till crash! the cruel <u>coulter</u> past   *cutter blade*
      Out thro' thy cell.

That wee-bit heap o' leaves an' stibble
Has cost thee monie a weary nibble!
Now thou's turned out, for a' thy trouble,
      <u>But</u> house or <u>hald</u>,   *without / land holding*
To <u>thole</u> the Winter's sleety dribble,   *endure*
      An' <u>cranreuch</u> cauld!   *hoarfrost*
                             (25–36)

The poet dramatizes the sudden destruction of the mouse's world so carefully built up to protect itself against the coming cold. The concrete images of the mouse's thoughts and work, with the bare fields and the nest of leaves and stubble, enable us to share her dismay along with the poet's regret. It seems she will now have little shelter from the "sleety dribble" of winter.

In the last two stanzas the poet broadens the scope of his reflections to humanity as a whole. He applies the lesson learned from the accident to common human experience and his own case in particular. The result is even more discomforting:

But Mousie, thou art no <u>thy-lane</u>,   *alone*
In proving foresight may be vain:
The best laid schemes o' Mice an' Men
         Gang aft <u>agley</u>,   *awry*
An' lea'e us nought but grief an' pain,
         For promis'd joy!

Still, thou art blest, compar'd wi' me!
The present only toucheth thee:
But Och! I backward cast my e'e,
         On prospects drear!
An' forward tho' I canna see,
         I guess an' fear!   (37–48)

Human planning, the poet concludes, is no more infallible than the mouse's. Both humans and animals are subject to the accidents of life, which may completely overturn their lives. Humans, however, have the additional burden of imagination, of a mind that looks forward and backward beyond the present to what has happened before and what may happen in the future. He offers himself as a particular example to be pitied by the mouse, as embodying one whose future seems bleak and uncertain. The plight of the mouse becomes the plight of the poet. It is a rather sudden shift in focus, for the reader is given no specifics about the poet's life to share. The concern for the mouse has turned into a concern with himself as a representative of humankind. Some readers, however, have found that this sudden shift undermines the poet's sympathy for the mouse. Others believe that it broadens the feeling to include all humanity. This is a good example of how poetry can be interpreted in different ways by different readers. A definitive interpretation is not always, or perhaps ever, possible. A poem, however, can still be a pleasure even if final judgments cannot be made about it.

In the next poem, "To a Louse," the poet descends even further on the scale of being. This bug would scarcely seem to be a poetic subject, but, as we will see, Burns is more interested in the louse's human connection than its own existence. The situation is again dramatic with the speaker in church watching as a louse climbs up the bonnet of a young lady sitting in front of him. He speaks to it, though obviously not out loud, admonishing the bug for its unaccountable boldness. Of course, he is amused by it as well, because it reveals a human foible that he wishes to expose, especially in this setting. Burns again uses the Standard Habbie stanza, but, despite its rigid form, he still manages to compose a colloquial and idiomatic dialogue using many Scots words.

In the opening stanza the poet registers his surprise at seeing a louse in such a place. He cannot believe its insolence and lack of respect for daring to appear at this time. This is a serious violation of decorum in a strict Presbyterian church service:

Ha! whare ye gaun, ye <u>crowlan</u> <u>ferlie</u>!	*crawling / wonder*
Your impudence protects you <u>sairly</u>:	*surely*
I canna say but ye <u>strunt</u> rarely,	*strut*
Owre gawze and lace;	
Tho' faith, I fear ye dine but sparely,	
On <u>sic</u> a place.	*such*
	(1–6)

The exclamatory opening is like some of John Donne's poems that record an emotional reaction to an event that needs then to be more fully explained to the reader. The tone here is one of surprise and scorn at the bug's boldness, as it walks proudly over the young lady's bonnet. It seems to know that it is safe from anyone trying to swat it at this time. The contrast between this vile bug and the fine "gawze and lace" of the bonnet is partly responsible for the speaker's shock. But the tone changes in the last two lines as the speaker seems to worry about the poor nourishment of the louse on such a body. The implication is that the young woman's blood is not as rich as would probably be found elsewhere. To use the word "dine" for the louse is to suggest, incongruously, that it is human, and the exclamation "faith" is amusingly appropriate (and ironic) in the context.

The second stanza returns to the speaker's verbal attack on the louse. He is still astonished at the brazenness of the bug, calling it names and bringing out some of the social implications of this scene:

Ye ugly, creepan, blastet <u>wonner</u>,	*wonder*
Detested, shunn'd, by saunt an' sinner,	
How daur ye set your <u>fit</u> upon her,	*foot*
Sae fine a Lady!	
Gae somewhere else and seek your dinner,	
On some poor body.	(7–12)

Here the speaker challenges the louse directly, saying that everyone hates it, both saints and sinners (again, appropriately amusing in the situation). As a kind of social pariah, it should not be so blatant about its presence on this fine lady. It is well to recall that at this time social distinctions were still clearly marked by clothing. The louse is acting as a kind of revolutionary, upsetting social rank as well as spiritual thoughts. At the end of the stanza, the speaker modulates his tone to suggest that the bug will no doubt find a better meal on a poor person, implying a concern for its welfare (but not much for the poor).

In the next stanza the speaker describes where the louse should go to suit its rank as well as find more nourishment: to the crowd of beggars, naturally, where plenty of fellow bugs may be found, and where it will not be bothered by fine combs that will disturb its nest. In the fourth stanza the speaker returns to the scene in the church with the bug in a new position on the bonnet:

> Now haud you there, ye're out o' sight,
> Below the <u>fatt'rels</u>, snug and tight,   *ribbon ends*
> <u>Na faith ye yet</u>! ye'll no be right,   *Confound you!*
>   Till ye've got on it,
> The vera tapmost, towrin height
>   O' Miss's bonnet.
>
> My sooth! Right bauld ye set your nose out,
> As plump an' gray as onie <u>grozet</u>:   *gooseberry*
> O for some rank, mercurial <u>rozet</u>,   *rosin*
>   Or <u>fell</u>, red <u>smeddum</u>,   *bitter / powder*
> I'd gie you sic a hearty dose o't,
>   Wad dress your <u>droddum</u>!   *buttocks*
>   (19–30)

Suddenly, the bug has disappeared beneath the ribbons on the lady's bonnet, so the speaker calls on it to stay there. Just as suddenly it reappears, making its way up the high, fashionable hat (modeled on a balloon that had recently flown over Edinburgh) to its peak, to the apparent dismay of the speaker. How can it do this, he wonders, in mock indignation at the boldness of the louse. It is ironic that the bug appears so fat and healthy, prompting the speaker to wish for some poison to deal with it definitively for its brazen violation of social decorum. His colloquial expression for killing it (meaning something like "cook your goose") is also amusing as well as alliterative.

After reiterating that he would not have been shocked to see the bug on a poor old woman or on an urchin's clothes, the speaker turns to address the young woman whose bonnet has drawn his attention. This alters the whole tenor of the poem to make it more satiric and moral. Here are the final two stanzas:

O Jenny <u>dinna</u> toss your head,	*do not*
An' set your beauties a' <u>abread</u>!	*abroad*
Ye little ken what cursed speed	
The <u>blastie</u>'s makin!	*creature*
<u>Thae</u> winks and finger-ends, I dread,	*those*
Are notice takin!	
O wad some Pow'r the giftie gie us	
To see oursels as others see us!	
It wad <u>frae</u> monie a blunder free us	*from*
An' foolish notion:	
What airs in dress an' gait wad lea'e us,	
And ev'n Devotion!	(37–48)

The speaker names the young woman directly and cautions her not to be too proud of her beauty or display it with too much boldness. She is, of course, not aware of the little bug crawling on her bonnet, which is the reason for all the pointing and winking among her neighbors. So the speaker prays for self-knowledge for all humans, that we might see ourselves from others' point of view, not just from our own limited perspective. This would teach us humility and perhaps even help us not to pretend to more piety than we truly feel. Thus does Burns, with humor and irony, draw a moral from this little scene but without too much pomposity or contempt for Jenny. She is merely an example of how we all could act when we ignore the perceptions of others.

Burns was also a remarkable narrative poet who was able to take traditional ballads and stories and put them into his own idiom. In "Tam o' Shanter: A Tale" he composes his own story with local place names and characters to create an amusing pseudo-gothic narrative from the superstitions and folklore of Scotland. It mixes realism, romance, and the uncanny with special art, all leavened with a delightful humor that can be ironic, but not sarcastic or harsh. It is a kind of moral tale in octosyllabic couplets in the eighteenth-century tradition, but with only a limited amount of half-serious moralizing. The pace of the plot is rapid and gradually increasing in tension, surprising in some of its turns, and somewhat ambiguous in its implications. Even the austere Wordsworth, who reportedly drank only water, enjoyed this story. It was also one of Burns's own favorites.

Burns sets the scene in Ayr, a market town near his home on the southwest coast, though he begins by describing actions common to practically any town in Scotland (and perhaps anywhere). It is late afternoon when the market is closing and everyone is ready to relax. It is time for socializing and conversation, and Tam joins in with relish:

When <u>chapman billies</u> leave the street,	*peddler fellows*
And <u>drouthy</u> neebors neebors meet,	*thirsty*
As market-days are wearing late,	
An' folk begin to tak the <u>gate</u>;	*road*
While we sit <u>bousing</u> at the <u>nappy</u>,	*boozing / ale*
And getting <u>fou</u> and <u>unco</u> happy,	*drunk / very*
We think na on the lang Scots miles,	
The mosses, waters, <u>slaps</u>, and styles,	*openings in walls*
That lie between us and our hame,	
Whare sits our sulky sullen dame,	
Gathering her brows like gathering storm,	
Nursing her wrath to keep it warm.	(1–12)

The narrator sets the scene by describing the general custom of the men who spend their time after work drinking with their friends and forgetting about the long trip home to an increasingly angry wife. Clearly, he sympathizes with this desire to escape from an otherwise dreary existence, using the first-person plural and characterizing the waiting woman in highly unflattering terms. We can easily visualize her at home, fuming over her husband's tardiness and taking pleasure in thinking about what she will say to him when he arrives. The pressure inside her is building, and she is not about to try to suppress it or excuse her husband.

Tam, meanwhile, despite his wife's warnings, has indeed spent the evening drinking in a pub. The narrator now appears to take the wife's side and blame Tam for his heedless behavior. Burns manages throughout the story to balance husband and wife, seeing the action from both points of view at different times:

O Tam! Hadst thou but been sae wise,	
As ta'en thy ain wife Kate's advice!	
She tauld thee weel thou was a <u>skellum</u>,	*good-for-nothing*
A <u>blethering</u>, blustering, drunken <u>blellum</u>;	*chattering / babbler*
That frae November till October,	
Ae market-day thou was nae sober;	
That <u>ilka</u> <u>melder</u>, wi' the miller,	*every / grinding of grain*
Thou sat as lang as thou had <u>siller</u>;	*silver, money*
That every naig was <u>ca'd a shoe on</u>;	*shod*
The smith and thee gat roaring fou on;	
That at the Lord's house, even on Sunday,	
Thou drank wi' Kirkton Jean till Monday.	
She prophesied that late or soon,	

Thou would be found deep drown'd in <u>Doon</u>;	*a small river*
Or catch'd wi' <u>warlocks</u> in the <u>mirk</u>,	*wizards / night*
By Alloway's auld haunted <u>kirk</u>.	*church*
	(17–32)

The narrator amplifies the way in which Tam has disregarded his wife's counsel. In the past she has warned him against too much drinking and treated him with contempt, the alliteration of her names for him (line 20) amusingly emphasizing her scorn. He has, however, continued to ignore her, so she predicts that he will probably drown in the river he has to cross to get home if he is not caught by witches or wizards. For the moment the story is about the relationship of man and wife at odds in a very human way. But this soon changes as the narrator turns to the story itself.

He describes in detail Tam's excessive drinking with his friend Souter Johnny, a cobbler. They are enjoying the pleasures of the tavern, with the fire burning brightly, the alcohol flowing freely, the stories more and more hilarious, and Tam flirting more and more with the landlady, while a storm brews outside. Tam feels on top of the world, but the narrator enters to offer a word of caution:

Kings may be blest, but Tam was glorious,
O'er a' the ills of life victorious!

But pleasures are like poppies spread,
You seize the flower, its bloom is shed;
Or like the snow falls in the river,
A moment white—then melts for ever;
Or like the borealis race,
That flit ere you can point their place;
Or like the rainbow's lovely form
Evanishing amid the storm.—   (57–66)

The series of similes from nature, indicating how transitory are the pleasures and beauty on earth, represents exactly what Tam has forgotten. Of course it is a common human failing to indulge oneself in the joy of the moment without worrying about the consequences, so the narrator's moralizing is perfectly appropriate, though his images are not very original. It is not harsh satire, but the truth about human weakness. Will Tam fulfill his wife's dire predictions as he heads home in the night? We are about to find out.

As Tam rides bravely out into the lonely, stormy night on his faithful mare Meg, he approaches the old ruined church at Alloway where, according to

legend, several violent events have occurred over the years. All of a sudden
he hears music and merriment, and sees a very strange sight: a group of
witches and wizards dancing various Scottish folk dances, with the devil himself presiding. Tam, emboldened by his drink, naturally stops to watch and
is entranced by the sight of the old men and women twirling around in
energetic motion:

Warlocks and witches in a dance;	
Nae cotillion <u>brent</u> new frae France,	*brand*
But hornpipes, jigs, <u>strathspeys</u>, and reels,	*slow Highland dance*
Put life and mettle in their heels.	
A <u>winnock-bunker</u> in the east,	*window seat*
There sat auld Nick, in shape o'beast;	
A <u>touzie tyke</u>, black, grim, and large,	*shaggy dog*
To gie them music was his charge:	
He screw'd the pipes and <u>gart</u> them <u>skirl</u>,	*made / screech*
Till roof and rafters a' did <u>dirl</u>.—	*rattle*
	(115–124)

This is not a formal French dance with slow movements and elegant gestures but
a vigorous series of steps practiced by the common people in the folk tradition.
The devil looks like a large hairy dog, but he incongruously plays a bagpipe with
great force. When the witches get too hot, they strip to their petticoats. No
wonder Tam is fascinated by the fantastic scene, though the narrator comments
that he could understand it better if the old women were young girls.

The scene becomes even more fascinating when Tam spies a "winsome
wench" (line 164) among the witches. Her petticoat is short and flying,
exciting Tam even more, as well as the devil. This brings about the climax of
the scene:

Her <u>cutty sark</u>, o' Paisley <u>harn</u>,	*short petticoat / yarn*
That while a lassie she had worn,	
In longitude tho' sorely scanty,	
It was her best, and she was <u>vauntie</u>.—	*proud*
Ah! little <u>kend</u> thy reverend grannie,	*thought*
That sark she <u>coft</u> for her wee Nannie,	*bought*
Wi' twa pund Scots ('twas a' her riches),	
Wad ever grac'd a dance of witches!	(171–178)

As Satan blows hard on the bagpipe, the young girl Nannie flings herself
about, causing Tam to lose his cool:

Tam <u>tint</u> his reason a' thegither,   *lost*
And roars out, "Weel done, Cutty-sark!"
And in an instant all was dark:
And scarcely had he Maggie rallied,
When out the hellish legion sallied.   (188–192)

Burns makes us see this young girl flaunting her best petticoat and young body in the company of old witches and wizards. Humorously and somewhat pathetically, he evokes the girl's grandmother having spent all her money on it and never thinking of the possibility that it could be worn at such an event, her pride in her granddaughter having been betrayed. Tam's reaction, too, is natural and impulsive, the result of his drinking and the girl's attractiveness. Then the chase begins.

According to Scottish superstition, the mare must reach the middle of the bridge to be safe from the witches, who could not cross a running stream. Meg gallops rapidly, but the fiends with their unearthly screams are right behind her. It seems doubtful she can make it, leading the narrator to comment on Tam's reckless folly, before describing the final outcome:

Ah, Tam! Ah, Tam! thou'll get thy <u>fairin</u>'!   *deserts*
In hell they'll roast thee like a herrin!
In vain thy Kate awaits thy comin!
Kate soon will be a woefu' woman!

❧

For Nannie, far before the rest,
Hard upon noble Maggie prest,
And flew at Tam wi' furious <u>ettle</u>;   *intent*
But little <u>wist</u> she Maggie's mettle—   *realized*
Ae spring brought off her master <u>hale</u>,   *whole*
But left behind her ain gray tail:
The <u>carlin</u> <u>claught</u> her by the rump,   *witch / grabbed*
And left poor Maggie scarce a stump.   (201–204; 211–218)

It is a comic ending to a fantastic story, though the narrator offers a kind of moral in the last short paragraph about the dangers of drinking and thinking too much about "cutty-sarks." Nannie has caught up with Maggie, who bolts away to the middle of the bridge, but her tail has been ripped off by the young witch before she could reach complete safety. Tam himself escapes without injury, though he will probably be scarred for life from his close encounter with these witches. Does he learn anything from it? We are not told if he does. But we are surely amused and delighted by it, nevertheless. Burns's blend of the supernatural and the realistic is unique, with the narrator providing a running commentary, all done with a light touch and a sympathetic heart.

We will end our look at Burns's poetry with another one of his famous songs, "John Anderson My Jo." Burns wrote many types of songs, from the patriotic to the bawdy and the sentimental. This is one filled with deep feeling but without his characteristic humor or sharp wit. I take it to be a woman's simple but memorable expression of her deep affection for her husband. Burns adapted it from an old bawdy song that is said to be still popular today, but he eliminated all the indecent elements to concentrate on the pathos of the relationship.

Its structure is simple with only two stanzas of eight lines each. In the first four lines of each, the woman talks about their relationship in the past; in the second four, she describes their present condition. The contrast between the two time periods is the main focus, but it is the continuing affection of the couple that binds them (and the stanzas) together. Here is the first one:

John Anderson my jo, John,	*joy, sweetheart*
When we were first acquent;	
Your locks were like the raven,	
Your bony brow was brent;	*bonny (handsome) / smooth*
But now your brow is beld, John,	*bald, receding*
Your locks are like the snaw;	
But blessings on your frosty pow,	*head*
John Anderson my jo.	(1–8)

The woman recalls their first acquaintance when her young man was dark-haired and smooth-browed, a handsome and vital youth. Her original attraction to him is still evident, but she also sees clearly the reality of the present. His brow is creased and his hair is as white as the snow, to suggest that the fire of life in him is growing cold. Nevertheless, she still asks for blessings on his head, however much he has aged, for her love lives on; he is still her joy.

In the second stanza, the speaker again contrasts the past and the present. In both she finds much to be thankful for, though she also faces time's ravages squarely:

John Anderson my jo, John,	
We clamb the hill the gither;	*together*

And mony a <u>canty</u> day, John,	*merry*
We've had wi' ane anither:	
Now we <u>maun</u> totter down, John,	*must*
And hand in hand we'll go:	
And sleep the gither at the foot,	
John Anderson my jo.	(9–16)

For the speaker, the past is represented by their sharing the freedom of a day in nature, climbing the surrounding hills and enjoying their time with each other. Climbing the hills could be understood metaphorically, of course, as surmounting the troubles and difficulties of existence. Their early life, in her memory, is one of vital energy and deep pleasure in mutual harmony. The contrast with the present is sharp, for, instead of climbing up, now they can only "totter down." Though they are clearly headed for the grave, they will walk (as best they can) together the rest of the way, and sleep at last united for eternity. Their love, she believes, has sustained them in life up to now and will forever into the future.

In this song Burns manages to keep the sentiment from being excessive by not having the woman lament their sad fate together, especially the hard facts of aging. It is, no doubt, an idealized picture of marital affection, but one that acknowledges the darker side of life and does not exalt the brighter side beyond belief. In his best verse Burns keeps the emotion of the subject under control through humor, the discipline of form, and a down-to-earth vision. Even in his best satires, where exaggeration is a normal part of the attack, he keeps close enough to the truth to remain believable. Perhaps the most appealing feature of his poetry is the lively enjoyment of life that shines through it. Burns himself certainly took a joy in living that he managed to capture in his verse, making it almost infectious. Some of this joy is carried in the sound of the verse. It would be helpful for readers to listen to his poetry read by a native of Scotland, whose lilt and burr will add significantly to its pleasure.

Like many of the earlier poets we have discussed, the range and variety of Burns's poetry, from the lyric to the narrative, dramatic, and satiric, are most impressive. Though he wrote in a language and tradition not very familiar to most of us today, Burns composed delightful poems in all modes, enabling us to take a continuing pleasure in their language, form, and ideas. There is no doubt he will remain a popular poet as long as English itself continues to be a living language.

Epilogue

Our reading of Burns's poetry takes us to the beginnings of the Romantic period, when an emerging group of young poets displayed a new interest in the inner experience of the individual, a heightened concern with nature, and an often radical politics (as Burns himself did in the democratic movements of the late eighteenth century). The Romantics retain a concern with traditional poetic forms, such as the sonnet and the ode, but they also create new forms like Shelley's blend of the sonnet and terza rima in the "Ode to the West Wind." They rarely, however, return to the heroic couplet, which had dominated the verse of the previous period. The first generation of the Romantic poets was already at work while Burns was alive, and some of them were influenced by him, especially in composing poems about the poor and the unfortunate. But that is another story, with its own interest.

Looking back over the two centuries of poetry we have covered, we can see much to interest us, even to teach us about ourselves and others, as well as about the past and our heritage. Our journey through these years has been filled with a variety of voices, events, characters, images, and forms. Of necessity, much has been left out, but that has allowed more time to explore some of the poems in depth, to see in detail how these poets have composed remarkable works from their concern with language, sound, rhythm, and meaning. They have treated many different topics from love to politics and religion, from the good life to death, and the many ways humans can cause problems for themselves and others. Even when they have chosen to write about the same subjects, their treatment has often differed radically from one poet to the next, in attitude, tone, and voice as they develop their own ideas and feelings. On occasion, they have probably surprised us with their unusual insights and perspectives, keeping us alert and challenging us in our own comfortable point of view.

Readers can now look back over the poetry of these two centuries with a renewed sense of its artistic power and grace, along with a greater understanding of the past. They will perhaps have discovered how writers two or three hundred years ago frequently addressed issues of continuing concern today, often with extraordinary insight. Falling in love, mourning the dead and dying, seeking spiritual guidance, exposing ethical lapses, and many more subjects they have written about are of permanent human interest. It should give readers a particular pleasure to recall some of the passages we have discussed that have had special meaning for them. If memorized, these passages can give further pleasure when recalled in the future. The strong bias today against learning by heart should not deprive us of the satisfaction of remembering lines of verse that express so well what we have felt (or feel) at different times but cannot articulate so effectively. Poets have much to teach us about the uses of language as well as about ourselves and our values.

Poetry is one of the glories of civilization, but it is also an integral part of most primitive societies. It seems to be a natural activity for human beings and has brought to many readers and listeners a deep and lasting pleasure as well as much significant meaning. Poetry will not make you rich, powerful, or attractive, it will not solve your personal problems or prevent bad things from happening to you, but it can enhance your satisfaction in life and contribute to a lasting measure of happiness. If you have not yet begun to mine this rich vein of enjoyment, passion, and insight, it is never too late to start. The work is not hard, you can proceed at your own pace, and the rewards are many and deeply fulfilling. Happily, there remain many more fine poems to explore and enjoy.

Further Reading

The following books may be of interest to a general audience. Many of the works will be found in the collections of local public libraries. Suggested readings for such writers as Milton, Pope, and Johnson represent only a small number in the vast and growing collections of general and specialized studies. Individual poets are listed in the order they are discussed in the text.

SELECTED GENERAL BOOKS ON POETRY

Bateson, F. W. *English Poetry: A Critical Introduction* (1950).
Brooks, Cleanth. *The Well-Wrought Urn: Studies in the Structure of Poetry* (1947).
Brooks, Cleanth, and Robert Penn Warren. *Understanding Poetry*, 4th ed. (1976).
Drew, Elizabeth. *Poetry: A Modern Guide to Its Understanding and Enjoyment* (1959).
Eliot, T. S. *On Poetry and Poets* (1957).
Gioia, Dana. *Can Poetry Matter?* (2002).
Heaney, Seamus. *The Redress of Poetry* (1995).
Jack, Ian. *The Poet and His Audience* (1984).
Leavis, F. R. *New Bearings in English Poetry* (1932).
Ricks, Christopher. *Allusion to the Poets* (2002).
Rosenthal, M. L. *Poetry and the Common Life* (1983).
———. *The Poet's Art* (1987).
Steele, Timothy. *All the Fun's in How You Say a Thing* (1999).
Vendler, Helen. *Coming of Age as a Poet: Milton, Keats, Eliot, Plath* (2003).

SELECTED BOOKS ON SEVENTEENTH- AND EIGHTEENTH-CENTURY POETRY

Barash, Carol. *English Women's Poetry, 1649–1714* (1996).
Doody, Margaret A. *The Daring Muse* (1985).
Erskine-Hill, Howard. *Poetry of Opposition and Revolution* (1996).
Fussell, Paul. *The Rhetorical World of Augustan Humanism* (1965).
Hammond, Gerald. *Fleeting Things: English Poets and Poems, 1616 to 1660* (1990).
Jack, Ian. *Augustan Satire* (1952).
Johnson, Samuel. *Lives of the Poets.* 2 vols. (1968).
Lewalski, Barbara K. *Protestant Poetics and the Seventeenth-Century Religious Lyric* (1979).
Miner, Earl. *The Metaphysical Mode from Donne to Cowley* (1969).
————. *The Restoration Mode from Milton to Dryden* (1974).
Price, Martin. *To the Palace of Wisdom* (1964).
Reid, David. *The Metaphysical Poets* (2000).
Scodel, Joshua. *The English Poetic Epitaph* (1991).
Sutherland, James. *A Preface to Eighteenth-Century Poetry* (1948).
Trickett, Rachel. *The Honest Muse* (1967).
Weinbrot, Howard. *Eighteenth-Century Satire* (1988).
————. *The Formal Strain: Studies in Augustan Imitation and Satire* (1969).

SOME ANTHOLOGIES OF SEVENTEENTH- AND EIGHTEENTH-CENTURY POETRY

Eighteenth-Century English Literature, ed. Geoffrey Tillotson, Paul Fussell Jr., and Marshall Waingrow (1969).
Eighteenth Century Poetry: An Annotated Anthology, ed. David Fairer and Christine Gerrard, 2nd ed. (2004).
Eighteenth-Century Women Poets, ed. Roger Lonsdale (1989).
The Metaphysical Poets, ed. Helen Gardner (1957).
The New Oxford Book of Eighteenth Century Verse, ed. Roger Lonsdale (1984).
The New Oxford Book of Seventeenth Century Verse, ed. Alastair Fowler (1991).
The Norton Anthology of English Literature, gen. ed. M. H. Abrams, assoc. ed. Stephen Greenblatt, 2 vols., 7th ed. (2000).
Seventeenth-Century Poetry: An Annotated Anthology, ed. Robert Cummings (2000).

INDIVIDUAL POETS

John Donne

More Poems by Donne

"Batter My Heart, Three-Personed God" (Holy Sonnet No. 14)
"The Canonization"

"Good Friday, 1613. Riding Westward"
"The Good Morrow"
"A Nocturnal upon St. Lucy's Day"
"Song" ("Sweetest love, I do not go")

Books about Donne

Bald, R. C. *John Donne: A Life* (1970).
Johnson, Samuel. *Lives of the Poets*. 2 vols. (1968).
Marotti, Arthur F. *John Donne, Coterie Poet* (1986).
Roston, Murray. *The Soul of Wit* (1974).
Sanders, Wilbur. *John Donne's Poetry* (1971).
Warnke, Frank J. *John Donne* (1987).

Ben Jonson

More Poems by Jonson

"A Celebration of Charis"
Epigrams: "To My Book," "To John Donne," "On Don Surly"
Epitaphs: "On My First Daughter," "Epitaph on S. P., A Child of Queen Elizabeth's
      Chapel"
Songs: "Slow, Slow, Fresh Fount," "Queen and Huntress"
"A Sonnet to . . . Lady Mary Wroth"

Books about Jonson

Leggatt, Alexander. *Ben Jonson: His Vision and His Art* (1981).
Peterson, Richard S. *Imitation and Praise in the Poems of Ben Jonson* (1981).
Riggs, David. *Ben Jonson: A Life* (1989).
Summers, Claude, and Ted-Larry Pebworth. *Ben Jonson* (1999).

Robert Herrick

More Poems by Herrick

"The Argument of His Book"
"His Farewell to Sack"
"His Prayer to Ben Jonson"
"His Return to London"
"Upon His Verses"

Books about Herrick

Deming, Robert. *Ceremony and Art: Robert Herrick's Poetry* (1974).
Rollin, Roger. *Robert Herrick* (1966).
Scott, George W. *Robert Herrick* (1974).

George Herbert

More Poems by Herbert

"Easter Wings"
"Jordan (2)"
"Prayer (1)"
"The Pulley"
"Redemption"
"The Windows"

Books about Herbert

Stewart, Stanley. *George Herbert* (1986).
Summers, Joseph. *George Herbert: His Religion and His Art* (1954).
Vendler, Helen. *The Poetry of George Herbert* (1975).

John Milton

More Poems by Milton

All of "Lycidas," *Paradise Lost*, and *Samson Agonistes*
"L'Allegro" and "Il Penseroso"
"On the Morning of Christ's Nativity"
Paradise Regained
Sonnets: "How Soon Hath Time," "On the Late Massacre in Piedmont," and "Methought I Saw My Late Espoused Saint"

Books about Milton

Brown, Cedric C. *John Milton, A Literary Life* (1995).
Evans, J. Martin. *Milton's Imperial Epic: "Paradise Lost" and the Discourse of Colonialism* (1996).
Flannagan, Roy. *John Milton: A Short Introduction* (2002).
Hughes, Merritt Y., ed. *Complete Poems and Major Prose* (1957).
Johnson, Samuel. "Life of Milton," in *Lives of the Poets*, vol. 1 (1968).
Lewis, C. S. *A Preface to "Paradise Lost"* (1942).
Low, Anthony. *The Blaze of Noon: A Reading "Samson Agonistes"* (1974).
Nicolson, Marjorie. *John Milton: A Reader's Guide to His Poetry* (1963).
Summers, Joseph. *The Muse's Method: An Introduction to "Paradise Lost"* (1962).

Andrew Marvell

More Poems by Marvell

All of "The Garden" and "An Horatian Ode"
"The Coronet"

"Damon the Mower"
"A Dialogue Between the Soul and Body"
"The Mower Against Gardens"
"The Nymph Complaining for the Death of Her Fawn"
"The Picture of Little T. C. in a Prospect of Flowers"

Books about Marvell

Berthoff, Ann E. *The Resolved Soul: A Study of Marvell's Major Poems* (1970).
Friedman, Donald. *Marvell's Pastoral Art* (1970).
Hunt, John Dixon. *Andrew Marvell: His Life and Writings* (1978).
Wheeler, Thomas. *Andrew Marvell Revisited* (1996).

John Dryden

More Poems by Dryden

All of "Mac Fleknoe," *Absalom and Achitophel*, and "Religio Laici"
"Alexander's Feast or the Power of Music"
Annus Mirabilis
The Hind and the Panther
Songs: "Why should a foolish marriage vow" (from *Marriage a la Mode*), "Ah how
      sweet it is to love" (from *Tyrannic Love*)
"To the Memory of Mr. Oldham"
Translated poetic tales: "Baucis and Philemon" (from Ovid's *Metamorphoses*),
      "Theodore and Honoria" (from Boccaccio's *Decameron*) in the *Fables*

Books about Dryden

Hoffman, Arthur. *John Dryden's Imagery* (1962).
Hopkins, David. *John Dryden* (1986).
Johnson, Samuel. "Life of Dryden," in *Lives of the Poets* (1779–1781).
Miner, Earl. *Dryden's Poetry* (1967).
Roper, Alan. *Dryden's Poetic Kingdoms* (1965).
Winn, James A. *John Dryden and His World* (1987).

Jonathan Swift

More Poems by Swift

All of "Verses on the Death of Dr. Swift" and "The Progress of Love"
"The Day of Judgment"
"Death and Daphne"
"The Progress of Beauty"
"The Progress of Poetry"

"A Satirical Elegy on the Death of a Late, Famous General"
"Stella's Birthday, 1721"

Books about Swift

Fischer, John Irwin. *On Swift's Poetry* (1978).
Jaffe, Nora Crow. *The Poet Swift* (1977).
Nokes, David. *Jonathan Swift, A Hypocrite Reversed* (1985).
Quintana, Ricardo. *Swift: An Introduction* (1955).
Schakel, Peter J. *The Poetry of Jonathan Swift* (1978).

Alexander Pope

More Poems by Pope

All the poems discussed in the text including "Eloisa to Abelard"
"Elegy to the Memory of an Unfortunate Lady"
"Epigraph Engraved on the Collar of a Dog"
"Epistle to a Lady"
"Epistle to Lord Burlington"
"Epitaph for Newton"
An Essay on Man
"The Universal Prayer"

Books about Pope

Brower, Reuben. *Alexander Pope: The Poetry of Allusion* (1959).
Fairer, David. *The Poetry of Alexander Pope* (1989).
Johnson, Samuel. "Life of Pope," in *Lives of the Poets* (1779–1781).
Mack, Maynard. *Alexander Pope, A Life* (1986).
Morris, David B. *Alexander Pope: The Genius of Sense* (1984).
Rogers, Pat. *An Introduction to Pope* (1975).
Sitter, John. *The Poetry of Pope's "Dunciad"* (1971).
Tillotson, Geoffrey. *On the Poetry of Pope*, 2nd ed. (1950).

Samuel Johnson

More Poems by Johnson

All of *London* and the *Vanity of Human Wishes*
"The Ant"
"An Epitaph on Claudy Phillips"
"Epitaph on Hogarth"
"Prologue Spoken by Mr. Garrick at the Opening of the Theatre Royal, Drury Lane"
"A Short Song of Congratulation"
Translation of Horace, *Odes*, Book 4, No. 7

Books about Johnson

Bate, W. Jackson. *The Achievement of Samuel Johnson* (1955).
————. *Samuel Johnson* (1977).
DeMaria, Robert. *The Life of Samuel Johnson* (1993).
Eliot, T. S. "Johnson as Critic and Poet," in *On Poetry and Poets* (1961).
Fussell, Paul. *Samuel Johnson and the Life of Writing* (1971).
Rogers, Pat. *Johnson* (1993).
Woodman, Thomas. *A Preface to Samuel Johnson* (1993).

Anne Finch

More Poems by Finch

"Adam Posed"
"The Atheist and the Acorn"
"The Introduction"
"The Spleen"
"To the Nightingale"

Books about Finch

Hinnant, Charles H. *The Poetry of Anne Finch* (1994).
McGovern, Barbara. *Anne Finch and Her Poetry* (1992).

Thomas Gray

More Poems by Gray

"Ode on a Distant Prospect of Eton College"
"Ode on the Death of a Favourite Cat"
"The Progress of Poesy"
"Sonnet on the Death of Mr. Richard West"

Books about Gray

Ketton-Cremer, R. W. *Thomas Gray: A Biography* (1955).
McCarthy, B. Eugene. *Thomas Gray: The Progress of a Poet* (1997).
Weinfield, Henry. *The Poet without a Name: Gray's "Elegy" and the Problem of History* (1991).

Oliver Goldsmith

More Poems by Goldsmith

All of "The Deserted Village"
"Retaliation"

Song: "When lovely woman stoops to folly" (from *The Vicar of Wakefield*)
"The Traveller"

Books about Goldsmith

Dixon, Peter. *Oliver Goldsmith Revisited* (1991).
Quintana, Ricardo. *Oliver Goldsmith* (1967).
Swarbrick, Andrew, ed. *The Art of Oliver Goldsmith* (1984).
Wardle, Ralph. *Oliver Goldsmith* (1957).

William Cowper

More Poems by Cowper

Various hymns such as "Light Shining out of Darkness" and "Oh, for a Closer Walk
        with God"
"On the Ice-Islands Seen Floating in the Germanic Ocean"
"The Poplar-Field"
The Task
"Yardley Oak"

Books about Cowper

King, James. *William Cowper: A Biography* (1986).
Newey, Vincent. *Cowper's Poetry* (1982).
Priestman, Martin. *Cowper's "Task"* (1983).

Robert Burns

More Poems by Burns

"Address to the Unco Guid"
"Afton Water"
"Auld Lang Syne"
"A Red, Red Rose"
"Robert Bruce's March to Bannockburn"
"Song: For a' that and a' that"

Books about Burns

Bentman, Raymond. *Robert Burns* (1987).
Bold, Alan. *A Burns Companion* (1991).
Crawford, Thomas. *Burns: A Study of the Poems and Songs* (1960).
Daiches, David. *Robert Burns* (1950).
Mackay, James. *A Biography of Robert Burns* (1992).
McGuirk, Carol. *Robert Burns and the Sentimental Era* (1985).

Index

About the Author

NICOLAS H. NELSON is Professor Emeritus of English at Indiana University. He has published several articles on poetry and philosophy.